Global Sustainability

Global Sustainability

Social and Environmental Conditions

Simone Borghesi
Department of Quantitative Methods and Economic Theory
University of Pescara

and

Alessandro Vercelli
Department of Economic Policy, Finance and Development
University of Siena

palgrave
macmillan

First published 2008 by
PALGRAVE MACMILLAN
Houndmills, Basingstoke, Hampshire RG21 6XS and
175 Fifth Avenue, New York, N.Y. 10010
Companies and representatives throughout the world

PALGRAVE MACMILLAN is the global academic imprint of the Palgrave Macmillan division of St. Martin's Press, LLC and of Palgrave Macmillan Ltd. Macmillan® is a registered trademark in the United States, United Kingdom and other countries. Palgrave is a registered trademark in the European Union and other countries.

ISBN 13: 978–0–230–54696–7   hardback
ISBN 10: 0–230–54696–X   hardback

This book is printed on paper suitable for recycling and made from fully managed and sustained forest sources. Logging, pulping and manufacturing processes are expected to conform to the environmental regulations of the country of origin.

A catalogue record for this book is available from the British Library.

Library of Congress Cataloging-in-Publication Data
Borghesi, Simone.
    Global sustainability : social and environmental conditions / by
    Simone Borghesi and Alessandro Vercelli.
       p. cm.
    Updated and revised English language version of : La sostenibilit?
    dello sviluppo globale / Alessandro Vercelli, Simone Borghesi.
    Roma : Carocci, 2005.
    Includes bibliographical references and index.
    ISBN 0–230–54696–X (alk. paper)
       1. Sustainable development. 2. Globalization–Economic aspects.
    I. Vercelli, Alessandro. II. Vercelli, Alessandro. Sostenibilit dello
    sviluppo globale. III. Title.
    HC79.E5B663 2008
    338.9′27–dc22   2008011108

10   9   8   7   6   5   4   3   2   1
17   16   15   14   13   12   11   10   09   08
Printed and bound in Great Britain by
CPI Antony Rowe, Chippenham and Eastbourne

Contents

List of Figures and Tables

Figures

List of Acronyms

ABB	Asea Brown Boveri Ltd
AIDS	Acquired Immune Deficiency Syndrome
BAU	Business as usual
C&C	Command and Control
CAFE	Corporate Average Fuel Economy
CFC	Chlorofluorocarbons
CG	Corporate governance
CH_4	Methane
CITES	Convention on International Trade of Endangered Species
CO_2	Carbon dioxide
CSA	Canadian Securities Administrators
CSR	Corporate Social Responsibility
DDT	Dichlorodiphenyltrichloroethane
DJSI	Dow Jones Sustainability Index
DM	Decision-maker
EIA	Energy Information Administration
EKC	Environmental Kuznets curve
EKR	Environmental Kuznets relation
EMAS	Eco-Management and Audit Scheme
EPA	Environmental Protection Agency
EU	European Union
EVA	Economic value added
FAO	Food and Agriculture Organization of the United Nations
FDI	Foreign Direct Investments
FIR	Financial Interrelations Ratio
GATT	General Agreement on Trade and Tariffs
GDP	Gross Domestic Product
GHG	Greenhouse gas
GLS	Generalized Least Squares
GMO	Genetically Modified Organisms
GT	The General Theory of Employment, Interest, and Money
$GtCO_2.e$	Gigatons of CO_2 emissions equivalent
HFCs	Hydrofluorocarbons
HIV	Human Immunodeficiency Virus
ICT	Information and Communication Technology
IEA	International Energy Agency

IMF	International Monetary Fund
IPCC	International Panel on Climatic Change
KC	Kuznets curve
kWh	Kilowatt-hour
N_2O	Nitrous oxide
NGO	Non-governmental organization
NO_x	Nitrogen oxide
OECD	Organization for Economic Co-operation and Development
OLS	Ordinary Least Squares
OPEC	Organization of Petroleum Exporting Countries
OTC	Over the counter
PCB	Poly-Chlorinated Biphenyls
PFCs	Perfluorocarbons
PM_{10}	Particulate matters (less than 10 microns in diameter)
R&D	Research and Development
RIH	Relative Income Hypothesis
SF_6	Sulfur hexafluoride
SME	Small-medium enterprise
SO_2	Sulfur dioxide
ST	Stakeholders theory
SVT	Shareholder value theory
TRIPS	Trade-Related Aspects of Intellectual Property Rights
UNDP	United Nations Development Programme
UNECE	United Nations Economic Commission for Europe
UNEO	United Nations Environmental Organization
UNEP	United Nations Environmental Programme
UNESCO	United Nations Educational, Scientific and Cultural Organization
UNICEF	United Nations Children's Fund
WB	World Bank
WBCSD	World Business Council for Sustainable Development
WHO	World Health Organization
WIPO	World Intellectual Property Organization
WTO	World Trade Organization

Preface

In this book we intend to discuss to what extent the post-war process of globalization may be considered consistent with the basic requisites of sustainable development. The approach that we have chosen for this purpose aims to be as rigorous as possible, avoiding prejudice and groundless simplification. We are fully aware that this is a difficult task. Both "globalization" and "sustainable development" are overworked and abused terms, full of polemic and emotional overtones. In spite – and partly because – of this, these two keywords have caught the attention not only of researchers but also of public opinion and mass media. The hot confrontation on these issues has also stimulated widespread interest in them but, at the same time, has polarized public opinion into two opposing camps: in favor or against globalization, and concerned or unconcerned with the requisites of sustainable development. Such a polarization has not helped the understanding of the ongoing processes nor the identification of the best policies to keep them under control. We should therefore abandon the sterile and misleading confrontation between unqualified arguments in favor or against globalization and try to give sounder foundations to the different points of view.

Since the book aims to give a *scientifically sound* contribution, why did we choose to combine in the very title two keywords (globalization and sustainable development) that are so highly controversial? First of all, because they raise issues that are strictly linked and complementary. Interest in globalization emerges from the need to appraise recent socio-economic processes in terms not only of local, but also of global determinants and implications. Similarly, interest in sustainable development arises from the need to appraise recent socio-economic processes not only from a short-term, but also from a long-term perspective. Taken together, therefore, the two keywords reflect the need of extending our analysis and policy concern beyond the "here and now". In other words, the same holistic role played by the concept of globalization from the spatial point of view is played by the concept of sustainable development from the temporal point of view. Both concepts express the awareness that we may understand the meaning and implications of current processes only by inserting them within their spatial (global) and temporal (long-run) contexts.

The second reason to relate globalization and sustainability lies in the causal influence of the first on the second. We believe that the issue of sustainable development became really topical as a result of the globalization of the environmental and social problems induced by the markets' internationalization. The analysis of the causal influence exerted by globalization on the sustainability of development helps clarifying which of its features have a positive impact on the environment, society and quality of life and which a negative impact. This suggests how economic, social and environmental policies might be redirected to eliminate, or at least mitigate, the adverse effects of current globalization while strengthening – at the same time – its positive influences on the sustainability of world development.

The analysis of the requisites for sustainable globalization is bound to engage us in a sort of patient restoration of a large mosaic of which we know neither the general design nor the details, while we can recover only a limited number of tesserae that require preliminary restoration before reassembling them in a meaningful whole. The basic tesserae are provided and validated by different scientific disciplines (such as economics, sociology, law and ecology) that are involved in the issues that we are going to discuss. As economists we rely mainly on economics and some of its specialized branches: environmental and international economics, industrial economics, finance, as well as growth and development theories. Within the limits of our competence, however, we also have to refer to other scientific disciplines such as law, social epidemiology, biology and sociology. These and other disciplines have much to say on the single tesserae of the mosaic and on how they can be restored but, generally speaking, they have so far avoided the crucial task of assembling them in a meaningful whole. This task was therefore left to the public opinion and hence mainly to the opinion-makers of mass media and political movements. It is our conviction, however, that scientific research should not sidestep this forbidding but crucial task. Otherwise, excessive weight would be given to the subjective opinion of those who, in the absence of firm arguments established by scientific disciplines, might be easily influenced by emotions and propaganda. Therefore, in this book we attempt to recover and reassemble the tesserae validated by scientific disciplines, accurately weighing the pros and cons of each assertion as in a process based on circumstantial evidence, setting aside personal prejudice and opinions as far as possible.

The task in hand is quite challenging. While we strive to take account of all relevant scientific information, we are aware that there are gaps in our coverage. In addition, as knowledge accumulates over time, the results we have attained so far are likely to require considerable updating or adjustment in the future. Our attempt at critical reconstruction and interpretation of facts aims thus mainly to suggest a method that can be further pursued in the future in the light of new and better knowledge. Only from the joint effort of many researchers belonging to the relevant scientific disciplines can there emerge in due time a persuasive critical reconstruction of facts and a well-designed policy strategy.

The structure of this work is the following. The book opens with an introductory chapter that deals with preliminary issues that we felt had to precede the rest of our argument. In the first section we introduce the definitions of globalization and sustainable development, their origins and evolution in the last two centuries. In the second section we outline a comprehensive preview of the interpretive appraisal of the book. In the third section we discuss the nature of the gap between the ideal textbook model of perfect competition and the real markets. This gap provides the ultimate foundations for many of the theoretical arguments underlying the interpretation, evaluation and policy suggestions advanced herein. The following four chapters investigate the main requisites of sustainable development with special reference to inequality and poverty (Chapter 2), environmental deterioration (Chapter 3), energy (Chapter 4) and health (Chapter 5). The sixth chapter focuses on the latter half of the 1990s in order to understand the impact on globalization of the so-called "new economy" and of the new international market regulations introduced by the World Trade Organization (WTO). The seventh chapter shifts the focus from the macroeconomic to the microeconomic point of view in order to analyze the impact of the recent process of globalization on the sustainability of corporations. For this purpose, we examine how the corporations' initiatives of self-regulation to consolidate their social responsibility affect their own sustainability as well as that of macroeconomic development. The eighth chapter investigates the nexus between the evolution of liberal doctrines since their classic exposition in Adam Smith (1776), and the evolution of the globalization process, including its impact on sustainable development. This allows us to point out how the history of markets (including their globalization) and the history of market theory with its policy implications (liberalism) have been strictly intermingled in the last two centuries. Chapter 9 ends the argument with a few concluding remarks. In the first section we summarize the argument developed in the book, while in the second section we discuss the main policy teachings that we are inclined to draw from our analysis. In the third section we discuss the "liberal dilemma" arising from the fact that any measure introduced to defend and expand the individual economic freedom may offer new pretexts for introducing limitations to it.

This book has two main purposes, each of which addresses a different audience. The first purpose, as we have mentioned above, is to provide an interpretation of the post-war process of globalization with special emphasis on the last quarter of the 20th century, in order to assess its sustainability. Though this theme is discussed with the maximum rigor we were capable of, we kept the technicalities to a minimum to ensure that our argument is accessible to a wide audience with a basic, though not necessarily professional, background in economics. The second purpose is to provide a fairly comprehensive textbook on globalization with special reference to its sustainability, or on sustainable development with special emphasis on the impact of globalization. We envisage it being used by undergraduates at the end of their studies in economics or at the beginning of graduate studies in development, international or environmental economics, as a premise for a more in-depth study of some of the issues discussed. Preliminary drafts of this book have been used by the authors as lecture notes for the course in environmental economics at the University of Siena since the academic year 2002–2003 and for the course in development economics at the University of Pescara since the academic year 2004–2005.

Acknowledgments

The first draft of this book was a translation of a book published in Italian: "La sostenibilità dello sviluppo globale", Carocci editore, Roma, 2005. The current draft has largely modified structure and contents of that book, trying to update and hopefully improve the arguments and their links.

We have utilized in this book ideas and excerpts from the following works, indicating in brackets the main chapters or sections in question:

Borghesi, S., 2001, The environmental Kuznets curve: a survey of the literature, in Franzini, M., Nicita, A. (eds), *"Economic Institutions and Environmental Policy"*, pp.201–224, Ashgate (Chapter 3).

Borghesi, S. and Vercelli, A., 2003, Sustainable globalization, *Ecological Economics*, vol. 44, no. 1, pp.77–89 (Chapters 1 and 3).

Borghesi, S. and Vercelli, A., 2006, Global Health, in Farina F., Savaglio E. (eds), *"Inequality and economic integration"*, pp.107–136, Routledge (Chapter 5).

Vercelli, A., 2004, Updated Liberalism vs. Neo-liberalism: Policy Paradigms and the Structural Evolution of Western Industrial Economies after W.W. II, in Arena, R. and Salvadori, N. (eds), *Money, Credit and the State: Essays in Honour of Augusto Graziani*, Aldershot, Ashgate (Chapter 8).

Vercelli, A., 2006, Globalization and Sustainable Development, in Basili, M., Franzini, M., and A. Vercelli (eds), *Environment, inequality and collective action*, Routledge (Chapter 1).

We thank the editors and the publishers of the above mentioned journals and books for their permission to re-utilize parts of the already published works. Of course, the passages borrowed from these works have been extensively updated and adapted within the framework of the book in order to avoid repetition and heterogeneity.

Preliminary drafts of single parts of the book have been presented during these last years at the Universities of Bergamo, Florence, Forlì, Milano Bicocca, Perugia, Pisa, Roma 3, Venice, the European University Institute, the Rio de Janeiro Federal University, the World Congress of the International Economic Association in Lisbon, the International School on Economic Research of the University of Siena, the Swiss

Society of Economics and Statistics at the University of Zürich, the Queen Mary College at the University of London. We would like to thank the participants to these seminars and conferences for stimulating discussions that have helped us to clarify ideas and improve the analysis.

In addition, Alessandro Vercelli wishes to thank the Financial Market Group of LSE where he has been hosted in the Fall Term of 2004 as visiting scholar, and the Queen Mary College of the University of London, where he has been hosted in the Fall Term of 2005 as "distinguished visiting fellow". Both institutions provided an excellent and stimulating environment for completing the book.

We would also like to thank Nicola Acocella, Riccardo Bellofiore, Andrea Cornia, Samuel Bowles, Lilia Costabile, Brigitte Granville, Maria Tinacci Mossello, Edward Nell, Lorenzo Sacconi, Alessandro Vaglio and two anonymous referees for their precious comments and bibliographic indications. Finally, we wish to thank Daniele Verdesca for his help in drafting Chapter 4, Arsenio Stabile and Martina Crociani for their help in drafting the list of references and the figures in the book.

1
Introductory Remarks: Definitions, Preview, Foundations

In the first part of this chapter we intend to give the basic definitions of globalization and sustainable development as well as some historical background that we believe essential for a full understanding of what we are going to say in the sequel. In the second part of the chapter we proceed to outline a preview of a few crucial arguments developed in the following chapters. In the third part we explicit the theoretical foundations underlying our arguments.

1 Definitions

In order to study the relationship between globalization and sustainable development we have first to clarify the meaning we attribute to these controversial concepts.

1.1 Globalization: definition and evolution

Since the late 1990s the economic and social implications of globalization have attracted increasing attention from both public opinion and mass media. In spite of the hot debate, or perhaps also because of this, there is no agreement on the very definition of globalization.[1]

In what follows we intend to focus exclusively on *economic* globalization. By economic globalization we simply mean the progressive integration of world markets induced by the liberalization of international exchanges of goods, services and productive factors. In a similar vein Bhagwati has recently defined economic globalization as "integration of national economies into the international economy through trade, direct foreign investment (by corporations and multinationals), short-term capital flows, international flows of workers and humanity generally, and flows of technology" (Bhagwati, 2004, p.3). Although this

1

definition is quite narrow, we wish to emphasize that economic global-ization is by no means reducible to free trade as in many economic studies. Single correlations between the degree of trade freedom and other desirable or undesirable features of development are insufficient for an evaluation of economic globalization. The latter cannot be reduced to one single variable. It is a complex historical process the characteristics of which may be somehow captured and assessed only by examining a multidimensional set of variables, interpreting their time patterns and correlations within the evolving historical context. Therefore, beside the strictly economic aspects mentioned above we should always keep in mind other political, social, cultural and institu-tional aspects of globalization some of which have been stressed in recent debate. In order to reach a sharper focus in our analysis, how-ever, we will deal with these aspects only insofar as they affect, or are affected by, what we have called *economic* globalization.

Although the process of economic globalization had a long gestation period,[2] we can give a fairly precise birth date to its take-off in the Con-temporary Era: the third decade of the 19th century, when the economic historians start to find a tendency of the prices of goods traded in differ-ent national markets to converge toward a single price (see O'Rourke and Williamson, 2000; Lindert and Williamson, 2003). In fact, given that a fundamental characteristic of a competitive market is a single price for a traded good, it is meaningful to speak of a real tendency towards a unified international market only when the empirical evidence shows a tendency of local prices to converge towards a single price. It was in that period that industrialization started to exert a pervasive influence in the direc-tion of increasing market freedom in the UK where it had first developed, and with a variable lag in other European countries as well as in their offshoots overseas (first of all in the USA). In the same period the liberal inspiration of economic theory, thoughtfully argued by Adam Smith and further developed by the other classic economists since the end of the 18th century, began to shape the markets, in a first time through scattered and timid interventions of liberalization of domestic and cross-border exchanges in the UK, and then in the other principal industrial-ized countries. Systematic liberal policies started to be adopted in the UK since 1846 when the "corn laws" were repealed,[3] and a bit later in the other countries that were more advanced in the process of industrial-ization. Free trade progressed until World War I, after which a phase of de-globalization that lasted about three decades set in. In this period, the two World Wars and the great depression of the 1930s fostered the adoption of inward policies in most countries.

Globalization did not bounce back until after World War II, but from then on it continued uninterruptedly up to the present time. This book focuses on the most recent post-war phase that can be divided into two periods. The first may be called the "Bretton Woods period", lasting from the end of World War II to the end of the '60s. In that period international markets were regulated by the International Monetary Fund (IMF), the World Bank (WB) and the other organizations set up during the peace conference held in Bretton Woods, which also established their underlying behavioral rules. After the collapse of the dollar exchange standard based on fixed currency rates in 1971,[4] a new international economic order gradually emerged that was based on floating exchange rates and a new policy philosophy. The latter, promptly adopted by the IMF and the WB, was further pursued by a new organization instituted in 1995 with the task of completing the liberalization of international exchanges: the WTO.[5]

After the end of the Second World War, the process of globalization was vigorously promoted by international organizations that supported the liberalization of trade across countries. In particular the GATT (General Agreement on Trade and Tariffs) progressively removed, or reduced, the tariffs and the other barriers to international trade, rapidly bringing back the extension of globalization to the level reached at the turn of the century before the period of de-globalization triggered by the First World War. The breakdown of the Bretton Woods system in the 1970s accelerated the process of international trade liberalization. The Uruguay Round of GATT progressively extended in the 1990s the range of goods freely exchangeable to most immaterial goods such as software, copyrights, patents and insurance. In the same period the growth of global markets was greatly enhanced by the diffusion of the information and communication technologies (see Chapter 6).

We wish to emphasize that the process of globalization of the world economy has continuously changed in the last two centuries and has become increasingly complex. The continuous evolution of the process of globalization and the marked differences between its local varieties explains why any attempt to achieve general conclusions on the features of globalization does not appear really meaningful and sound. We have to distinguish different "modes of globalization" that are affected by various economic, technological, demographic, social, and policy factors. In order to avoid vacuous generality or ungrounded generalizations, we are thus going to distinguish between different phases of globalization and differentiated impacts on specific aspects of economic life in different countries or groups of countries. In addition we wish to emphasize that the evaluation of the impact of different modes of globalization on the crucial economic, social and environmental variables, is relative to the point of view chosen. In this book we are going to analyze the multi-faceted impact of globalization exclusively from the point of view of sustainable development.

1.2   Sustainable development: definition and foundations

Let us now introduce the concept of sustainable development.[6] We will adopt, as is customary, the now-famous definition introduced in 1987 by the so-called "Brundtland Report": "Development is sustainable if it satisfies present-day needs without compromising the capacity of future generations to satisfy their needs" (WCED, 1987, p.43). This definition gained instant popularity and rapidly became a crucial reference in the debate on the limits to economic growth and development. Attention was first focused on the environmental equilibrium of the biosphere, ignoring almost completely the social aspects whose crucial importance, however, have become increasingly recognized as of late. In fact, as it was stressed by the Brundtland Report itself, the rationale underlying sustainable development "implies a commitment to social equity between generations which for consistency's sake must be extended to equity within each generation" (*ibidem*).

The *inter*-generational condition of sustainability is meant to guarantee that the choice freedom of future generations is not compromised by myopic decisions of the preceding generations. We will adopt the convention of calling this prerequisite of sustainability as the *environmental condition*, given that the real freedom of future generations will depend to a large degree on the state of the natural environment they inherit. In practical terms, this means that the indices of environmental deterioration should not worsen any further with time, as this would jeopardize the ecological equilibrium of the biosphere. Of course, this minimal requirement of environmental sustainability is not sufficient if the current state of the biosphere lies beyond the threshold of ecological resilience.

The *intra*-generational condition of sustainability is meant to guarantee equal opportunities to all participants in market competition. This prerequisite is met only when there is sufficient initial equality among competitors, i.e. equal access to all significant economic options. We adopt the convention of calling this criterion of sustainability the *social* condition of sustainability, given that it depends to a large degree on indices such as the magnitude of income inequality and the incidence of poverty. A crucial role is played by poverty, since it may severely reduce the potential access to economic opportunities. An extreme consequence of poverty, apart from the dire eventualities of death and diseases, is malnutrition that seriously reduces the psychophysical efficiency of the victims whose access to economic opportunities is therefore severely limited (people in the world suffering from undernourishment are estimated to be still about 854 million; see FAO, 2006). In practical terms, this means that in order to achieve sustainability, these social indices should not worsen any further with time. Also in this case, the minimal requirement of social sustainability is not enough if the current indices are inconsistent with the social stability of the development process.

The two conditions of sustainable development that we have just defined are founded on ethical principles of equity, freedom, and equal opportunities, which are not necessarily in contrast with more prosaic, yet vital, economic objectives. Equal access to all the basic economic opportunities is, after all, a fundamental condition of efficiency. It is the only way to reasonably guarantee that the "winners" of the always renewed "economic competition" in the market are actually the best participants, those capable of adding the maximum value to society.[7] Thus the conflict between ethics and economics should not be considered inevitable as far as long-term sustainable development is concerned. This conflict emerges mainly when the time period for economic decisions becomes increasingly confined to the short term (see Chapters 5 and 6).

As we have seen, the recent growing concern for inequality, poverty and environmental degradation has sound ethical and economic foundations. From the ethical viewpoint, this concern has a common root in the violation of the crucial ethical principle of equal *ex ante* opportunities for each citizen. *Ex post* inequality is not necessarily a problem *per se*: if one accepts a meritocratic point of view it is in principle acceptable that more active and productive people have, to some extent, higher rewards. In the real world, however, the rich have greater opportunities than the poor (e.g. easier access to higher education), so that the difference in productivity (and earnings) is affected by the difference in initial opportunities. Inequality between citizens, therefore, cannot be light-heartedly accepted when it reflects differences in *ex ante* opportunities. Similarly, sustainable development should be interpreted in its broadest sense as development that gives "equal opportunities" to all generations. This does not imply that we have to guarantee every generation, nor every individual, exactly the same level of income and wealth, but rather that we should try to guarantee the same basic set of initial options (Chichilnisky, 1997; Vercelli, 1998b).

An increasing level of inequality, poverty and environmental degradation may be a matter of concern also for economic reasons, since each of these trends would have negative consequences on the performance of the economy. The latter strictly depends, *ceteris paribus*, on the extension of the option set of economic agents. In particular, a wider set could include superior options that would improve the utility as well as the performance of economic agents with a positive fall-out on social welfare. Since poverty often implies a restriction of the option sets of agents, it also reduces their potential contribution to economic efficiency and wealth. A constrained opportunity set excludes from market competition people that may have better specific skills whose exploitation would improve market performance. Among poor people who could not afford a good education there are potentially excellent scientists, technicians, managers, and so on; no doubt, a proper use of these under-exploited resources would improve the efficiency and performance of the economy.

Apart from this general argument, there are further specific reasons for believing that inequality and environmental deterioration may worsen the performance of a market economy. As several works have pointed out (e.g. Alesina and Perotti, 1996; Benhabib and Rustichini, 1996) high levels of inequality may cause social and political tensions that often have negative effects on income growth.[8] Socio-political unrest threatens property rights, and therefore tends to discourage investment in the country. Anger about inequality, moreover, may lead to riots and strikes that tend to reduce the average number of working hours and thus the total production of the economy. Interestingly, these social tensions are more likely to arise in a period of recession than of prosperity. Indeed, when the economy grows, the poor may be also better off, but in a recession they are likely to suffer relatively more than the rich. Though they are likely to lose less money than the rich, they may lose their jobs as well.

Similarly, environmental degradation might have adverse effects on production by increasing workers' health problems and thus reducing their productivity (see Chapter 5). Ecological degradation, moreover, reduces land and forest productivity in the long run. This may give rise to a "poverty-environment trap" since the poor often rely on natural resources as their main source of income: environmental degradation tends to worsen the conditions of the poor, which – in turn – leads them to exploit natural resources even more to secure their day-to-day survival.

Summing up, both ethical and economic reasons should induce public opinion and policy-making authorities to be concerned about the social and environmental requisites of sustainable development.

But does current globalization worsen these problems, or does it potentially solve them? To answer this question, the next section starts to examine the impact of globalization on the conditions of sustainable development.

2 A preview

In this section we present an outline of the main arguments that we are going to develop in order to answer the question "is post-war globalization consistent with the requisites of sustainable development?" The answer to this question will also provide insights on how to answer a second related question: "is the current process of globalization sustainable?" We start by examining the empirical correlation between globalization and the rate of growth of per capita income in order to verify whether it is detectable a long-run link between them. Having ascertained that globalization offers crucial opportunities for accelerating the pace of economic growth, we wonder whether the kind of development that is likely to be promoted is consistent with the main requisites of its sustainability. We proceed thus to analyze the impact of globalization on the social condition and the environmental condition of sustainability in a long-term perspective. We then move towards a tentative causal analysis of the impact of globalization on sustainable development in different historical phases and circumstances in order to evaluate whether the empirical correlations detected are to be considered spurious or grounded on genuine causal mechanisms. We start our analysis from a long-run global perspective with the intention of narrowing progressively its scope to focus mainly on the most recent phase of globalization.

2.1 The relationship between globalization and growth of per capita income

Most economists maintain that market globalization tends to enhance income growth (see, e.g., among many others, Bhagwati, 2004; Wolf, 2004). According to many studies, the empirical evidence supports this theoretical assumption. Frankel and Romer (1999), for instance, estimate that the elasticity of per capita income with respect to the trade-GDP (Gross Domestic Product) ratio ranges between 0.5% and 2%. According to Dollar and Kraay (2002) growth rates accelerated in developing countries that increased their trade-GDP ratio over the past 20 years, whereas growth rates fell on average in developing countries that experienced a declining trade-GDP ratio. Lindert and Williamson (2003) show strong empirical evidence that open economies grow faster than closed ones and that growth rates increase with the degree of openness. Similar results emerge in the studies by Irwin and Tervio (2002) and by Collier and Dollar (2002).[9]

If we interpret the kernel of globalization, as we do here, as a progressive extension and deepening of markets, this is hardly surprising. We know since the seminal contribution of Adam Smith (1776) that such a process favors a progressive division of labor that fosters efficiency and productivity of labor and capital. In particular, as the process goes on, the economic agents may exploit growing opportunities of scale and scope economies.[10] Economic theory pointed out further channels through which globalization may foster growth. Liberalization of capital flows can increase portfolio risk diversification and thus allow more investments in risky and remunerative projects that increase the country's growth rate (Obstfeld, 1994). Similarly, financial openness to foreign banks may reduce the cost of investments in the country and thus enhance its growth rate (Baldwin and Forslid, 2000). In a globalized world, moreover, trade flows and foreign direct investment (FDI) can contribute to diffuse production techniques and technological know-how across countries, increasing domestic investment, efficiency and productivity in the receiving countries.

We should moreover emphasize that the outward orientation of a country stimulates trans-boundary and domestic competition, challenging domestic monopolies and sheltered positions. In addition it encourages the adoption of policies that assure the establishment and consolidation of macroeconomic stability, while under fixed or sticky currency exchange regimes inflation would sooner or later jeopardize exports and boost imports.

Since population growth is relatively stable and to great extent exogenous, the positive effects on the growth of income tend to be transmitted to the growth rate of per capita income (as, for example, in the United Kingdom and in the United States). We can therefore conclude that, generally speaking, the correlation between the degree to which a country participates in the process of globalization and its rate of growth of per capita income does not seem to be spurious, although in each single case its sign and strength depends on the structural and institutional characteristics of the economy as well as on its policy strategies.

2.2   The social condition of sustainable development

The empirical evidence examined by economic historians *prima facie* suggests that, since the third decade of 19th century, income inequality showed a tendency to grow as the process of globalization spread and took root. In particular the important study by Bourguignon and

Morisson (2002) shows that their index of inequality "among the world citizens" increases from 1820 to 1992 with the only exception of a mild reduction in the period 1950–1960 that is too short to affect significantly the upward trend (see Figure 1.1). This has been interpreted by a few observers as a proof that, since globalization has characterized economic development for much of the period, it tends to increase inequality. The interpretation of this positive long-term correlation, however, is not as obvious as it seems at first sight.

To examine how and to what extent globalization may affect inequality, we have to distinguish inequality within countries from inequality between countries. The two components of world inequality, in fact, may depend on different factors[11] and require different policy responses.

As soon as we decompose the overall inequality index in its two components within and between countries, the picture becomes much more complex. First of all we see that the growing trend of global inequality (i.e. between world citizens) registered by Bourguignon and Morisson (2002) depends essentially on the index of inequality between countries. In addition, a more accurate analysis of the behavior of this index

Figure 1.1   Inequality of individual incomes, 1820–1992

Theil coefficients of inequality

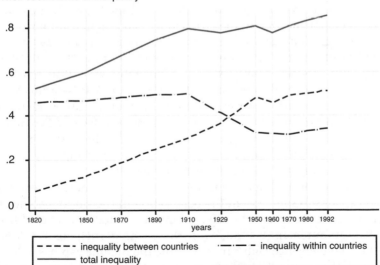

Source: Authors' elaboration on Bourguignon and Morisson (2002).

immediately falsifies the existence of a positive correlation between globalization and inequality between countries in the 20th century. Inequality between countries increased rapidly in the period 1910–1950 when globalization receded most of the time at a sustained pace. On the contrary, it diminished between 1950 and 1960 when the post-war process of globalization restarted with impetus, while it grew very slowly afterwards when globalization progressed at a sustained pace. The behavior of this index suggests that we cannot consider globalization as a major determinant of the inequality trend between countries, at least not in the 20th century. This is consistent with economic theory. As we maintained in section 2.1, globalization may increase the inequality between countries to the extent that it gives better opportunities of growth to the countries that actively participate in the process, opportunities from which the other countries that remain at the margin of the process are excluded.[12] At the same time, however, the spreading of competitive markets through countries has an equalizing effect between the participating countries to the extent that there is free movement between them not only of goods and services but also of productive factors and technology.[13] In the long period the second effect should predominate over the first, the more so the more the process of globalization extends to further countries. Economic historians show that the first process of globalization in the 19th century was very intense but had sizable effects on a restricted number of countries (European countries and their main overseas offshoots) while the second process of globalization in the 20th century had a significant impact on a much larger and growing group of countries (Toniolo, 2005). This could eventually trigger an inversion of the trend towards diminishing inequality between countries. Such a favorable evolution has been already detected by a few empirical studies (see, e.g., Sala-i-Martin, 2002). Not all the scholars, however, agree that between-countries inequality stopped growing since World War II. This is partially due to different data and methods of measurement.[14] In any case, the inequality between countries is still close to its maximum value in the Contemporary Era and calls for policy measures designed to improve the trend.

The degree of participation in the international market integration thus explains to some extent the polarization in the world income distribution that is observed today: countries isolated or excluded from globalization remain behind, while those who participate in it join a sort of "convergence club". In fact, while the income gap has reduced between the most industrialized countries, only a few nations – mainly in Europe and South-Eastern Asia – were able to join this "convergence club". On the contrary, the income distance with respect to the leading economies has further increased for many countries placed in other world areas. Thus, to quote just one Asian example, the per capita income of Bangladesh fell from 10% to 5% of the US per capita income in the period 1960–2000 and similar results apply in the same period to Latin America (e.g. Argentina from 45% to 35% of the US per capita income), Eastern Europe (e.g. Poland from 37% to 26%) and Africa (e.g. Nigeria from 6% to 2%). In the rest of the book we are going to ignore the likely, but weak, differentiated and evolving consequences of globalization on between-countries inequality focusing instead on within-country inequality.

The influence of globalization on within-country inequality seems, on the contrary, much more consistent with the empirical evidence. Bourguignon and Morisson (2002) find that the within-country Theil index of inequality registers a mild increase when globalization proceeds (first and second phases of globalization) and a sharp reduction when it recedes in the intermediate period. It is not difficult to suggest a plausible explanation of this correlation. To the extent that a country participates in the process of globalization, the additional impulse to growth tends to augment inequality because the diffusion of the ensuing increments in personal incomes takes time. The acceleration of development initially boosts profits in the most dynamic sectors and only later affects, and not always to the same degree, wages and employment in the same sectors. The diffusion of these increases to other sectors requires further time and is often incomplete. The same holds for the spatial spread of development from the most dynamic regions of a country to other areas. In the period of de-globalization (1915–1945) the spirit of cooperation and solidarity in the face of wartime troubles favored vigorous redistribution policies during the two World Wars (Sen, 2000, p.54). A similar phenomenon occurred as a consequence of the New Deal policies adopted by the United States and other industrialized countries to combat the drastic effects of the Great Depression in the 1930s. Analogously, in the Bretton Woods period the systematic adoption of social security measures inspired by the principles of the welfare state managed to obtain a further moderate reduction of inequality in many countries. The almost continuous succession of these periods interrupted for a long interval of time (1915–1970) the progressive increase in within-country inequality that began with the globalization process set off in the 1820s. Inequality started to grow again by the mid-1980s in most Organization for Economic Co-operation and Development (OECD) countries, including the United Kingdom and the United States (see Burniaux, *et al.*, 1999; Brandolini, 2002; Forster and Pearson, 2002; Atkinson, 2003; Brandolini and Smeeding, 2007). This was partly due to the great increase in higher-level incomes and the fact that weakened redistribution policies have not succeeded in completely compensating for the trend of growing inequality.

The average long-term trend of within-country inequality is in any case not particularly significant since it is very moderate and, after all, the final value of the series is slightly inferior to the initial value. In addition, an average global index such as that of Bourguignon and Morisson (2002) conceals different patterns of particular groups of countries. For this reason in this book we focus on the correlation between inequality and per capita income in single industrialized countries. This investigation turns out to be more revealing and has been extensively studied.

The implications of globalization for within-country inequality can be assessed more precisely on the basis of a significant research stream that has examined the available empirical evidence in different countries through rigorous econometric analyses. This enlightening literature began in 1955 with the publication by Kuznets of an article suggesting the existence of an inverted-U empirical relationship between per capita income and inequality (Figure 1.2). If this relationship, which has been

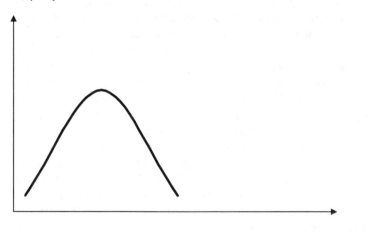

Figure 1.2   The Kuznets Curve

called "Kuznets curve", were generally valid, the process of globalization would eventually become sustainable from the point of view of within-country inequality, at least in the long term (see, e.g., Lomborg, 2001).

The theoretical plausibility of the Kuznets hypothesis is based on the structural characteristics of development. The latter typically entails a progressive concentration of population in urban centers where the distribution of income and economic opportunities is generally more unequal than in rural areas. The process of local penetration of development requires time and thus creates temporary income gaps even when there is the prospect of a homogeneous result. Nonetheless, the same process creates a "growing pressure of political and legal decisions affecting higher-level incomes" (Kuznets, 1955, p.9) which manifests itself in increasingly effective redistribution measures such as progressive income taxation.

Later studies seemed to initially confirm the Kuznets hypothesis (see Ahluwalia, 1976 and Robinson, 1976), but empirical support for it has progressively weakened since the '70s. The deterioration in the econometric fit of the Kuznets curve can be explained in the light of the historical trend of the data examined above, keeping in mind the existence of a temporal delay of a few years between the emergence of a change in the trend and the availability of data documenting it. The hypothesis proposed by Kuznets and the first studies corroborating it found support in the general attenuation of within-countries inequality occurring between the two wars and continuing in different forms during the Bretton Woods period. Since the 1980s, however, the econometric studies have increasingly reflected the widespread rise in within-countries inequality in many OECD countries since the late 1970s (see Chapter 2 for a more detailed analysis of these issues).

Some observers object that in order to evaluate the social effects of globalization we should focus on poverty rather than inequality. The eradication of poverty is considered a priority because it jeopardizes the survival and wealth of many people, while an increase in inequality is often claimed to be a side effect of growth that is seen as the crucial instrument to reduce poverty.[15] According to what Bhagwati himself "with some immodesty" called "the Bhagwati hypothesis and prescription", countries seem to have a similar distribution of income regardless of their structural and policy peculiarities so that any feasible strategy meant to reduce significantly poverty has to rely on the increase of the average income of the country, i.e. growth of per capita income (Bhagwati, 2004, p.54). Since globalization gives important opportunities to accelerate growth, the conclusion often drawn is that "globalization is good for the poor". This conclusion has been further supported by recent statistical and econometric studies (see in particular Dollar and Kraay, 2002). The weak point of this reasoning is that the impact of growth on poverty is significantly conditioned by its consequences on inequality. As a matter of fact, Bourguignon and Morisson (2002, p.733) show that, "had the world distribution of income remained unchanged since 1820, the number of poor people would be less than 1/4th than it is today and the number of extremely poor people would be less than 1/8th of what it is today". We may hope to be able to reduce rapidly the number of poor people only by promoting growth and, at the same time, a reduction in inequality. On the contrary, inegalitarian growth is unlikely to be sustainable in the long period. In this book, therefore, we consider both the reduction of poverty and the reduction of inequality as important requisites of sustainable development and crucial targets of economic policy.

Turning now to the evolution of poverty in the era of globalization, the optimists emphasize that the percentage of poor people over the world population diminished constantly from an appalling 94.4% in 1820 to a still dreadful 51.3% in 1992 (Bourguignon and Morisson, 2002, pp.731–732; see Figure 1.3).[16] Some authors claim that these

Figure 1.3   The long-run trend of poverty (< $2 a day)

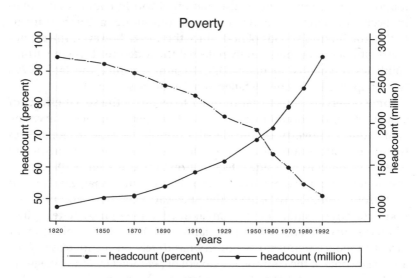

Source: Authors' elaboration on Bourguignon and Morisson (2002).

trends would be compatible with sustainable development because the percentage of poor people tends to converge towards zero (see, e.g., Lomborg, 2001, p.72). This assertion is not consistent with the available evidence, because in the meantime the absolute number of poor people continued to increase from 997.8 million in 1820 to 2,800.5 million in 1992 (see Figure 1.3). These figures show that the reduction in the percentage of poor people was impressive but not rapid enough to reduce the absolute number of poor people so that, *rebus sic stantibus*, it is not necessarily true that their percentage will tend to vanish. The percentage of poor people diminished in the last two centuries mainly because the population grew at a very high rate. The sharp reduction of population growth that is under way could even stop and reverse the declining trend of the percentage of poor people unless the latter will be further reinforced (according to some authors, this could happen by the second decade of this century). In addition, the optimism on the reduction of the poor rate seems to ignore the existence of a threshold of social instability beyond which the social fabric tends to disintegrate and the "social contract" binding citizens to their institutions tends to deteriorate. In our opinion, the current number of poor people in many countries is still persistently beyond this threshold. Finally, the reduction of the absolute number of poor people since the early 1980s is restricted only to the area of South-East Asia, while it increased almost everywhere.

Optimists underline that the percentage of extremely poor people (who earn less than $1 a day) diminished from 83.9% in 1820 to 23.7% in 1992. They also underline that, though the number of extremely poor people increased from 886.8 million in 1820 to 1,293.8 in 1992 (see Figure 1.4), it diminished after 1950 (when it was about 1,376.2 million people) and particularly in the last few years, decreasing up to 986 million people in 2004 (World Bank, 2007a). This result, however, cannot be considered as particularly satisfactory. First, the absolute number of poor people (that earn less than $2 a day) continued to increase also after 1950 from 1,805.6 to 2,800.5 million in 1992 (see Figure 1.3) and only in the very last few years their number has experienced a slight reduction (to 2,556 million in 2004) (World Bank, 2007a). Second, in a long period perspective a given purchasing power ($1 or $2 per day) may become an index of increasingly worse poverty through time since, with the progressive extension of markets and the reduction of population in rural areas, the opportunities of auto-consumption and barter progressively diminished through time. In addition, the decreasing

Figure 1.4   The long-run trend of extreme poverty (< $1 a day)

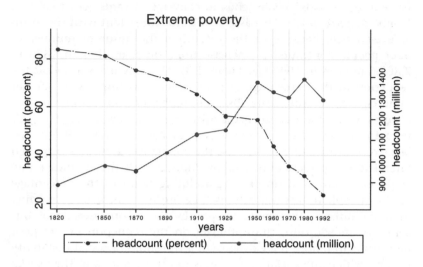

Source: Authors' elaboration on Bourguignon and Morisson (2002).

diffusion of poverty (as measured by the rate of poor people over the population) tends to isolate poor people even more from the rest of society. This increasing isolation may reinforce their feelings of frustration and anger against more advantaged people (see Chapter 5 on that). Therefore, a permanently high (or, even worse, increasing) *number* of poor people in society is not only ethically unacceptable, but also economically undesirable and politically unsustainable, since it may nurture violence and social conflicts that destabilize the macroeconomic system, and implies the need for high social transfers that could have alternative uses. Finally, as noted above, poverty causes an enormous waste of potential human resources. This is particularly true when the social protection net is inadequate. In the last 20 years the widespread weakening of the social protection net, the privatization of education and health services and the systematic search for more flexibility in the labor market have reduced the access of the less affluent classes to many fundamental economic opportunities. We can therefore conclude this first part of the analysis by noting that the trends of the globalization process after the Second World War, and in particular in the last two decades, cannot be considered fully compatible with the social requisites of sustainable development.

2.3 The environmental condition of sustainable development

We may now raise the question whether in the post-war period the trends of globalization were compatible with the environmental condition of sustainability. The question is difficult to answer as we do not have sufficiently long and comprehensive historical series on global environmental quality to make reliable statistical correlations.[17]

We must settle for an analysis of statistical correlations between per capita income and some specific indices of environmental deterioration for which we have adequate historical series. At the beginning of the 1990s some researchers observed that the curves representing these correlations typically go up and then down (Figure 1.5) exactly like the Kuznets curve (one of the first authors to notice this empirical trend was Panayotou, 1993). For this reason this alleged economic regularity came to be called "environmental Kuznets curve".

Two main explanations for this behavior have been put forward. It has been observed that in the first phase of industrial development the production structure undergoes radical changes, gradually reducing the percentage of the domestic income produced by agriculture and increasing that of heavy industry (steel, chemicals, etc.), which is much more polluting. There is typically a subsequent shift of production and

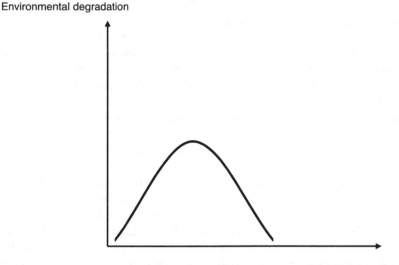

Figure 1.5   The Environmental Kuznets Curve

labor to light industry and services which are less polluting and consume less energy, improving the aggregate indices of environmental stress. Furthermore, while in the first phase of industrial development environmental quality is seen as a luxury, in a more mature phase of industrialization environmental quality starts to be considered crucial in improving the overall quality of life. The final users of goods and services then exert growing pressure on their suppliers to enhance the environmental quality of productive processes and goods offered. Voters simultaneously exert growing pressure on their political representatives to reinforce environmental policies. Due to the changes in the productive structure and preferences of economic agents, it is reasonable to assume that there exists a threshold of per capita income beyond which the indices of environmental deterioration tend to decrease. If this hypothesis were verified, the resulting message would be optimistic: to the extent that the process of globalization accelerates per capita income growth, it tends to reduce environmental deterioration, at least in the long term.

Further econometric research done along the lines of the "environmental Kuznets curve" initially supported the hypothesis that most significant indices of environmental deterioration were characterized by a behavior of this type (see Shafik, 1994), while later research raised serious doubts about its validity (see, e.g., the survey by Borghesi, 2001). The hypothesis was corroborated for some indices regarding problems whose effects are local, such as access to sewers and to drinking water, or the concentration in the atmosphere of sulfur dioxide (SO_2) or suspended particles, but not for indices of environmental problems whose effects are global, such as carbon dioxide (CO_2) emissions, or could be transferred elsewhere, such as solid urban waste treatment.

Even in cases where the data were compatible with the virtuous inversion implied by the environmental Kuznets curve, it is not clear whether in developing countries the hoped-for turning point will come before the threshold of ecological stability is crossed.[18] We must therefore conclude that the empirical evidence does not corroborate the hypothesis that the recent globalization process has brought about, or is due to produce, a general improvement in the environmental sustainability of development. Furthermore, some indices show a particularly worrisome N-shaped curve: after an improvement in the '80s and early '90s, the trend has recently switched again towards deterioration (as in the case, for example, of coliform bacteria). This is likely to be related to the recent weakening of environmental policies recently observed in many countries.[19]

While lacking sufficiently long and reliable historical series regarding global environmental deterioration, we can concentrate on some logical prerequisites of sustainable development, based on analytical considerations, which can direct economic and environmental policies towards reinforcing sustainable development. In particular, it may be demonstrated that the maximum sustainable growth rate of per capita income can be positive only if the intensity of environmental deterioration decreases at a rate that exceeds the population growth rate (see Chapter 3). We can essentially count on two factors to respect this crucial condition of sustainable economic growth: i) that technological progress be orientated towards a growing environmental compatibility of products and productive processes; ii) that consumers increasingly privilege products and services linked to better environmental quality. These two processes have been at work for some time, but they are rather slow so that they rarely manage to compensate for the effects of demographic growth. It is therefore necessary to speed them up with suitable environmental policy measures. This is particularly true for developing countries with higher demographic growth rates and fewer possibilities of reducing environmental deterioration.

The process of globalization has had an ambiguous influence on the environmental prerequisite of sustainability. From a technological point of view it favored the transfer to developing countries of "clean" technologies created by more advanced countries but also of toxic and radioactive waste and more polluting obsolete technologies rejected in developed countries. Regarding the cultural impact on preferences and behavior of developing countries, the process of globalization has led to a deceleration of demographic growth and heightened environmental awareness, but also fueled consumerism with its attendant woes of pollution and waste of natural resources.

2.4   Towards a causal analysis

The analysis provided so far has sought to reconstruct the evolution of empirical correlations between globalization and sustainable development in the post-war period.

With respect to the social condition of sustainability, the Bretton Woods phase managed to come closer to sustainability as a result of the narrowing of poverty (at least in percentage terms) and within-country inequality.[20] The phase which has taken over in the last two decades (i.e. in the so-called Washington Consensus period) has drifted away from social sustainability to the extent that the previous trend towards less within-country inequality has been reversed while the number of poor people increased (from 2,457 to 2,556 million people between 1981 and 2004) (World Bank, 2007a).

As for the environmental condition of sustainability, neither of the two periods has completely passed the test of sustainability. The systematic adoption since the 1970s of increasingly rigorous environmental policies has led to the improvement of some significant environmental indices. We have seen, however, that this is not true of all of them. Furthermore, most recent data show a worrying slowdown, and in some cases an inversion, of the trend towards better environmental quality.

As is well-known, the existence of a statistical correlation between two variables does not necessarily imply a causal relationship between them.[21] Thus we need a deeper analysis in order to base causal inferences on consolidated theoretical foundations and to identify precise effect-generating mechanisms. What follows is a tentative first step in this direction.

The most convincing argument supporting globalization is based on the fundamental theorems of welfare economics which demonstrate how, with an initial distribution of resources and under well-defined conditions that are not very realistic (see section 3 of this chapter and Chapter 8), a perfectly competitive market determines an optimal allocation of resources corresponding to maximum social welfare.[22]

We could assert that the *raison d'être* of economic globalization is to unify local markets into a single competitive market in order to allocate world resources in the best possible way and to maximize the well-being of the global community. If this is the goal, however, the process of post-war globalization has shown some basic failures. The application of this argument to global markets requires an adaptation of the conditions mentioned above. First of all the theorems of welfare economics require free movement across countries of goods and services as well as productive factors. Looking at the recent globalization process from this point of view, we can identify some significant anomalies.

As for the mobility of goods and services, developed countries have continued to maintain strict protectionist measures in sectors such as agriculture and textiles in which developing countries have a higher export potential. As pointed out in an Oxfam (2002) report, these protectionist measures dump costs on developing countries that are almost twice as much as what the latter receive as foreign aid. In addition, developed countries often react to spontaneous increases in imports from developing countries with new tariffs by calling on, often surreptitiously, anti-dumping laws (see Stiglitz, 2002).

Secondly, as far as productive factors are concerned, labor has undergone growing restrictions of movement in the last 20 years, while both theory and experience demonstrate that migratory movements are a formidable "last-resort" instrument for equalizing incomes across countries. Obviously, the preceding considerations do not exonerate us from doing everything in our power to bring development to countries with high emigration flows so as to offer effective alternatives to emigration. This is the only acceptable way for a civilized country to stem immigration flows. Moreover, unjustified administrative or police restrictions would risk putting a constraint on the economic growth of the countries due to the lack of labor power in certain areas or sectors.

Movements of capital, on the other hand, have been almost completely liberalized without discriminating between speculative and entrepreneurial flows. This has produced a few benefits, such as an increase in FDI in developing countries, but has given rise to serious problems such as accentuated financial instability.[23] The sharp increase in flows of speculative capital ("hot money") in an era of floating exchange rates has contributed to destabilize economies at the first hint of a crisis and made it more difficult to control them. The flows of "hot money" shifting very rapidly from one country to another have increased tremendously since the 1970s, jeopardizing the effectiveness of any type of economic policy. As summarized by Chomsky (1999, p.29): "in 1971, 90% of international financial transactions concerned the real economy – either commercial or long-term investments – and 10% were speculative. In 1990, the percentages were turned upside down...with daily flows frequently higher than the entire reserves in foreign currency of the seven major industrial powers". In addition: "of the 1,300 billion dollars which feed daily global transactions, only a small part is linked to movements of productive capital, from savings of a country that are transformed into investments in another country" (Tobin, 1999).

Moreover, recent econometric studies show that in the existing international markets, that are structurally imperfect and lack international regulatory institutions enforcing effective controls, contrary to pure theory the capital flows tend to move from poor countries towards rich ones (this empirical trend is often called the "Lucas paradox" after the name of the author who emphasized it: see Lucas, 1990).

The growing difficulties of the globalization process in complying with the requisites of sustainability are clearly linked to these structural anomalies. They also depend on the evolution of economic and environmental policies. Indeed, the sustainability of development in the last 20 years has been jeopardized in many countries by excessive faith in unfettered markets, causing a weakening in the social protection net and redistribution policies. The weakening of the welfare state, the progressive privatization of education and health services, the reduction of progressive taxation and the systematic increase in the flexibility of labor relations have led to greater internal inequalities, while protectionism towards developing countries, reduction in international aid and the restriction of migratory labor flows have led to greater income inequality between countries. By the same token, progress made in the 1980s and early 1990s regarding environmental sustainability is currently being undermined in many countries by weakening environmental policies. The difficulty of implementing the Kyoto agreements after its signature in 1997 is just one of the relevant examples.

Regarding the philosophy of regulation in international markets, the present one has a far different influence on markets with respect to what took place in the period following the Bretton Woods agreements. The latter were conceived in an era in which the limitations of the market economy, as witnessed in the Great Depression of the 1930s, were still deeply impressed in the collective memory. Thus an apparatus of institutions and regulations was set up to control international markets for the prevention, or at least attenuation, of market "failures".

This regulatory apparatus was based on the following main institutional principles: i) a system of fixed exchange rates to stabilize expectations of international operators; ii) the GATT rounds, an international negotiating table aimed at the progressive liberalization of the exchange of goods, services and productive factors; iii) the IMF, with the task of preventing, through anti-cyclical financial interventions, local deficits of aggregate demand to spread deflationist impulses into other economies; iv) the WB, with the task of financing structural interventions to eliminate poverty. This regulatory structure did to some extent succeed in mitigating problems linked to poverty and inequality by promoting a certain degree of compliance with the social condition of sustainability. The same cannot be said of the environmental condition of sustainability, mainly because of a still very low public concern for environmental issues.

The recent redefinition of the system of international markets has significantly altered the regulatory system and thus its impact on sustainable development. The new regulatory system of international markets in place since the early 1980s, commonly called the "Washington consensus", can be summarized in the following way: i) a system of flexible exchange rates which deregulated the exchange market and set off a process of systematic deregulation of markets; ii) the creation in 1995 of the WTO so as to complete the liberalization of the exchange of goods, services and capital; iii) the concession of financial support from the IMF to countries in difficulty subject to their adoption of structural measures aimed at deregulating and privatizing national markets and at introducing monetary and budgetary austerity measures; iv) a *de facto* subordination of structural interventions of the WB to previous approval from the IMF, aimed to verify compliance with its policy directives in the recipient countries.

Within the new regulatory system it is possible to identify a few causal mechanisms that may explain the recent worsening of the social condition of sustainability. In particular, the WTO has often interpreted the trade constraints introduced by local laws or international agreements, even those with genuine social or environmental purposes, as non-tariff barriers incompatible with free trade and forced their elimination (see Chapter 6). The same organization has also extended the range of its authority to sectors such as the defense of intellectual property rights (TRIPS [Trade-Related Aspects of Intellectual Property] agreement) which entails a considerable redistribution of wealth from (usually poor) countries using patents to (usually rich) countries which register most patents (see Legrain, 2002, and Tisdell, 2001). The low transparency of decision-making and the real difficulty of guaranteeing the active participation of member countries, especially developing ones, has at times led to biased rulings (see Esty, 2001, and Francioni, 2002).

In addition, in the last 20 years the IMF has progressively modified its original (broadly speaking "Keynesian") philosophy of intervention to a new stance favoring privatization and deregulation. In addition it has often recommended restrictive budget policies in situations where there was a lack of aggregate demand (Stiglitz, 2002). These policies are based on the conviction that unfettered markets are able to self-regulate themselves and resolve any sort of economic problem in the best possible way. Economic theory from Adam Smith onwards has often disputed this position, stressing the nature and significance of the limitations of markets as well as the necessity to regulate them to avoid their "failures" (see Chapter 8). Theory and historical experience have also shown the important repercussions of state failures. It is therefore necessary to keep in mind both aspects of the dilemma without forgetting that failure on the part of public authorities can be linked to processes of regulation as well as of deregulation. A recent example of the latter phenomenon is the privatization process in Russia in the 1990s (see Stiglitz, 2002). In many cases this has led to significant increases in structural unemployment as well as to the suspension of monetary transfers aimed at supporting low-income families and environmental protection. Generally speaking, the goal of monetary stability has often overridden the original key-objective of full employment.

Thus far we have considered a few major macroeconomic aspects of sustainability. We intend to consider also a few equally important microeconomic aspects. The economy as a whole can be sustainable only if it is based on a network of sustainable enterprises. Empirical research suggests that the longest-lasting and, in the medium-long term, most profitable businesses are those with a longer time horizon that at the same time pay closer attention to the interests of all stakeholders.[24] This is also confirmed by the recently introduced indices which synthesize the stock market performance of the most sustainable companies. These indices perform not worse than the general ones, as can be seen from a comparison between the *Dow Jones Sustainability Group Index* and the general Dow Jones index (see Chapter 7). The recent globalization process has jeopardized businesses' social responsibility and thus their sustainability in the medium/long term. The growing geographical dispersion of productive processes has made it more difficult to ensure active participation and control on the part of stakeholders. There has also been a progressive shortening of the time horizon of decision-making in markets unified by Internet and deregulation and showing an increasing degree of imitation (often called herd behavior). This has induced many enterprises to focus on impressive short-term results even at the expense of their sustainability in the long term. Short-termist firms are the main responsible for a third category of economic failures that we suggest to call "corporate failures" (see Chapters 7 and 9).

To sum up, the new regulatory system of national and international markets that has emerged in the last 20 years has weakened the social sustainability of development and is unable to assure the environmental sustainability of development. The empirical correlations that we have identified seem to be fairly supported, albeit inconclusively, by precise causal mechanisms, some of which have been touched upon. Analysis of the data at our disposal does not justify either catastrophic pessimism or quietist optimism. The process of globalization since 1820 has been instrumental to an extraordinary increase in per capita incomes and world population but has not always been fully successful in solving the social and environmental problems raised by economic development. Social and environmental policies have been enacted to attenuate these problems by consolidating the sustainability of world development. These problems persist, however, and their solution entails more vigorous and far-sighted policy interventions (see Chapter 9).

3 Foundations

In this final section of the introductory chapter we wish to outline the theoretical foundations of the main arguments developed in the subsequent chapters, briefly and very partially anticipated in the preceding section.

3.1 The virtues of an ideal market of perfect competition and its limits

As anticipated in section 2, the main economic argument in favor of free markets and their globalization lies on the claim that an unfettered perfect-competition market is the most efficient way of coordinating the economic activity of rational individuals (the evolution of liberal ideas based on this proposition is reconstructed and discussed in Chapters 8 and 9). In this perspective, we could assert that the economic rationale of globalization is that of unifying the local markets into a single competitive market in order to realize the optimal allocation of world resources and to maximize the welfare of the world population. In this section we intend to discuss this crucial claim from the point of view of the contemporary theory of competitive markets and economic policy.

In the second part of the 19th century, virtues and limits of markets have been discussed mainly on the basis of the Paretian approach to the general equilibrium model. Pareto was the first economist who realized that the path-breaking contribution by Walras to general equilibrium theory permitted a much more rigorous scrutiny of the soundness of the invisible-hand argument. He started thus a research program meant to clarify this point, a program that progressed quite slowly because of the conceptual complexity and mathematical sophistication involved in the related issues.

Pareto succeeded in providing a first clarification of the scope and limits of the invisible hand in a general equilibrium model by introducing the famous criterion of optimality that is still routinely used in the economic literature (Pareto, 1906). He maintained that a general equilibrium position realizes the optimal allocation of resources within a given society in the sense that it is impossible to improve the welfare of one agent without reducing the welfare of another agent (what was subsequently called a Pareto optimum). On the basis of this precise, though limited, concept of social optimum, he pointed out that in a

general equilibrium model the efficiency issue concerning the allocation of resources is sharply severed from the fairness issue concerning
the initial and final distribution of resources. The efficient allocation
implemented by the model is relative to the initial distribution of
resources. The model implies an efficiency frontier characterized by a
continuum of equilibria corresponding to different initial distributions
of resources. The fairness of the final distribution of resources between
the economic agents is thus crucially dependent on the fairness of
the initial distribution of resources. Some economist claimed that the
re-allocation of resources performed by a general equilibrium model is
in principle fair as the income produced accrues to the factors of production in proportion to their marginal productivity (Wicksteed, 1894;
Clark, 1899). Even if we accept this controversial argument,[25] it is clear
that the marginal productivity of a certain factor depends on the initial
distribution of resources among factors. In particular the productivity
of the labor exerted by a certain person depends on her initial wealth
that affects the access to economic opportunities. A lower education,
for example, may exclude an agent from the most desirable economic
opportunities and reduce the efficiency of her choices in the implementation of the accessible opportunities. In this broader sense, the
efficiency of allocation is not independent of the fairness of the initial
distribution of resources. There are reasons to believe, in particular,
that a more egalitarian initial distribution would affect the technological coefficients in such a way to shift outward the efficiency frontier.
This has been a common conviction expressed by the most eminent
exponents of economic liberalism (see Chapter 8).

As we have anticipated in section 1.1 the argument in favor of a fair
amount of initial equality very often advanced by classical and updated
liberalism does not require initial equality of wealth but only equal
access to economic opportunities. This criterion of fairness does not
forbid a meritocratic distribution of income proportional to the quality
and quantity of individual effort but, in principle, imposes a constraint
also on the final distribution of wealth. In a multiperiod approach, the
final distribution of wealth in a certain period becomes the initial distribution of the following period. The requirement of equal initial
opportunities posits a constraint also on the distribution of income
within each period described by the general equilibrium model.

Finally, the pursuit of efficiency by a perfect-competition market may
itself bring about serious distributive problems. In fact it may easily
lead to what economists call a "corner solution", i.e. an equilibrium in
which certain economic resources obtain a null, or very low, price

(Schotter, 1985, pp.66–80). This is not a problem from the point of view of the mathematical calculus or of the strictly economic allocation of resources but may have highly undesirable social consequences. The wage offered to certain categories of labor may be too low to justify their employment or could remain below the poverty level (working poor). This is because from the point of view of a perfect-competition market it is not efficient to employ these categories of labor at a higher wage. Unskilled workers in developing countries, for example, may be considered so abundant by the market that their "shadow wage" is zero or near-zero. The pure *laissez-faire* principle maintains that in such a situation the labor force emarginated from the labor market should just retrain itself to become more desirable to the market. Emarginated workers, however, may not have sufficient wealth to invest in their skills. This explains why a series of measures have been introduced to cope with these serious problems: unemployment benefits, gratuitous training schemes, and other social benefits (see Chapter 8). Notwithstanding all these measures, a "rational" response of emarginated workers may be to allocate part of their time in illegal activities. This explains why crime is correlated with unemployment and poverty, the more so the weaker are the social provisions for unemployed and/or poor people. This may be interpreted as an endogenous negative externality of competitive markets that updated liberalism struggled to minimize (see Chapter 8).

Summing up, the existing knowledge on the model of perfect competition suggests that in principle such a model deals well with allocation problems but is unable to take care by itself of distribution problems. A second limit of the model is that there is no reason to believe that the equilibrium of the system described by the model is unique. We know, on the contrary, that the generic case is that of multiple equilibria. A further limit is that, even if we are able to demonstrate that its equilibrium is unique, it is not necessarily stable. There are several important markets that are fairly *unstable* from three different points of view. Competitive markets tend to be *institutionally* unstable in the sense that they tend to lose their competitive nature in consequence of the exploitation of scale and scope economies, due to monopolist and oligopolist practices or to the discretionary power of agents outside the equilibrium position. In addition, markets may be *dynamically* unstable in the sense that they do not easily recover the equilibrium position whenever they are displaced from it by a shock. Finally, markets may be *structurally* unstable in the sense that a small shock may alter the qualitative characteristics of their dynamic behavior.[26]

We have discussed so far some crucial limits of the ideal model of perfect competition without questioning its presuppositions. From the interpretive point of view we are mainly interested, however, in the properties of the real markets which are quite different from those of the ideal model of perfect-competition market. Economic liberalism never denied the existence and relevance of the gap between the ideal market of perfect competition and real markets which, for the sake of brevity, we are going to call "market gap". The strategy adopted to cope with this problem has typically been that of assuming the ideal model of perfect competition as a target to approach through policy under the implicit, but crucial, assumption that the smaller the market gap, the smaller are the allocation distortions and the ensuing loss of social welfare (see Proposition 5 in the Appendix to Chapter 8).

3.2   The market gap

As mentioned above, a competitive market realizes the optimal allocation of economic resources among alternative uses only under very stringent assumptions underlying the abstract model of perfect competition. The trouble is that real markets do not comply with these conditions. It could be claimed, however, that in principle the process of globalization pushed the real markets closer to the abstract model of perfect competition by enhancing their extension and thickness, and that for this reason it improved their economic and financial efficiency. This argument, however, cannot be pushed too far since the global market gap is still very large for a host of reasons:

i) Markets are *incomplete*; in particular most future markets are missing. It is true that a missing market may be established through apt interventions that remove the cause of its absence (for example, undefined property rights on a certain good) or introduce a surrogate for it by means of ad hoc devices (such as Arrow securities). It can be argued, however, that in principle markets cannot be fully completed, in particular as far as future markets are concerned. As one of the most profound thinker on the properties of competitive markets, maintained:

> A complete general equilibrium system, as in Debreu (1959), requires markets for all contingencies in all future periods. Such a system could not exist. First, the number of prices would be so great that search would become an insuperable obstacle; that is, the value of knowing prices of less consequence, those on events remote in time or of low probability, would be less than the cost so that these markets could not come into being. Second, markets conditional on

privately observed events cannot exist by definition (Arrow, 1987, p.209).

The optimal intertemporal allocation of resources cannot be realized by the real markets even if they were fairly competitive, not only because most future markets are missing but also because the more expectations refer to the distant future the more they are liable to be systematically incorrect, as an unavoidable consequence of the intrinsic unpredictability of complex phenomena.

ii) The *uncertainty* intrinsic in the working of markets raises serious problems. The ideal model of perfect competition is consistent only with weak forms of uncertainty whenever the expected values of the relevant variables may be represented by fully reliable additive probability distributions. This is reasonable only when the observed stochastic processes are quite familiar to the decision-makers (DMs) and may be assumed to be stationary (Lucas, 1976). In all the other cases the uncertainty over the expected values of the relevant variables is likely to distort significantly the allocation of resources. In particular more radical forms of uncertainty imply that the expectations of economic agents are in general neither correct nor rational (see, e.g., Vercelli, 2005).

iii) The costs and benefits not registered by markets, called *externalities*, bring about sizeable distortions in the allocation of resources, even in perfect-competition markets. In the real world the economic externalities are ubiquitous because markets are incomplete preventing a correct registration of all the costs and benefits of economic decisions, and because the property rights on goods and resources are not always well defined, as is typical with many environmental resources such as the global commons (water, air, biodiversity, etc.).

iv) The *transaction costs* that the economic agents have to bear to finalize desired exchanges and contracts are often quite considerable. These costs are involved by the decentralized exchange of private property rights. In particular the costs necessary to match demand and supply may involve significant material costs, such as travel costs, or immaterial costs, such as those involved by the gathering and elaboration of information about the main characteristics of potential demand and supply. As Niehans (1987, p.676) argues, "in modern economies a substantial, and probably increasing, proportion of resources is allocated to transaction costs". The more a market economy develops the more the contractual clauses of exchanges have to be made explicit. This implies increasing transaction costs as contracts are drawn up by lawyers, records have to be kept, and compliance needs to be enforced through legal action. Transaction costs inevitably reduce, *ceteris paribus*, social welfare as they reduce the set of consumption options and suppress exchanges that would otherwise have been mutually beneficial.

v) The rationality of real economic agents is bounded from the cognitive, operational and pragmatic points of view. The ideal perfect-competition market requires that the rationality of the agents is unbounded in each of these dimensions. In fact, the invisible-hand argument requires that each agent maximizes the individual objective function. This is possible only if the DM never makes systematic errors, either cognitive or pragmatic, a condition that requires access to unlimited information and an unbounded capability to calculate the consequences of each choice for each possible state and to realize promptly the option chosen in practice. This implies heroic cognitive requirements: a "true" representation of reality and correct expectations (apart from the purely stochastic errors admitted by the rational expectations hypothesis). Otherwise, the agents are liable to make systematic errors that bring about sub-optimal choices. These individual deviations from the invisible-hand prescriptions may be propagated and determine non-uniqueness and instability of equilibrium.

In addition, when rationality is bounded, even if the agents effectively maximize their own perceived objective function, it is possible that they neglect a better option that could be reached only in a cooperative way by apparently violating the principle of individual maximization. The main argument to prove this point is the well-known prisoner's dilemma.[27] In this sense, rationality has been often considered "the Achilles heel of the free market argument" (Schotter, 1985, p.47). This situation is typical whenever public goods and/or externalities are involved in the choice.

A further delicate implication of unbounded rationality is complete, and therefore symmetric, information for the DMs. When cognitive rationality is bounded, information may be asymmetric. In this case, individual maximization may lead to unethical and socially inefficient behavior (moral hazard) that leads to sub-optimal social welfare. In such a situation, whenever the ethical standards are weak and/or heterogeneous, the only alternative is that of regulating the markets.

Taking into due account the limits of the ideal model of perfect competition discussed in the preceding section and the much wider and deeper limits of the real markets discussed in this section, we have to draw the conclusion that for sound reasons global markets cannot be left fully unregulated. Regulation is in principle necessary for (a) maintaining and perfecting competition, (b) approaching equilibrium as much as possible in order to optimize the allocation of resources, (c) assuring full employment, maintaining a distribution of resources sufficiently fair in order to guarantee equal access to economic opportunities and to minimize social evils such as poverty and malnutrition, (d) improving intertemporal allocation of resources (in particular the intergenerational distribution of resources), (e) reducing uncertainty and mitigating its effects, (f) internalizing externalities. These interventions should take account that the economic agents are characterized by bounded rationality and partly endogenous preferences, so that their reaction to policy interventions is difficult to forecast.

This general perspective on the properties of competitive markets and the need of minimal but efficient regulation applies in particular in the environmental and social spheres that are crucial for sustainable development because:

i) *Uncertainty* is particularly serious since the interaction between the biosphere and economic development is extremely complex.[28] The same may be claimed for the social consequences of economic development. This implies, in particular, an overvaluation of short-run costs and benefits to the detriment of long-run sustainability of the world development.

ii) Markets for environmental resources are highly *incomplete* since property rights on natural resources are often undefined. As for the civil rights and the quality of life, a reduction to marketable goods would be extremely narrow. In addition, most future markets are missing leaving without a benchmark the long-term intergenerational considerations crucial for sustainability. The allocation of environmental and social goods is thus bound to be sizably distorted in the absence of an apt regulation of markets.

iii) For the above reasons *externalities* are bound to have a crucial role in this field. Strong uncertainty and the lack of markets prevent a fair assessment of environmental costs and benefits by the actual system of unregulated markets. Property rights may be partially substituted by pollution marketable permits but the transaction costs for establishing them are initially very high and are unlikely to be borne spontaneously by unregulated markets.

iv) *Instability* may be specifically important in the environmental and social fields. Because of its long-term nature, for example, environmental investment is not considered a priority when a crisis develops or whenever the relevant prices are volatile. For example the marked volatility of the price of oil has discouraged serious long-term investment for substituting its use with renewable and/or less polluting sources of energy.

The trouble with the argument developed so far is that, if market failures require some amount of regulation, the failures of regulation are no less harmful. Both the experience and the theoretical analysis of bureaucratic and political processes have shown that the failures of regulation, often called "state failures", are systematic and may be worse than those of the markets. In addition, the failures of regulation are much more visible than the market failures that they are supposed to mend. In consequence of this, disillusionment on the efficiency of regulation has been so strong that an irrational faith has spread, particularly since the 1970s, on the unlimited power of unregulated markets. The ensuing process of deregulation has been successful in dismantling many degenerated forms of regulation and should go on to pursue this specific purpose, but in a few important cases it has gone too far, dismantling also the necessary forms of regulation such as those that set environmental, health, humanitarian and ethical standards. In addition, the relationship between regulators and regulated agents happened to be a sort of evolutionary game: regulated agents always try to elude the rules set by the regulators who must therefore continuously update these rules. Therefore a continuous process of re-regulation must accompany the process of deregulation meant to dismantle obsolete or inefficient rules in order to introduce the most efficient necessary rules in the evolving context. Of course the regulation of markets must be kept to a minimum level in order to avoid as far as possible the disruptive potential of regulation failures but cannot be altogether absent.

The main troubles with globalization arise precisely because the regulation of global markets is inefficient and is exerted in an unsatisfactory way. The local regulating institutions have been progressively displaced and weakened by the process of globalization. As for international organizations, the system of UN institutions has succeeded to some extent in defending, sometimes upgrading, the humanitarian, social, and environmental standards of economic activity but the active and democratic participation of people from member countries (particularly in developing countries) was wanting because of their institutional structure and increasingly frequent de-legitimizing action on the part of some powerful member countries that, for example, do not pay regularly their fees. Furthermore, the international institutions appointed at Bretton Woods to regulate the post-war world economy (IMF and WB) have been increasingly criticized for the questionable criteria of their interventions. While, however, the system of active *regulation* of global markets has been progressively weakened and delegitimized, the process of their *deregulation* has been progressively strengthened by the GATT agreements that culminated in the Uruguay Round and in the institution in 1995 of the WTO. In the first years of its activity (1995–99) the WTO contributed greatly to accelerating the deregulation of global markets, but its power, which proved to be quite effective, was exerted without the necessary transparency, accountability, and active participation of the stakeholders.

A model of regulation of global markets that relies mainly on their systematic deregulation, privatization, and the widespread elimination of humanitarian, social, and environmental standards is inconsistent with the social and environmental sustainability of development at the world level. This does not imply that globalization should be stopped or reversed. Inward-oriented policies (in particular the abuse of protectionist measures) may shield production and employment in the short period from external shocks only at the cost of shrinking the opportunities for domestic enterprises to innovate and increase productivity, and of enhancing at the same time harmful regulation by local authorities. This is borne out by the history of the 20th century. The retreat from globalization starting with World War I, reinforced by the 1930s crisis, and protracted by World War II, badly affected all regions and in particular developing countries. Similarly, in the 1970s and 1980s the Latin American and African countries that adopted inward-oriented policies lagged behind world growth, while the countries of Asia that adopted in the same period outward-oriented policies became some of the most dynamic in the world economy.

A viable model of sustainable globalization, however, requires a radical reform of the institutions with the responsibility of regulating global markets. This reform should assure their transparency and accountability, as well as the democratic participation of member countries and stakeholders, and the progressive upgrading of ethical and environmental standards of global economic activity.

2
Inequality, Poverty and the Kuznets Curve

1   Globalization and inequality within countries: the role of factors endowment

In this chapter we intend to analyze in some more detail the impact of globalization on within-country inequality. Income distribution became more unequal after liberalization in four large countries that account by themselves for much of the world population, namely China, India, Indonesia and Russia (Lindert and Williamson, 2003). Inequality increased mainly in globalizing countries with large regions cut off from the globalization process, such as rural and hinterland China or rural India. In some cases access to trade reforms and benefits was limited to an extremely small minority, as in Russia where only a few oligarchs took part in the internationalization process (Flemming and Micklewright, 2000). These observations suggest that the differential access to the process of globalization largely contributed to increasing inequality.

Despite the rise of inequality in the large economies mentioned above, the population-weighted general index of within-country inequality has increased only slightly since the 1960s (see Chapter 1). In the post-war period, in fact, within-country inequality has followed different and sometimes opposite patterns in different countries. It is difficult to find a general explanation for these differences. An interesting hypothesis relates them to the standard factor endowment trade theory by Heckscher-Ohlin (Wood, 1994). This well-known model, in fact, predicts that in each globalizing country the process of commodity market integration should increase income for the abundant factor and reduce it for the scarce factor. Since unskilled labor is relatively more abundant in the South, globalization should increase unskilled wages relatively to skilled wages and returns on property, thus lowering inequality in developing countries. The opposite applies in the North where skilled labor is relatively more abundant, so that globalization is expected to increase wage dispersion. The Heckscher-Ohlin model, therefore, implies a negative correlation between globalization and inequality in the South and a positive one in the North. Given the positive relationship between globalization and per capita income discussed above, this seems also to imply a convex relationship between per capita income, measured on the horizontal axis, and income inequality, measured on the vertical axis (see Figure 2.1).

The empirical evidence, however, gives only limited support to this conjecture. In some countries, the data seem consistent with the predictions of the model. For instance, several studies have observed a sharp rise in wage inequality in the UK and the USA since the early 1980s (see Chapter 1 and Freeman and Oostendorp, 2000). Similarly, three East Asian countries (Korea, Singapore and Taiwan) showed a decline in wage inequality in the 1960s and 1970s after liberalization. Empirical evidence for other countries, however, is at odds with what the theory would lead us to expect. Wage gaps, in fact, increased in several Latin American countries during the 1980s following their liberalization process. The different timing and historical context in

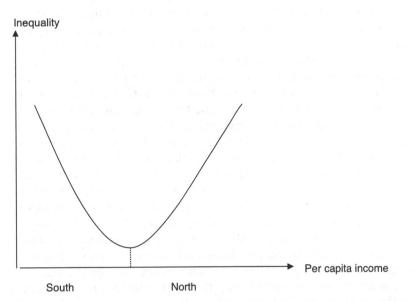

Figure 2.1   Inequality-income relationship derived from the Heckscher-Ohlin model

which liberalization occurred may explain the different effect of free trade on inequality in Latin America compared to East Asia (Wood, 1997). The Mexican liberalization, for instance, took place at the same time as the entry into the world market of China and other Asian countries with a relatively more abundant pool of unskilled workers than Mexico. The rise of inequality in Mexico in that period is, therefore, consistent with the simple Heckscher-Ohlin model. But the latter is generally insufficient to account for the empirical evidence. Income distribution is affected by many other factors beyond those underlined by the standard trade theory (O'Rourke, 2001). For example, the increasing wage dispersion in Latin American countries might depend on the evolution of education in those countries, on political events reducing the power of trade unions and therefore of unskilled workers or on the introduction of new technologies that weakened them even further in favor of skilled workers.

2   The Kuznets curve

Many empirical studies have tried to estimate the impact of trade liberalization on intra-national inequality. While they arrive at conflicting results as regards the sign of the trade coefficient, most of them find that openness has a limited direct impact on within-country inequality.[29] By increasing per capita income, however, trade liberalization may also have an indirect effect on inequality through income growth, as is claimed by the literature on the Kuznets curve (henceforth KC for the sake of brevity). As mentioned in Chapter 1, Kuznets (1955) observed that inequality tends to increase during the early stages of growth to decrease later on, describing an inverted-U shaped relationship between per capita income (on the horizontal axis) and income inequality (on the vertical axis) (see *retro* Chapter 1, Figure 1.2). It is interesting to notice that the direct and the indirect effects of trade liberalization on inequality might run in opposite directions. In other words, the direct impact of globalization on inequality described by the factor endowment theory suggests that inequality should decrease in developing countries and increase in developed countries. This effect, however, might be counterbalanced by the indirect impact of globalization upon inequality through income growth that would tend to increase inequality in the South and decrease it in the North, as described by the KC.

The KC was very popular during the 1970s when it was taken as one of the very few empirical regularities of the economy (Ahluwalia, 1976; Robinson, 1976). Later contributions, however, started to question the evidence brought forward in its support. Kuznets himself recognized that his hypothesis, while compatible with the data examined, had yet to be fully confirmed and expressed the desire that it be corroborated by further research: "in winding up my work, I am painfully aware of the scarce reliability of the information I have presented. This study consists of possibly 5% empirical information and 95% speculation, part of which boils down to pure wishful thinking" (Kuznets, 1955, p.26).

The data currently available on inequality were, and still are, scarce and sometimes unreliable, especially in developing countries, because the data collection is difficult and costly. In the data set on inequality collected by Deininger and Squire (1996), for instance, only a low percentage of the data are evaluated as "high-quality" by the authors. Inequality data, moreover, present international and intertemporal comparability problems because of definitional differences across countries and over time. Beyond that, some authors found that different inequality indices may give different results (Anand and Kanbur, 1993). Others pointed out that income explains only a small part of the variance of inequality that depends also on other development-related variables such as secondary school attendance and past population growth (Papanek and Kyn, 1986; Fishlow, 1995).

Some of the results in the literature, moreover, might be biased by the failure to account for the feedback effects that inequality may have on income growth. Early contributions on the KC considered, in fact, income growth as an exogenous process, whereas more recent studies have shown that growth is endogenously affected by inequality. For instance, as we will see in Chapter 5, inequality affects health that in its turn impinges on growth. Moreover, high inequality generates tensions between social classes and/or ethnic groups that cause strikes (reducing the total number of working hours and thus the GDP), discourage foreign investments and, in the worst cases, may also contribute to civil wars, as occurred in Africa. Finally, high income disparities tend to lower social cooperation, which can adversely affect the supply of public services. Therefore, even in the few cases in which the KC is robust to the use of different inequality indices and additional explanatory variables, these possible feedback effects of inequality on income growth may prevent the economies from running along the curve. Many econometric studies have confirmed that higher inequality can have negative effects on income growth (Perotti, 1996; Barro, 2000; Easterly, 2001). If inequality gets sufficiently high along the KC, this can slow down income growth or even prevent it from persisting. As a consequence, the desired shift to the declining part of the KC can take longer or even become impossible if inequality has recessive effects that move the economy back along the horizontal axis. This is particularly likely to occur if inequality overcomes the threshold level above which social stability falls apart.

Furthermore, several works claimed that the KC applies fairly well to cross-country studies, but fails in time-series analysis, therefore it does not necessarily describe the evolution of single countries over time (Clarke, 1992; Li *et al.*, 1998). The studies that used time-series analysis to investigate the income-inequality relationship on a country-by-country basis found little support for the KC hypothesis (e.g. Deininger and Squire, 1996; Bruno *et al.*, 1998). More generally, cross-country regressions have been criticized in the empirical growth literature for their ad hoc specifications and for the limited robustness of the estimations (see Banerjee and Duflo, 2003). Therefore, as Piketty (2005, p.7) has argued, more can be learnt by examining historical case studies than by analyzing "the reduced-form, cross-country regressions routinely run by economists during the 1990s, from which it is fair to say that we did not learn very much".

Finally, in several developed countries that are more free-market oriented (particularly Canada, the UK and the US) the top income shares have followed a U-shaped evolution over the last century rather than a Kuznets-type path (Atkinson, 2003; Piketty and Saez, 2003 and 2006). Income inequality decreased dramatically in most countries between the two World Wars due to the solidaristic policies meant to fight the social effects of war and the great depression and to the severe shocks to capital holdings (destruction, inflation, bankrupts, fiscal pressure to finance the wars) that caused a large reduction of top income shares. In the post-war period, the income share accruing to the richest decile in developed countries remained stable or slightly decreased because of the introduction of tax progressivity and the strengthening of welfare state policies, but since the 1970s it rose again up to pre-war levels in the English speaking countries, thus describing a U-shaped curve (see *retro* Chapter 1). This was mainly due to the weakening of social insurance transfers and the progressive diffusion of neoliberal policies. In particular, there was a surge in the income of the top executives whose average salary increased dramatically with respect to the wages of unskilled workers so that top salary earners have now replaced top capital earners at the top of the income distribution.

These results, together with the methodological pitfalls discussed above, lead us to believe that the quadratic relationship between inequality and per capita income suggested by the KC is not generally sound. If so, the globalization process cannot be considered as socially sustainable in the long run in the absence of appropriate policy interventions, since the economic growth that this process tends to generate in the participating countries does not necessarily reduce inequality within them.

As anticipated in the preceding chapter, the early success of the KC may be explained as a fairly accurate description of an historical pattern observed from the beginning of 19th century to the 1960s rather than as a genuine economic regularity.

In order to have a more comprehensive vision of the social sustainability of the globalization process, in the next section we examine its effects on poverty. Although the latter is closely related to inequality, it concerns other important aspects that are overlooked in the inequality debate and that can be considered as complementary to the ones discussed so far.

3 Globalization and poverty

The impact that the world economic integration process may have on poverty is currently the object of a particularly hot debate both in the academic field and outside it. To get a deeper understanding of the complex mechanisms underlying this relationship, it is important to identify some of the main channels through which globalization may affect poverty.

In general, trade and financial openness may generate a virtuous exposure to external competition. This increases the country's efficiency and productivity, leading to growing per capita income that may benefit also the poor sectors of the population (see *retro* Chapter 1). A similar positive impact may derive from an easier access to technological progress and from better opportunities for human capital accumulation that globalization may produce. The current globalization process, however, may also hurt the poor in several ways. A higher degree of financial openness, for instance, tends to increase the country's exposure to volatile shocks, which may lead to higher interest rates, lower per capita income and thus possibly also higher poverty rates. Moreover, the growing tendency to abrupt reversal of capital flows that has characterized the recent financial integration can increase the country's macroeconomic instability with negative effects on its domestic output. This is more likely to happen in developing countries (where poverty rates are very high) since their financial systems are poorly regulated and their relation to the world capital market is generally pro-cyclical as they borrow during the upward swings of the economic cycle while they face credit constraints during the recessions. Like financial openness, also trade openness can damage the poor, at least in the short period. Opening the domestic market to foreign competitors, for instance, may force some firms out of the market, increasing unemployment and poverty, especially if the industrial structure is still fragile and the imperfect mobility across sectors hampers the reallocation of labor towards the most export-oriented sectors. Similarly, the possible access to technological progress and the learning-by-doing process emphasized by the supporters of globalization may vanish if the country is unable to attract technology-intensive productions due to lack of infrastructures and human capital. This problem is particularly serious in developing countries where credit market imperfections generate severe borrowing constraints that prevent poor individuals from the acquisition of the necessary labor skills.

Two main features seem to emerge from this brief overview of the theoretical debate. In the first place, globalization may have in principle both positive and negative effects on poverty. Since these consequences are often likely to coexist, we need to test empirically which of the two effects tends to prevail in different countries and circumstances. In the second place, most of the arguments in favor and against globalization underline an indirect impact of the world integration process on poverty through income growth, similar to the one on inequality discussed above. Therefore, if we accept the evidence that globalization tends to increase the average per capita income of the participating countries (both in absolute levels and in terms of growth rates), then the empirical issue to be examined is whether and in what measure this larger income is made available to the poor. A clear-cut positive answer has been given by Dollar and Kraay (2002) who have investigated the impact that economic growth may have on poverty in a large sample of developed and developing countries over the period 1950–1999. Taking the income share of the poorest quintile as dependent variable, their regression estimations find that the incomes of the poor rise proportionally with average incomes: a 1% increase in the average per capita income translates into a similar increase in the per capita income of the poorest 20% of the population so that the share of income of the poorest quintile does not vary with average income. This result seems *prima facie* particularly robust as it holds over time, across different geographic regions, across countries with different income levels, and even when accounting for openness to trade (their proxy for globalization) and a variety of other "pro-growth policies" (i.e. low inflation, moderate government size, sound financial development, respect for the rule of law). From these results it is tempting to draw the following conclusions: (i) growth is good for the poor (as the title of the article explicitly states) and thus also globalization is good for them as it increases economic growth; (ii) "a basic policy package of private property rights, fiscal discipline, macroeconomic stability, and openness to trade on average increases the income of the poor to the same extent that it increases the income of other households in society" (Dollar and Kraay, 2002, pp.218–219); (iii) changes in income are unrelated to changes in inequality, thus contradicting the KC hypothesis.

The empirical evidence of this contribution and the conclusions drawn by the authors had a large echo in the media (see, for instance, *The Economist*, 2000; Dollar, 2000; Wolf, 2000). They have provoked, moreover, a harsh debate among prominent economists which contributed to further increasing the distance between advocates and opponents of the current globalization process. This critical point of view is well represented by the severe critiques moved to Dollar and Kraay (2002) in a reply published by the Center for Economic and Policy Research (Weisbrot *et al.*, 2001). The authors argue that the contribution by Dollar and Kraay (2002) misses the main point. The principal finding of the paper that growth on average benefits the poor as much as anyone else in society (conclusion (i) above) is what one would reasonably expect. Nevertheless, "there are plenty of instances in which the poor...have been left behind in the era of globalization – even where per capita income has grown" (Weisbrot *et al.*, 2001, p.2).

Moreover, the results of Dollar and Kraay (2002) are less robust than it appears at a first glance. Most of their empirical tests (including those on pro-growth policies) are statistically insignificant (Weisbrot *et al.*, 2001). Although the analysis of Dollar and Kraay (2002) is carefully done, this does not allow reliable inferences and policy conclusions from the performed tests. Even if one accepts in principle the existence of a positive correlation between economic growth and the income of the poor, it cannot be claimed that the policy package adopted by the WB and the IMF as defined by Dollar and Kraay (2002) has always contributed to the economic growth of the countries in which it was applied. As Weisbrot *et al.* (2001) pointed out, economic growth has slowed down in the period 1980–1998 as compared to the period 1960–1980 in every region except East and South Asia where growth was driven by the extraordinary economic performances of China and

India. The fast growth of these two large countries, however, cannot be ascribed to the IMF and WB policies. In fact:

> ...[the Bank or Fund] are understandably reluctant to claim credit for China, which maintains a non-convertible currency, state control over its banking system, and other major violations of IMF/Bank prescriptions. (Weisbrot *et al.*, 2001, p.3)

The Chinese experience is particularly interesting when compared to that of Russia. Both countries have moved from a centralized to a market economy, but in Russia incomes have decreased by one-third during the 1990s, whereas in China – where the transition to the market economy has been more gradual – they have increased by 135% (Stiglitz, 2006).

The critique moved by the authors thus mainly concerns the policy implications drawn by Dollar and Kraay on the basis of their conclusion (ii) above. In our opinion, however, also their third conclusion (i.e. inequality unrelated to income growth) might need some further specification. As mentioned above, Dollar and Kraay (2002, p.196) use "a particular measure of inequality", the first quintile share. Although this share is closely related to the Gini index of the whole distribution, it might provide too narrow a picture of the overall income distribution. In fact, as it can be easily proved (see Box 2.1), even if the first quintile share does not vary with average income, the overall distribution might get more unequal as average income changes. This would occur, for instance, if the average income growth accrues more to the richest portion of the population than to the middle class and even more if the increase in the average income is accompanied by regressive transfers from the middle to the top class. Thus, focusing only on the bottom quintile of the population may lose important information on what happens in the rest of the distribution.

The bottom quintile of the population, moreover, is a relative poverty line as it defines who is poor relative to the income distribution of the whole community. Focusing attention only on this measure, therefore, does not provide any information on absolute poverty, the other component of poverty one should look at. Interestingly enough, if one adopts an absolute poverty line as the dollar-a-day criterion to define the poor, it turns out that the elasticity of incomes of the poor with respect to average incomes is less than one (Ali and Elbadawi, 2001). Although even this methodology is not immune from critiques, in our opinion it may provide some important insights

Box 2.1

Let us suppose that there are only five individuals (or, equivalently, five equally numerous groups of individuals) in the population. We will call them P (poor), LM (lower-middle), M (middle), UM (upper-middle) and R (rich) to denote their position in the income ranking in increasing order from the poorest to the richest. Let us assume that the initial total income Y of the whole community is equal to 100 and is distributed among the five agents as follows:

$$Y_P = 10; \ Y_{LM} = 15; \ Y_M = 20; \ Y_{UM} = 25; \ Y_R = 30.$$

In this case, the average per capita income $\bar{Y}$ is obviously equal to 20, while the first quintile share is 0.1 (i.e. Y_P/Y). As it is well-known, the Gini coefficient G is equal to the average of all the pairwise income differences among the agents divided by twice the average income, that is:

$$G = \frac{\sum_i \sum_j |Y_i - Y_j|}{2N^2 \bar{Y}}$$

where N is the number of individuals in the population.

Computing all the pairwise income differences between the five (groups of) individuals in the population and replacing N and $\bar{Y}$ with the correspondent values (5 and 20, respectively), the Gini coefficient associated with the income distribution described above is: $G = 0.2$.

Let us now suppose that total income doubles ($Y = 200$) and so does also the income of each individual in the community. Assume, however, that there is a redistribution of 10 units from agent M to agent R. If so, the new income distribution among the five individuals will be:

$$Y_P = 20; \ Y_{LM} = 30; \ Y_M = 30; \ Y_{UM} = 50; \ Y_R = 70.$$

As it can be seen, the income of the poor has grown in the same proportion (i.e., by 100%) as average income (that has obviously also doubled: $\bar{Y} = 40$) and the first quintile share has remained constant ($Y_P/Y = 0.1$). However, the Gini index underlying the whole income distribution is now higher (i.e. the new distribution is more unequal) due to the regressive redistribution from the middle to the richest class. In fact, from the formulation of the Gini coefficient indicated above, we now have: $G = 0.24$.

The theoretical possibility that the Gini coefficient increases though the first quintile share is constant is confirmed by a closer look at the data. For instance, according to the values reported as "high-quality data" by Deininger and Squire (1996), in the United Kingdom the first quintile share remained constant (equal to 0.0932) between 1966 and 1984, while the Gini coefficient increased from 25.3 to 25.8 in the same period.

especially in the less developed countries where the share of people below the absolute poverty line is often higher than the bottom quintile, so that the latter measure does not offer an exhaustive picture of the situation of the poor.

4   A poverty Kuznets curve?

A different perspective on the consequences that the world economic integration may have on poverty can be obtained by examining its effects on the ratio of the poor rather than on their income. Taking the headcount index as poverty measure, interesting results emerge when accounting for possible non-linearities in the globalization-poverty relationship. Agenor (2003), for instance, finds that trade openness (measured by the average tariff rate) has a statistically significant negative effect on the headcount index when performing linear cross-country regressions, whereas a different, concave relationship emerges when both the linear and the squared value of a composite index of globalization are entered in the estimated model, such that an increase in the globalization index initially raises and then lowers the headcount index. The turning point of this concave curve, moreover, gets lower when a two-step procedure is used to account for possible indirect effects of globalization on poverty through higher growth rates and lower inflation and variability in the exchange rate. This empirical pattern seems to suggest the optimistic conclusion that the world economic integration may eventually solve the social problems that it generates at the early stages of development and that these problems might not be that high: the lower the turning point, the lower the maximum poverty rate that can be achieved along the curve. If so, the globalization process could be socially sustainable in the long run provided we let it achieve that threshold level of what he calls the poverty-globalization "Laffer curve" beyond which the beneficial effects of globalization on poverty should tend to prevail.

In our opinion, it would be more appropriate to call this relationship a poverty-globalization "Kuznets curve". In fact, the estimated relationship does not seem to have much in common with the Laffer curve apart from the shape (but in that regard there are plenty of other inverted-U relationships between economic variables in the literature). On the contrary, the curve has two possible theoretical similarities with the KC: the close link existing between the notions of poverty and inequality and the policy implications drawn by the authors from the shape of the curves. The link between inequality and poverty is implicitly recognized by Agenor (2003) himself when he considers the possible causes for non-linearities in the globalization-poverty relationship. As he argues, the skilled-unskilled wage differential may initially rise with openness because firms substitute unskilled workers with imported capital, increasing unemployment and poverty, but it would then fall when higher investments in human capital (and possibly subsidies to skill acquisition) gradually increase the supply of skilled labor. If this argument were true it would describe a bell-shaped relationship of globalization not only with poverty but also (and above all) with inequality.

As to the policy implications that can be drawn from the shape of the curve, Agenor (2003, p.39) concludes that "paradoxically, globalization may hurt the poor in some countries not because it went too far but rather because it did not go far enough". If so, openness should be further increased in these economies to reach the favorable part of the curve where poverty would get lower. This point of view closely recalls the one originally prevailing in the KC literature that economic growth should be accelerated to overcome the turning point as soon as possible and thus enjoy decreasing inequality.

In our opinion, however, referring to the KC literature and learning from its evolution would induce a more cautious approach and might also shed light on some problems that currently affect the author's analysis. Although Agenor's contribution is certainly quite stimulating, like most contributions in the KC literature it suffers from insufficient data reliability and sample size problems (as recognized by the author himself). And we know from the KC literature how deeply the results may change according to the quality of the data and the dimension of examined samples. Agenor's analysis focuses only on 11 developing countries. Given the low number of observations at disposal (30 at most) and the high number of explanatory variables and fixed effects included in the analysis, the author is left with an extremely low number of degrees of freedom (10 at most), which may heavily affect the reliability of the results.

Even disregarding these problems and assuming – for the sake of the argument – a quadratic relationship between globalization and poverty in developing countries, one cannot exclude that the curve shape may change as soon as we take account of developed countries. Similarly to inequality, in fact, the poverty ratio has increased in several developed countries in the last two decades or so (Baldini and Toso, 2004). This suggests that poverty might rise again with further increases in per capita income, a possibility that cannot simply be dismissed without further empirical investigations. If so, an N-shaped (rather than a bell-shaped) relationship would better describe the link between globalization-driven growth and poverty as well as between growth and inequality, so that the KC and the "poverty KC" (or whatever one may want to call it) would be only part of a more complex, cubic relationship.

Finally, the bell-shaped relationship found by Agenor (2003) is based on cross-country estimations. As mentioned above, however, the KC literature has shown that the similar bell-shaped relationship observed in the inequality-growth context was very sensitive to the kind of econometric analysis adopted in the estimations and tended to disappear when passing from cross-country to time-series analyses. This casts some doubts on the effective capacity of poverty to follow an inverted-U pattern as the globalization index increases within single countries over time.

Many other studies have recently looked at the evolution of poverty over time. As we have seen in Chapter 1, there seems to be a large consensus in the literature on the fact that the world poverty ratio has been (and is currently) moving along a downward trend (Bourguignon and Morisson, 2002; Chen and Ravallion, 2004; Sala-i-Martin, 2002). Their estimations, however, show huge differences according to the sample and methodology that have been used. According to Sala-i-Martin (2002) the poverty rate was only 5% in 2000, whereas Chen and Ravallion (2004) estimate that it was around 21.3% in 2001 if we take the $1-a-day poverty line and up to 52.9% if we consider $2 a day as poverty line.[30] While the common declining trend that emerge in these studies can induce a moderate optimism on the future evolution on poverty, the huge differences among their results cause suspicions on data reliability. In any case, the uncertainty on the true level of the current poverty rate makes these results of little guidance for policy-makers.

Some interesting insights on the poverty trend can also be learnt by decomposing data by different geographical areas. Most of the reduction in the world poverty rate recorded in the last two decades has occurred in the South-Eastern Asia where India and, above all, China have experienced a dramatic decrease of the poverty rate. In China the percentage of those below $1 a day has fallen from 63.8% to 16.6% in the period 1981–2001, while the percentage of the population below $2 a day has passed from 88.1% to 46.7% (Chen and Ravallion, 2004). A different picture, however, emerges for all the other world areas. The population rate below $1 and $2 a day has remained basically constant or substantially increased in the Sub-Saharan Africa as well as in Eastern

Europe/Central Asia. And even where the poverty rate has slightly decreased (Middle East/North Africa and Latin America/Caribbean), the number of those below $2 a day has grown.

Summing up, currently available data seem to suggest that globalization may benefit the poor as much as the other sectors of the population and may reduce the poverty ratio at the world level. These results, however, should be treated with caution for the limited evidence and the scarce reliability of the data at disposal; for the large differences in the results of different studies and in the trends of different world areas; and for the persistent high number of poor people that still account for about 40% of the world population.

5 Concluding remarks

In this chapter we have discussed the impact that globalization has had on two crucial and related aspects of social sustainability: within-country inequality and poverty.

Within-country inequality has grown in many countries after trade liberalization. This increase can be partially explained by the differential access to the globalization process that has characterized different regions within these countries (e.g. urban vs. rural areas). Within-country inequality, however, is more sensitive to income growth and socio-economic policies than to trade liberalization in itself, therefore its trend changes according to the nation taken into account.

Given the positive effect of globalization on the per capita income of participating countries, many have looked with renewed interest to the KC to evaluate the consequences of market integration on income distribution. And, despite a growing agreement among economists on the possible shortcomings of the KC, this relationship is beginning to play a crucial role also in the current debate on the effects of globalization on poverty. While most contributions recognize that increasing openness may have contrasting effects on inequality and poverty, it is often believed that the beneficial consequences of globalization will prevail in the long run. From this point of view, a possible increase in inequality and poverty should be considered only as a temporary phenomenon, as suggested by the shape of the KC. The limitations of the KC analysis and the evidence at disposal, however, do not seem to support this conclusion. In the last decades inequality and poverty have increased in many developed countries that are very open to international trade and have high levels of per capita income. If so, they should not be regarded as short-run negative consequences of globalization that in the long-run economic growth is able to solve once and for all. Inequality and poverty, moreover, are heavily affected not only by income growth, but also by country-specific factors such as geographical, historical, political and institutional aspects. Therefore, although it is tempting to give time-series interpretation to cross-country evidence, little can be learnt on inequality and poverty within countries from pooling observations from different nations.

These considerations must not lead to neglect the large improvements that have been achieved during globalization on specific aspects of the income distribution problem. While the world income distribution has become more polarized, the percentage of poor people at the global level has substantially decreased following the huge poverty reduction in China and India, the most populated countries in the world. The prevailing optimism generated by the observed reduction in the world poverty rate, however, has partially neglected the increase in the absolute number of the poor since the beginning of the globalization process. As Kanbur (2001) has pointed out, the lack of attention to this equally important aspect of poverty explains much of the disagreement on the poverty impact of the recent globalization process and many of the critiques moved by large sectors of public opinion to the present features of globalization. The absolute number of the poor is crucial from the ethical point of view and has a large influence on the perception that public opinion has of poverty. In fact, it is the increasing number of poor people (though more dispersed in a wider population) that can be met everyday on the way, especially in big urban centers, that generates that sense of social insecurity often reported in modern societies. This feeling is stronger the larger is the income gap between poor people and the rest of the society. Therefore, a persistently high (or, even worse, increasing) number of poor people together with the increasing polarization of the income distribution discussed in this chapter may generate an explosive mix that undermines social stability in the long run, causing diffidence towards the others and contributing to the overall degradation of social capital.

Social stability, moreover, is crucially influenced not only by the number of the poor but also by their localization. If the poor tend to concentrate in a few suburban areas, this is more likely to generate social tensions and riots, as shown also by the recent episodes of urban fights in France that originated in the *banlieue* and then extended to many cities all over the country. Therefore, even if the poverty rate has diminished at the country level, it may well increase in specific areas with high concentration of poor people and low life quality standards, which may further increase the feeling of isolation suffered by the poor and their anger towards the rest of society.

The opposite trends in the poverty rate and in the number of the poor, moreover, may also contribute to explain the contrasting feelings and opinions that people (and economists) have on the capacity of globalization to reduce poverty. Paraphrasing what Kuznets claimed about modern economic development, it is surprising how much the poverty rate has decreased at the world level. But it is also astonishing how many people still experience poor life standards despite the enormous and ever-increasing technological progress that mankind has achieved over time.

A long way is still to go to defeat poverty. In this effort globalization can be a powerful instrument by increasing growth, but specific policies, both at the national and at the international levels, are also needed to spread its benefits to the poorest sectors of the world population. In particular, the globalization process should be extended to ensure that the countries that have been left behind can actually benefit from market integration. This may be achieved by lowering or removing the trade barriers of developed countries to increase imports from developing countries. While some developing world regions (e.g. Eastern Asia, Eastern Europe and Mexico) have increased their market share in the industrialized countries, this share was halved between the 1980s and 1990s for the world's 48 least developed countries (mainly African and Southern Asiatic countries). The reduction of Northern trade barriers is particularly important in two specific sectors, agriculture and the textile industry, that account respectively for about 15% and 20% of exports from developing countries. These sectors are important sources of economic growth for developing countries that still lack sufficient capital and technology to shift their production towards high-technology products. From this point of view, the suspension in July 2006 of the "Doha Round" of WTO agricultural negotiations is a matter of serious concern for the developing countries. As a matter of fact, the Doha Development Agenda was intended to promote the interests of developing countries and thus also possibly stop or reverse the progressive deterioration in the agricultural export performance of the developing world that has been observed during the past few decades (Senior, 2008). Although negotiations were resumed in February 2007, a full agreement between the contrasting interests of developed and developing countries in the agricultural negotiations is still far from being reached, mainly because of the developed countries' resistance to cut their farm subsidies.

A more generalized and consistent deregulation of world trade, however, is not enough to ensure the sustainability of world development. The regulation of international markets should be radically reformed by establishing a minimal but efficient set of enforceable rules. These rules should be managed in a non-bureaucratic and accountable way and ensure the active and democratic participation of all countries in the decision-making process.

The regulation process mentioned above should include among its crucial targets that of coordinating and promoting active policies to strengthen the social sustainability of development. Though far from being exhaustive, among these policies we may recall here at least those that promote higher health and education levels. As we will argue below (see Chapter 9), these policies are extremely important in reducing inequality and poverty, particularly in the recent phase of globalization characterized by the increasing mobility of information and the unparalleled speed of its world-wide diffusion. Inadequate education (e.g. lack of computer literacy) may prevent access to such information and thus also to the opportunities that it creates, while inadequate health may hinder the acquisition of the skills that are necessary to exploit these opportunities.

3
Sustainability Conditions and the Environmental Kuznets Curve

1 Introduction

In this chapter we intend to discuss to what extent it is possible to identify specific causal mechanisms that connect the process of globalization to that of global environmental deterioration.

The globalization of economic and financial activity that started in the early 19th century has increasingly undermined the environmental equilibria of the biosphere not only at the local level (deforestation, desertification, pollution of rivers and seas, urban smog, and so on) but also increasingly at the global level (global warming, depletion of the ozone layer, loss of biodiversity, exhaustion of crucial natural resources, and so on). Although the trend of liberalization has experienced ups and downs, the negative externalities of globalization have continued to accumulate. The acceleration of globalization after World War II has made environmental degradation clearly visible, raising the issue of the environmental sustainability of economic development at the world level.

Human activities often involved undesirable environmental effects even in the distant past, mainly wherever people were spatially concentrated for habitation or work. In the ancient world and in the Middle Age, however, environmental problems were mainly local, most of them affecting fairly restricted areas. In the classical period (Greek, Hellenistic and Roman) many problems raised by urban concentrations were tackled and solved: towns and cities introduced sewers to carry off refuse liquids, built aqueducts for distributing safe water, paved roads to avoid dust and mud, and so on. Other environmental problems proved to be much more intractable and irreversible. For example, the extensive and systematic exploitation of North African forests for building and re-building large commercial and military fleets easily destroyed by storms and wars, resulted in irreversible deforestation of this once very fertile area, accelerating the northward expansion of the Sahara desert. Also in this case, however, the environmental problems were circumscribed to a particular region and could be solved just by transferring the dwellings or the activities elsewhere.

The process of globalization, starting with the great explorations of the 16th and 17th centuries and strongly accelerating since the industrial revolution at the turn of the 18th century, has led to the gradual globalization of environmental problems and progressive awareness of their crucial importance. The ships of explorers opened the way to a network of commercial routes around the world, which progressively extended trade, and consequently production and distribution of goods, around the globe. Natural resource scarcity at the world level began to emerge only after the economic and demographic boom triggered by the first industrial revolution at the end of the 18th century. The growing impact of global markets upon economic activity since the 1820s accelerated the process of commodities and factor market integration, which concurrently increased the pace of worldwide economic growth and natural resource depletion. By the end of the 19th century it began to be understood that the worldwide exhaustion of crucial natural resources could jeopardize the continuation of growth. Widespread awareness of the global nature of pollution emerged later, when the demographic explosion triggered by the industrial revolution virtually eliminated under-populated lands and connected the ever larger spots of pollution in an almost seamless web over land and sky. The temporary retreat from globalization, during the World Wars and the period in between, reduced the impact of global markets on economic development but did not interrupt the growth of world population, technical change, and global infrastructures (transport, telecommunication, energy networks, etc.). In addition, global environmental problems were seriously aggravated by extensive war destruction and damage. After World War II the process of market globalization resumed a steady pace and increasingly affected the environmental and social sustainability of world development.

The globalization of environmental problems has undermined the viability of their traditional solution: just "moving away" towards a new unspoiled environment. The problems raised by resource scarcity used to be circumvented by migrating, founding colonies, looking for new sources of vital resources (minerals, food, clean water, etc.) and extending commerce to distant lands. In particular, nomadic populations overcame resource exhaustion and pollution by continuous migrations to new unspoiled habitats. But as soon as it became clear, quite recently, that there were limited untapped natural resources left, their sustainable exploitation turned out to be a necessary prerequisite for further economic development (a crucial contribution to a greater awareness of these problems came from the epoch-making publication in 1972 of *The limits to growth* by the Club of Rome).

The modern globalization process of the world economy has been and continues to be in its essence a process of progressive market expansion around the globe. The globalization of trade, propelled by the increasing efficiency of transports since the industrial revolution (steamships, railroads, cars, aircraft, and so on), has progressively affected the production and distribution of goods in an increasingly wider area of the globe. The international mobility of goods has been enhanced by the increasing mobility of capital and, to some extent, labor. As a result, the economic and financial decisions became increasingly ruled by market laws rather than by alternative principles which were very influential in traditional communities, including ethical principles (solidarity, equity, reciprocity, etc.). Increasing market expansion and power have produced desirable consequences such as the increasing efficiency of productive and financial processes, the accelerating growth of world production and average per capita income, the worldwide access to global resources. However, it has also been *accompanied* by a few undesirable phenomena such as increasing inequality between nations for much of the time and, to some extent, within nations, an increasing number of poor people (at least up to the last decade), a widening gap between the North and the South of the globe, loss of cultural diversity, exhaustion of natural resources, and pollution at the world level. The correlation between globalization and undesirable phenomena such as those just mentioned, that has been often ignored or de-emphasized in the past, is now at the center of public debate. It is very difficult, however, to assess whether these and other undesirable phenomena, which have accompanied the recent process of globalization, are actually *caused* by some intrinsic feature of the process of globalization or by some external or extrinsic feature that may be removed. Unfortunately, the heated debate on these issues has taken too often, at least in the mass-media, the misleading form of a poll for or against globalization, i.e. whether to stop and/or reverse the process of globalization or allow it to proceed along the existing lines. In our opinion, the negative phenomena associated with globalization are often avoidable consequences of the way in which globalization has been managed, while the reversal of globalization is to some extent possible, but does not seem to be the right solution to the problems. The episode of de-globalization occurred between the two World Wars confirms its possibility, but its consequences are not encouraging as they involved a global economic depression and appalling conflicts between industrialized countries.

2   The environmental Kuznets curve

In order to study the impact of globalization on the environmental requisites of sustainability, we have to take into account four basic categories of causal mechanisms depending on technological, economic, demographic and cultural factors. The diffusion of mechanization during the industrial revolution increased the exploitation of natural resources used as inputs in industrial production, as well as the deterioration of their quality as a consequence of pollution. Since then, successive waves of technological innovation have raised new environmental problems along with new opportunities for solving them (see Chapter 6). The ensuing acceleration of economic growth progressively increased the size of industrial activity that favored a progressive increase in per capita income (see Chapter 1). This also led to a steady increase in world population that increased the stress on environmental resources and proved to be a crucial factor of environmental deterioration. Finally, the new cultural values introduced by the industrial revolution and progressively spread all over the world by free markets considered nature as a mere means for satisfying human needs rather than a value in itself as it was common in pre-industrial cultures (Bhagwati, 2004).

An empirical analysis of the impact exerted by these four causal factors requires extensive evidence in order to assess to what extent they may be interpreted in genuine causal terms. Unfortunately, the required empirical analysis is almost completely absent. Some hints, however, may be found in the literature on the relationship between economic growth and environmental quality that has been the object of a large debate for many years. This debate goes back to the controversy on the limits to growth at the end of the 1960s. At one extreme, environmentalists as well as the economists of the Club of Rome (Meadows *et al.*, 1972) argued that the finiteness of environmental resources would prevent economic growth from continuing for ever and urged a zero-growth or steady-state economy as the only solution to avoid dramatic ecological scenarios in the future. At the other extreme, some economists (e.g., Beckerman, 1992) claimed that technological progress and the substitutability of natural with man-made capital would have reduced the dependence on natural resources and allow an everlasting growth path.

This debate lacked reliable empirical evidence to support one argument or the other, remaining on a purely abstract level for a long time (Shafik, 1994). This also reflected the difficulty to define how to measure environmental quality. Given the absence of a unique criterion of environmental quality, several indicators of environmental degradation have been used in the literature to measure the impact of economic growth on the environment. Different indicators, however, yield different empirical results. The World Development Report (World Bank, 1992) was one of the first studies to emphasize this issue. As shown in the Report, some indicators of environmental degradation (e.g. CO_2 emissions and municipal solid wastes) increase with income, which implies that economic growth tends to worsen these ecological problems (World Bank, 1992, Figure 4, p.11). However, other indicators (such as the lack of safe water and urban sanitation) fall as income rises, indicating that – in these cases – growth can improve environmental quality. Finally, there exists a number of indicators (e.g., SO_2, particulate matters and nitrous oxides (N_2O) emissions) that show an inverted-U relationship with income, so that environmental degradation gets worse in the early stages of growth, but eventually reaches a peak and starts declining as income passes a certain threshold level (see retro Figure 1.2). This inverted-U relationship has been defined "Environmental Kuznets Curve" (henceforth EKC) by analogy with the KC discussed before.

Although the EKC literature started almost four decades after the seminal paper by Kuznets (1955), it followed the same path of the KC literature, passing from initial enthusiasm for what was considered as a genuine empirical regularity to a much more cautious appraisal of the plausibility and robustness of the curve and the possibility to draw policy conclusions from it. Despite the critiques to the EKC hypothesis that emerge from the most recent contributions, this alleged empirical regularity still plays a crucial role in the environmental policy debate, as witnessed by the ever-increasing number of studies on this issue.[31] To get a deeper understanding of its theoretical plausibility and empirical robustness, therefore, we have to examine the main theoretical arguments underlying the EKC hypothesis.

3 Conceptual background of the EKC: the effects of growth on the environment

We may distinguish three main channels whereby income growth affects the quality of the environment (Grossman, 1995). In the first place, growth exhibits a *scale effect* on the environment: a larger scale of the economic activity brings about *per se* more environmental degradation. This occurs because increasing output requires that more inputs, and thus more natural resources, are used up in the production process. In addition, more output also implies increased waste and emissions as by-product of the economic activity, which contributes to worsen the environmental quality. In the second place, income growth can have a positive impact on the environment through a *composition effect*: as income grows, the structure of the economy tends to change, gradually increasing the share of cleaner activities in the GDP. In fact, environmental degradation tends to increase as the structure of the economy changes, shifting from agriculture to industry (Panayotou, 1993). But it starts falling with the second structural change from energy-intensive heavy industry to services and technology-intensive industry. Finally, "green" technological progress accelerates with economic growth since a wealthier country can afford to spend more on research and development. This leads to a more rapid substitution of obsolete and dirty technologies with cleaner ones. This is known as the *technique effect* of growth on the environment.

The existence of an inverted-U relationship between environmental degradation and per capita income suggests that the negative impact on the environment of the scale effect tends to prevail in the initial stages of development. However, it is eventually outweighed by the positive impact of the composition and technique effects that tend to lower the emissions level. The *income elasticity of environmental demand* is often invoked in the literature as the main reason to explain this process. As income grows, people achieve higher living standard and care more for the quality of the environment they live in. The growing demand for a better environment induces structural changes in the economy that tend to reduce the degradation of the environment. On the one hand, the increased environmental awareness and the ensuing "greener" consumer demand contribute to shift production and technologies toward more environmental-friendly activities. On the other hand, it can induce the implementation of enhanced environmental policies by the government (such as stricter ecological regulations, better enforcement of existing policies and higher environmental expenditures). This also contributes to shift the economy towards less polluting sectors and technologies. Hence, the demand for a better environment and the induced policy response may be considered as the main theoretical underpinnings behind the decreasing path of the EKC (Grossman, 1995, p.43).

Another argument has been advanced in the literature to explain the bell-shaped environment-income pattern. As some authors have suggested, for those natural resources that are traded in markets, the existence of an endogenous *self-regulatory market mechanism* might prevent environmental degradation from continuing growing with income (World Bank, 1992; Unruh and Moomaw, 1998). In fact, growth is often associated with high exploitation of natural resources at the early stages of development due to the relative importance of the agricultural sector. This tends to reduce the stock of natural capital over time. The consequent increase in the price of natural resources reduces their exploitation at later stages of development as well as the environmental degradation associated with it. Moreover, higher prices of natural resources can also contribute to accelerate the shift toward less resource-intensive technologies (Torras and Boyce, 1998). Hence, not only induced policy interventions, but also market signals could explain the alleged shape of the EKC.

4 The empirical evidence on the environment-income relationship

The discussion developed so far has pointed out which are the main conceptual arguments that make the EKC pattern plausible from a theoretical viewpoint. However, does empirical evidence really support this pattern and for which indicators is it observed? Given the lack of long time-series for environmental data, most empirical studies have addressed this question by adopting a cross-country approach. The present section examines the results and the main limitations of these studies and indicates in the single-country approach an alternative method that should be further developed in the future.

4.1 Cross-country studies

The empirical literature on the EKC has grown exponentially in the last few years. Recent studies have tried to overcome the limitations of early contributions by using new data sets, new functional forms, more refined econometric techniques and additional explanatory variables. Both early and more recent studies on the EKC, however, address the following common questions: (i) is there an inverted-U shape relationship between per capita income and environmental degradation?; and (ii) if so, at which income level does environmental degradation start declining? As we will see, both questions have ambiguous answers. In general, given the absence of a unique environmental indicator, the estimated shape of the curve, as well as its possible turning point, depends on the kind of index that is taken into account. In this regard, it is possible to identify three main categories of environmental indicators that have been used in the literature: air quality, water quality and other environmental quality indicators.

As to *air quality indicators*, the evidence in favor of an EKC is strong, but not overwhelming. There is a consensus in the literature to distinguish between local and global air pollutants (e.g., Grossman, 1995; Barbier, 1997). The measures of urban and *local* air quality (SO_2, suspended particulate matters, carbon monoxide and N_2O) generally show an inverted-U relationship with income. This outcome that emerged in all early studies seems to be confirmed by more recent works (Panayotou, 2000; Dinda, 2004). However, there are relevant differences across indicators as to the turning point of the curve. In fact, carbon monoxide and especially N_2O show much higher turning points than SO_2 and suspended particulate matters. Moreover, there are also large differences across studies that focus on the same indicator. For instance, Selden and Song (1994) estimate a turning point for suspended particulate matters that is three times higher than that found by Shafik (1994) and similar large differences occur in the case of SO_2.[32]

As distinct from local air pollutants, the literature generally finds no evidence of an EKC whenever emissions have little direct impact on the population. In particular, both early and recent studies find that emissions of *global* pollutants such as CO_2 either monotonically increase with per capita income or start declining at income levels well beyond the observed range. Moreover, as Cole *et al.* (1997) have recently pointed out, even in those studies that find a peak (however high) in the CO_2 curve, the alleged turning point has very large standard error. This implies that the estimates of the CO_2 turning point are quite unreliable, casting doubts on the possible downturn of the CO_2 curve. This is in principle fully consistent with the theoretical arguments discussed above to explain the EKC: differently from local air pollutants, CO_2 creates global rather than local disutility; therefore people make little pressure for environmental intervention since the global warming problem generated by CO_2 has an international nature and can be transferred elsewhere.[33]

As for *water quality indicators* the empirical evidence on the EKC is even more mixed than in the case of the air quality indicators. When a bell-shaped curve applies, however, the turning point for the water pollutants is generally higher than that of the air pollutants. Water quality can be measured by three main categories of indicators: (i) concentration of pathogens in the water (indirectly measured by faecal and total coliform bacteria), (ii) amount of heavy metals and toxic chemicals discharged in the water by human activities (lead, cadmium, mercury, arsenic and nickel) and (iii) measures of deterioration of the water oxygen regime (dissolved oxygen, biological and/or chemical oxygen demand). Although there is evidence of an EKC for some indicators (especially in the latter category), many studies reach conflicting results as to the shape and peak of the curve (see Borghesi, 2001).

In addition, it is interesting to underline that several authors (Shafik, 1994; Grossman and Krueger, 1995; Grossman, 1995) find evidence of an N-shaped curve for some indicators: as income grows water pollution first increases, then decreases and finally rises again. Thus, the inverted-U curve might correspond just to the first two portions of this more complex pattern. The existence of an N-shaped curve seems to imply that at very high income levels, the scale of the economic activity becomes so large that its negative impact on the environment cannot be counterbalanced by the positive impact of the composition and technology effects mentioned above. The emergence of this shape of the curve in recent years is likely to signal also a weakening in the relevant environmental policies.

Finally, in the absence of a single reliable measure of environmental quality, many *other environmental indicators* have been used to test the EKC hypothesis. For most of these indicators there seems to be only weak evidence of a Kuznets-type story. Both early and more recent studies (Shafik, 1994; Cole *et al.*, 1997; Dinda, 2004) find that those environmental problems that have a direct impact on the population (such as access to urban sanitation and clean water) tend to improve steadily with growth. On the contrary, when the environmental problems can be transferred elsewhere (as in the case of municipal solid wastes) the curve does not fall even at high income levels. As to deforestation, the empirical evidence is a matter of debate in the literature. Some studies find an inverted-U curve for deforestation where the peak of the curve occurs at relatively low income levels (e.g., Panayotou, 1993), whereas others conclude that "per capita income appears to have little bearing on the rate of deforestation" (Shafik, 1994, p.761). Finally, even when an EKC seems to fit the available evidence (as in the case of traffic volumes and energy use), the relative turning points are often far beyond the observed per capita income range.

Summing up, from the cross-country studies three main stylized facts appear to emerge that provide a tentative answer to our initial questions: (i) only some indicators (mainly air quality measures) follow an EKC; (ii) an EKC is more likely to appear when the pollutant in question has a direct impact on the population rather than when its effects can be shifted elsewhere or in the future; (iii) in all those cases where an EKC is empirically observed, there is still no agreement in the literature on the income level at which environmental degradation starts decreasing.

4.2   From cross-country to single-country studies

As the section above has pointed out, cross-country studies suggest that the EKC can be a valid description of the environment-income relationship only for a subset of all possible indicators. However, Roberts and Grimes (1997) have provided an argument that questions the existence of the EKC even for those indicators that seem to follow this pattern. They observe in particular that the relationship between per capita GDP and carbon intensity has changed from linear in 1965 to an inverted-U in 1990. How can we explain the modification in the curve shape over the last 30 years? The Kuznets-type curve that we observe for carbon intensity today is the result of the environmental improvements in the developed countries in these last decades and "not of individual countries passing through stages of development" (Roberts and Grimes, 1997, p.196). The data show that carbon intensity has fallen steadily among high income countries in the period 1965–90, whereas it has increased among middle- and low-income nations, with a marked increment in the latter group (see Chapter 4). Therefore, the EKC that emerges in the cross-section analysis "may simply reflect the juxtaposition of a positive relationship between pollution and income in developing countries with a fundamentally different, negative one in developed countries, not a single relationship that applies to both categories of countries" (Vincent, 1997, p.417). In general, pooled estimations implicitly assume that the curvature and turning points are identical for all countries, whereas the environment-income relationship can vary a lot among the different cross-section members. For this reason, Vincent (1997) claims that the cross-country version of the EKC is just a misleading statistical artifact and that it should thus be abandoned.

More useful insights on the EKC hypothesis could be obtained by analyzing the experiences of individual countries at different levels of development as they develop over time (Stern *et al.*, 1996). These considerations have given birth to a new line of research based on single-country analyses. This econometric approach achieves some surprising results that cast serious doubts on the reliability of the indications emerging from cross-country studies. Vincent (1997) has examined the link of per capita income with a number of air and water pollutants in Malaysia from the late '70s to the early '90s. Two main conclusions emerge from this single-country study. First, cross-country analyses can fail to predict the income-environment relationship in single countries, as it occurs in the case of Malaysia. Second, none of the pollutants examined by Vincent shows an inverted-U relationship with income. Contrary to the cross-section analyses, several measures indicate that increments in the per capita income level may actually worsen environmental quality. It can be argued that the results achieved by Vincent heavily hinge on the specific features of the country in question and cannot be extended to other countries. However, De Bruyn *et al.* (1998) reach similar conclusions analyzing other individual countries over time. More specifically, they estimate the pattern of several air pollutants (SO_2, CO_2 and N_2O) in four OECD countries (Netherlands, West Germany, UK and USA) between 1960 and 1993 and find that the emissions are positively correlated with per capita income growth in almost every case. Similar results emerge in the longitudinal analysis performed by Roca *et al.* (2001) for Spain on six air pollutants during the period 1980–96. At the beginning of the observed period Spain was already rich enough to lie on the downward part of an alleged cross-sectional EKC. Therefore, Spanish emissions should have decreased during the period of observation for the EKC hypothesis to be confirmed. On the contrary, the authors find that only SO_2 per capita emissions decrease with per capita income, whereas there is no evidence of correlation between higher income and lower emissions for all other pollutants. These conclusions are questioned by Carson *et al.* (1997) who find the opposite result in a single-country study on the Unites States. Using data collected by the Environmental Protection Agency (EPA) from the 50 US states, Carson *et al.* (1997) find that per capita emissions of air toxics decrease as per capita income increases.

In conclusion, all current single-country studies seem to suggest that *the EKC need not hold for individual countries over time*. In addition, different works reach conflicting results as to the effects of growth on the environment. Therefore, further research will be necessary to understand the evolution of environmental degradation relative to income in a single country over time. In particular, both Vincent (1997) and Carson *et al.* (1997) studies are still *cross-regional*, therefore they are also subject to the critiques addressed against the cross-country approach mentioned above. In fact, cross-country studies implicitly assume that all countries will follow the same pattern in order to infer the environment – per capita income relationship of a single country over time. As mentioned above, this assumption does not seem to be supported by empirical evidence. Analogously, in order to infer the environmental degradation of the whole country over time, cross-regional studies implicitly assume that all regions within the same nation follow the same pattern. For some countries, however, regional differences can be very significant. The environment-income relationship thus can differ not only across nations, but also across regions of the same country. Hence, although current single-country studies tend to go in the right direction, a time-series approach – as the one adopted by De Bruyn *et al.* (1998) and Roca *et al.* (2001) – seems more appropriate than a cross-regional one to examine individual countries over time and this is the line of research that single-country analyses should further develop in the future.

5   Policy implications of the EKC

The shape of the environment-income relationship has critical policy implications. The alleged form of the EKC has lead some authors to conclude that the current process of environmental degradation might be only a temporary phenomenon and that it is possible to "grow out" of the environmental problems in the long run (Beckerman, 1992; Radetzki, 1992; Shafik, 1994). If so, policy-makers should promote faster growth rates to overcome the income turning point as soon as possible. As pointed out above, however, several limitations seem to restrict the reliability of current results for policy aims. We already mentioned the reason why the use of cross-sectional studies (both cross-country and cross-region) restricts the validity of the evidence at disposal. Beyond that, it is possible to identify several further drawbacks (e.g. data problems, use of reduced-form models, limitations of econometric techniques, inconsistency among different versions of the EKC and so on) that adversely affect much of the literature and should induce to use the available results with particular caution for policy aims.

Even if we neglect the flaws of the empirical studies and accept the EKC as a stylized fact for the sake of the argument, there are several reasons to question the conclusion that in the long-run economic growth will automatically solve the environmental problems that it brings about in its initial phases. As Panayotou (1993) has underlined, a policy that devotes most resources to growth is not necessarily an optimal one. In fact, achieving the downturn of the EKC may be a very long process that takes decades, the more so the longer one waits for intervention. In fact, emissions and consequent environmental degradation often tend to cumulate over time. Therefore, postponing any environmental intervention to later stages of growth may build up prohibitively high abatement costs. If so, even those damages that are physically reversible could become economically irreversible.

The literature on the EKC has given large emphasis to the income level at which the turning point occurs. The height of the curve, however, might be even more important than this. In fact, if the level of emissions or concentrations corresponding to the vertex of the parabola is above some threshold level, we might enter that "shadow area" where damages are difficult to reverse (Figure 3.1). This implies that environmental degradation may become irreversible before we reach the top of the curve. If so, it might be impossible to operate in the future along the alleged decreasing path of the EKC. This is a possibility that cannot be neglected, especially because empirical evidence suggests that the EKC is not stable, but tends to shift and change its shape over time (Roberts and Grimes, 1997). For all these reasons, a policy of "wait and see" based on an uncritical reliance on the EKC might have vast negative effects on the environment in the future. On the contrary, we should intervene to "tunnel through" the curve (Munasinghe, 1999), building a bridge that allows to move from the upward to the downward portion of the EKC without waiting until environmental problems reach their peak level. As Panayotou (1993)

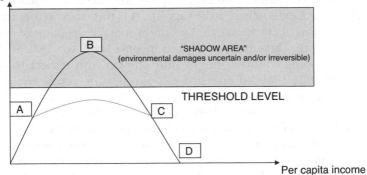

Figure 3.1 "Tunnelling through" the Environmental Kuznets Curve

has argued, several policies can be implemented to flatten the curve out. For instance, eliminating policy distortions (e.g., subsidies to energy and agrochemicals) or enforcing property rights over natural resources might both serve this purpose. Similarly, transferring pollution abatement technologies to the South of the world could also substantially lower the EKC. As shown by Anderson (2001), in fact, a dramatic reduction could occur in the peak of the EKC with respect to the projections of the literature, if developing countries were to introduce technological progress on pollution abatement at a much earlier phase of development than the industrialized countries in the past.

These considerations are particularly important for the developing countries that are currently on the upward part of the curve. There are good reasons to believe that these countries might not be able to repeat the same path as the one followed by developed countries in the past. In the first place, as Unruh and Moomaw (1998, p.222) have claimed:

> "...it is not certain whether 'stages of economic growth' is a deterministic process that all countries must pass through, or a description of the development history of a specific group of countries in the 19th and 20th centuries that may or may not be repeated in the future".

In the second place, the environmental conditions in which the South is developing today are much different from the ones faced by the North in the past. In fact, the current stock of greenhouse gases (GHGs) in the atmosphere inherited from the past by the newly developing countries is certainly higher than the correspondent stock met by the developed countries at the early stages of their development. As the so-called "stock externality" issue suggests, it is this stock, rather than the current flow of emissions, that produces most of the damage from global warming. Therefore, for a given income level, the EKC of the newly developing countries might shift upward with respect to the EKC of the industrialized ones if we could measure actual environmental degradation rather than emissions on the vertical axis.

Finally, Roberts and Grimes (1997) point out another reason why the South might be unable to follow the Northern path. In fact, some of the environmental improvements in the North were made possible by relocating more polluting, energy-intensive industries to the South (Hettige *et al.*, 1992). The South, however, will be unable to find some other countries where these productions can be shifted in the future.

As a consequence, the EKC seems inadequate to predict the future evolution of the environment-income relationship: industrialized countries may have moved along an inverted-U pattern in the past, but this does not imply that developing countries will or should follow the same pattern today. Moreover, even if we transferred the less polluting, energy-saving technologies from the North to the South, this might not necessarily improve the environmental quality in the latter unless it is accompanied by other socio-economic reforms. In fact:

"even identical industries operating in non-wealthy countries face obstacles making them less efficient in energy and carbon terms, such as poor roads, inefficient energy sources and local shortages of well-educated high-tech workers". (Roberts and Grimes, 1997, p.196)

These considerations call for an international environmental policy that is different from the one developed in the Kyoto Protocol. According to that agreement, the North has to bear most of the burden of cutting emissions, while the South has been left free to pollute. This policy reflects the belief (partially nourished by a misinterpretation of the EKC) that the developing countries have to grow first so that this will automatically lead them to solve their environmental problems in the future. Increasing pollution in the developing countries, however, might have adverse effects on the developed nations. In fact, issues like global warming are irrespective of the country where emissions occur: one unit of pollutant equally contributes to the greenhouse effect wherever is emitted.

Sustainability should be addressed at all levels of development to achieve an effective solution to global environmental problems (Roberts and Grimes, 1997). This does not mean that the South should introduce the same higher environmental standards of the North from the beginning, but should ensure that environmental interventions as well as social reforms (such as increased education and inequality reduction) accompany the financing policies of the development assistance agencies in the South. This is particularly important if we want that developing countries do not simply mimic the past experience of industrialized nations, but rather learn from it. Policy-makers should therefore avoid simplistic recommendations based on the EKC. More specifically, the possibility that environmental degradation may eventually fall as income grows (as suggested by the alleged decreasing portion of the EKC) should not be taken to imply that the current phase of globalization – by moving the economies along the horizontal axis of the EKC – will auto-matically guarantee their sustainable development in the long run. For this reason, in the next section we propose an alternative, more general approach to determine some basic conditions for long-run environmental sustainability and examine how globalization may influence these con-ditions in order to clarify to what extent different phases of globalization may be considered as environmentally sustainable.

6   A suggested step forward: from the Environmental Kuznets Curve to the Environmental Kuznets Relationship

As mentioned before, three different versions of the EKC can be iden-tified according to the dependent variable on the vertical axis: per capita degradation (d_p), degradation intensity (d_y) or total degradation (D). As emerged from the review of the EKC literature, however, the available evidence gives only limited support to the EKC hypothesis, no matter

Figure 3.2   Scatter diagram of CO_2 emissions intensity in 2005

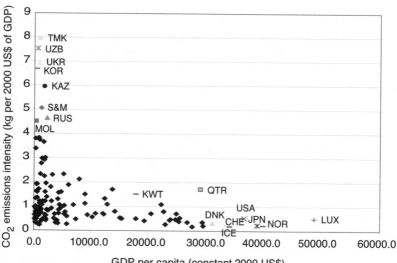

Legend: CHE = Switzerland; DNK = Denmark; KAZ = Kazakhstan; KOR = Korea; KWT = Kuwait; ICE = Iceland; JPN = Japan; LUX = Luxembourg; MOL = Moldavia; NOR = Norway; QTR = Qatar; RUS = Russia; S&M = Serbia & Montenegro; TMK = Turkmenistan; UKR = Ukraine; USA = United States of America; UZB = Uzbekistan.

Source: Authors' elaboration on IEA data (IEA 2006, Key World Energy Statistics).

which version one may adopt. Moreover, as shown in the Appendix, even when the empirical evidence is consistent with the EKC hypothesis for a certain dependent variable (D, or d_y, or d_p), this does not imply that it is also consistent with it for another dependent variable. In general, using one version of the EKC leads to results that are different from the one emerging in the other two variants. For instance, the scatter diagram for cross-country CO_2 emission intensity in 2005 (Figure 3.2) reveals extremely high values of this variable in the former Soviet Union countries. On the contrary, the pollution impact of these regions does not emerge if we look at cross-country per capita emissions of CO_2 in the same year (Figure 3.3). In this case, the outliers are mainly the oil producers that have high emissions and low population levels.

In order to use the EKC for constructive purposes, therefore, we have to relax the constraints of its narrow specification and reformulate it as a more general relationship that clarifies the logical link between the three

Figure 3.3 Scatter diagram of CO_2 per capita emissions in 2005

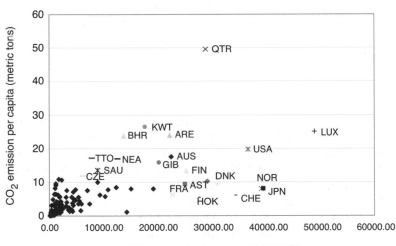

Legend: ARE = United Arab Emirates; AUS = Australia; AST = Austria; BHR = Bahrain; CHE = Switzerland; CZE = Czech Republic; DNK = Denmark; FIN = Finland; FRA = France; GIB = Gibilter; HOK = Hong Kong; JPN = Japan; KWT = Kuwait; LUX = Luxembourg; NEA = Netherlands Antilles; NOR = Norway; QTR = Qatar; SAU = Saudi Arabia; TTO = Trinidad and Tobago; USA = United States of America.

Source: Authors' elaboration on IEA data (IEA 2006, Key World Energy Statistics).

dependent variables appearing in the Kuznets literature (d_y, d_p and D). We suggest to call it the "environmental Kuznets relation" (EKR). As for the dependent variable, in our opinion total environmental degradation is the most convenient choice since long-term global sustainability strictly depends on it. As D increases, the conditions of environmental sustainability are bound to be violated sooner or later, either because some components of the comprehensive sustainability index will exceed the specific assimilative capacity of the environment or because the exploitation of a certain renewable resource exceeds its natural growth.

Let us now clarify the logical nexus between the independent variable (per capita income, y) and the three dependent variables that appear in the EKC literature (d_y, d_p and D). To this end we define the following identity:

$$(1) \qquad\qquad D = P \, y \, d_y$$

where D measures global environmental degradation, P measures world population, $y = Y/P$ measures per capita income, and $d_y = D/Y$ measures the intensity of environmental degradation. As Daily and Ehrlich (1992) have pointed out, it may be difficult to estimate the environmental impact of the last two factors separately. It is sometimes useful, therefore, to summarize them by a fourth factor through the following identity:

$$(2) \qquad\qquad d_p = y \, d_y$$

where d_p measures per capita environmental deterioration. These two identities clarify the logical nexus between the independent and the dependent variables that appear in the EKC literature. In addition, they provide a bridge with the well-known IPAT model originally proposed by Holdren and Ehrlich (1974). The IPAT model tried to identify the environmental impact (I) of a population as the product of three factors: population size (P), its affluence (A) measured in terms of per capita consumption, and the damage per unit of consumption determined by the technology used (T). Differently from that model, here we consider income rather than consumption per person as a measure of a population's affluence. This allows us to derive a general relationship between environmental degradation and per capita income encompassing the different functional forms examined in the empirical literature.

Finally, these two identities may help us to understand the nexus between the four causal mechanisms mentioned above (see p.54): P represents the demographic factor, y (given P) the economic factor,

d_y the technological factor, and d_p the nexus between the economic and the technological factor. The cultural factor mentioned above remains implicit in these indexes and can be made explicit only through a structural analysis that goes beyond the scope of the present chapter.

It should be stressed that these two identities are, by definition, unfit for a causal analysis but fix important constraints that any causal analysis has to comply with. A proper causal analysis could start from an equation of the following kind:

(3) $$D = aP + by + cd_y + fz$$

where the variables are measured in their logarithms, z represents a vector of relevant exogenous variables, while a, b, c, and f are empirical coefficients.

Equation (3) may be estimated to evaluate how total environmental degradation reacts to changes in the single explanatory variables and thus how it changes over time.

In order to achieve a sound process of sustainable globalization, total environmental degradation D should not increase over time. To this end we may derive from equation (1) the following identity:

(4) $$D^* = P^* + y^* + d_y^*$$

where the star above each variable indicates the logarithmic derivative (i.e. the rate of growth) of the variable. It is clear from this identity that global environmental deterioration tends to increase *ceteris paribus* with per capita income unless the sum of demographic growth and degradation intensity is negative and higher in absolute terms than per capita income growth. Therefore, we may set the following condition of long-term global sustainability:

(5) $$P^* + y^* \le - d_y^*$$

In other words, global environmental deterioration does not increase if and only if the degradation intensity growth is sufficiently negative to offset the (*ceteris paribus*) negative effect of population growth and per capita income growth. Both per capita income and population tended to increase at the world level within the post-war process of globalization. It follows that the only way to achieve a process of sustainable globalization relies on a reduction of deterioration intensity sufficient to offset the negative implications of demographic and economic growth. This is what is happening in a few countries and economic sectors as a consequence of technological change and consumption evolution that are reshaping the structure of economic activity in a direction more consistent with economic sustainability. However, the velocity of reduction of degradation intensity is, generally speaking, clearly insufficient to stabilize environmental degradation and must be accelerated through specific policies. These policies should be directed to shift downwards, i.e. in a more favorable direction, the relationship between D and y. This may be clarified through equation (3) where D depends on y and

$$aP + cd_y + fz$$

are shift factors. A reduction of demographic pressure and/or of degradation intensity would shift the relationship between D and y downwards.

The relationships examined above may also shed some light on the conditions of sustainable globalization in a more disaggregated approach. In particular, we may better understand why industrialized countries rather than developing countries seem to follow an EKC pattern. In the industrialized countries demographic growth is around zero, and the technological and cultural mechanisms that tend to reduce deterioration intensity may be sufficient, for certain indexes, to reduce aggregate degradation. In the developing countries, on the contrary, demographic growth is typically quite high while the reduction of environmental degradation is rather slow for technological and cultural reasons, and this may help to explain why the empirical evidence is unable to find in these countries the negative correlation between per capita income and environmental deterioration necessary to assure sustainability. It is important to underline that most of the world's population lives in developing countries. Using the classification adopted by the World Bank (2007b), in the year 2006 low-income and lower-middle income countries accounted for around 71% of the world's total population (see Figure 3.4). Since these countries generally lie on the increasing portion of the EKC, one can reasonably expect that the global environmental degradation will tend to increase with further economic growth in the next decades unless proper interventions are made to implement the shift factors described above.

We may conclude that the causal relationship between globalization and global environmental degradation is quite complex and ambiguous. While so far there has been a clear prevalence of negative causal effects for most indexes of environmental degradation, especially in developing countries, it is possible to reinforce the positive effects and at the same

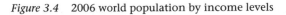

Figure 3.4   2006 world population by income levels

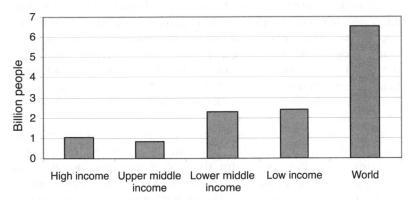

Source: Authors' elaboration on World Bank data (World Development Indicators, 2007b).

time reduce the negative effects of globalization on the environment through appropriate policies to implement a viable process of sustainable globalization.

7   Globalization and the environmental Kuznets relation

In this chapter we have considered the impact of the recent process of globalization on the sustainability of world development in the light of the literature on the EKC. This curve seems to suggest that the process of globalization may render the world development more sustainable simply by pushing the world economy towards the decreasing part of the bell-shaped curve. Globalization, in fact, increases per capita income of the countries that actively participate in this process and spreads the technological knowledge of the most advanced economies, which contributes to reducing environmental degradation intensity. The interpretation of the empirical evidence discussed in this chapter, however, seems on the whole to be inconsistent with these optimistic conclusions. In particular, the process of globalization pushes developing countries upwards along the rising part of a hypothetical EKC, i.e. in the direction of diminishing sustainability, while there is often no clear-cut evidence that we can rely on a peak beyond which a healthy descent may start. Moreover, even when the empirical evidence supports the existence of a peak, this may be reached if and only if the average income growth is higher than the average population growth for a sufficiently long time. Since the average income growth is relatively low in some of the poorest developing countries, this implies that their demographic growth should be kept under control. Finally, recent changes in the institutional regulation of the globalization process have not helped to corroborate its sustainability. The indiscriminate deregulation of world trade is progressively sweeping away many of the environmental constraints introduced by international institutions, countries and multilateral agreements (Esty, 2001; Tisdell, 2001). This sort of deregulation has contributed to accelerating the rate of growth of participant countries but has undermined its sustainability.

On the other hand the globalization process could *in principle* contribute to shift downwards the environment-income relationship in a more sustainable direction. Within the process of globalization it is possible to modify the shape and position of the EKR, thus improving the ecological sustainability conditions. The increasing mobility of information that characterizes the current phase of globalization rapidly disseminates images of environmental disasters that may occur even in distant countries. This is likely to make people more aware of ecological problems worldwide than in the past and tends to create "global" public opinion pressure for intervention. It has been noted, in fact, that while most of the people concerned with these issues come from industrialized countries, they express concern for environmental problems occurring both in the North and the South of the world. Globalization, therefore, may create a pressure for ecological policies even in countries where lack of democracy hinders the ability of people to express their preferences on such issues. This "global" pressure, therefore, takes place even when a country is still relatively poor and might lead to significant interventions to mitigate environmental degradation at an earlier stage of growth than predicted by the turning point of the EKC.

This potential positive effect of globalization on the environment has remained so far mainly unexploited and the available empirical evidence suggests that the *current* process of globalization is environmentally unsustainable in the long run unless we introduce new institutions and policies able to govern it. For this purpose, it is necessary to encourage participation in the process of market integration on the part of those countries and regions that have been excluded from the globalization process to date. Moreover, developing countries should introduce ecological policies and have access to the environmental-friendly technologies of the industrialized countries from the very first stages of their economic development. In any case, the process of deregulation should comply with the environmental and social constraints that buttress the sustainability of world development.

The policy measures briefly mentioned above are just tentative examples of interventions that may help in implementing the conditions of sustainability that we have tried to clarify in this chapter. It is our hope that a further clarification of the conditions of sustainable globalization may help policy-makers to reform the process of globalization in the direction of its long-term sustainability. To this end, the approach we have tentatively sketched here must be developed in many directions. First of all, the conditions of sustainable globalization should integrate in a more satisfactory way the conditions of environmental sustainability with those of social sustainability. Secondly, the conditions of sustainability must be disaggregated from the sectoral and spatial viewpoints in order to separate and better understand the impact of technological and cultural changes. Finally, extensive empirical work is needed to identify the relevant causal mechanisms underlying the influence of globalization on sustainable world development.

Appendix
Limitations of the EKC Studies

Data problems

The first and most obvious limitation of the studies on the EKC is the lack of good data on environmental indicators. Even when such data are available, in some low-income countries they appear to be unreliable because of data collection problems. Moreover, the existence of definitional differences across countries raises problems of data comparability, which cast serious doubts on the cross-country approach (Shafik, 1994; Carson *et al.*, 1997). One important consequence of the shortage of data is that many studies use *estimates rather than actual measures* of environmental indicators. Such estimates are based on rates of conversion from economic data "both of which can be unreliable, especially in developing countries" (Kaufmann *et al.*, 1998). In some cases (e.g., CO_2) the estimations are computed by applying emission coefficients to national consumption of various kinds of fuel. In other cases (e.g., SO_2 and other air pollutants) they are calculated by multiplying national consumption "by coefficients that reflect the contemporaneous abatement practices in each country" (Grossman, 1995, p.24).

Beyond *data quality and comparability*, current studies might also suffer from *sample selection bias*. In fact, the monitoring stations that collect data on pollution are often set where pollution is potentially more severe. Thus, for instance, most stations are in towns or along rivers that are suspected to have high pollution. Therefore, the results are likely to reflect local conditions and, in some circumstances, pollution might be overestimated. On the other hand, developed countries collect most of the available data. However, a large contribution to global pollution comes from many developing countries for which data are not available that generate high emissions per unit of GDP. Hence, the sample selection made in cross-country studies might underestimate pollution, especially as far as the emissions intensity is concerned.

Reduced-form models

Both cross- and single-country studies are based on *reduced form models*. As De Bruyn *et al.* (1998) point out, these models allow to directly estimate the influence of income on the quality of the environment. However, they give no indication about the direction of causality, namely whether growth affects the environment or the other way around. In other words, reduced-form relationships "reflect correlation rather than a causal mechanism" (Cole *et al.*, 1997, p.401). In reality, environmental quality is likely to have a feedback effect on income growth (Stern *et al.*, 1996; Pearson, 1994). In fact, the environment is a relevant factor of production in many underdeveloped countries that heavily rely on natural resources as a source of output. Any environmental degradation in these countries thus is likely to reduce their capacity to produce and hence to grow. Moreover, several studies point out that high pollution levels can reduce the workers' productivity and thus the output of the economy (see Chapter 5). Hence, a *simultaneous-equations model* would be more appropriate to deepen our understanding of the environment-income relationship.

Limitations of the econometric techniques

Beyond the problems mentioned so far, there are also other limitations that restrict the validity of current EKC studies (both cross- and single-country). One of the main criticisms concerns the *choice of specific functional forms* to estimate the environment-income relationship. Most of the literature has examined reduced-forms where the environmental indicator is a quadratic or cubic function of income. Neither the quadratic nor the cubic function can be considered a realistic representation of the environment-income relationship. In fact, as Cole *et al.* (1997) have stressed, a cubic function implies that environmental degradation will eventually tend to plus or minus infinity as income grows over time. Similarly, a quadratic concave function implies that environmental degradation could eventually tend to zero (or even become negative) at sufficiently high income levels, which is not supported by empirical evidence. Another drawback of the quadratic function is that it is a symmetrical function, that is, the uphill portion of the curve has the same slope as the downhill part. This implies that, when income overcomes some threshold level, environmental degradation will decrease at the same rate as it previously increased. This is also very unlikely to occur. In fact, many forms of environmental degradation can be very difficult to undo. For instance, most pollutants tend to cumulate and persist for a long time, therefore their reduction is generally much harder and takes much longer than their generation. Hence, as Pearson (1994, p.212) has argued, more sophisticated techniques of curve fitting should be investigated in the future to avoid that imposing a specific functional form may determine our findings.

The use of unrefined econometric techniques concerns not only the choice of the regression models, but also the estimation method. This is another reason that should induce to treat the empirical evidence of some studies with caution. For instance, most of the early studies used Ordinary Least Squares (OLS) estimations without correcting for heteroscedasticity and autocorrelation of the residuals. However, as Carson *et al.* (1997) point out, the variance of the error terms can differ across countries or regions. Moreover, the residuals are also likely to be auto-correlated because of possible common shocks (e.g., the oil shock) that affects several countries simultaneously (Unruh and Moomaw, 1998). In all these cases, OLS estimates of the standard errors turn out to be biased. This weakness, however, concerns mainly the early studies and it has been generally corrected in most of the recent contributions by using Generalized Least Squares (GLS) estimates.

Inconsistency among different versions of the EKC

Another problem that arises in the empirical literature is the choice of the scaling factor to be used in the regression model. While all studies agree on using per capita GDP (i.e., the ratio y between total income Y and the population level P) as the independent variable on the horizontal axis, one can distinguish three main variants in the literature as to the dependent variable: (i) total emissions (D), (ii) emissions per capita ($d_p = D/P$), (iii) emissions intensity, namely, per unit of GDP ($d_y = D/Y$).

If a given environmental indicator follows an EKC path when measured in terms of per capita degradation, that indicator cannot show a similar EKC pattern in terms of degradation intensity and vice versa, so that the two variants of the EKC are inconsistent.

To show that this is the case, let us assume that there exists an EKC in terms of per capita degradation (Figure 3.5):

(6) $$d_p = ay + by^2$$

where $b < 0$ (since the EKC is a concave parabola) and $a > 0$. This latter condition derives from the former condition on b, since the income value at the vertex of the parabola (i.e., $-a/2b$) must be strictly positive. Notice that we have set the vertical intercept of the parabola (6) equal to zero. This follows from the simplistic assumption that if there is no production (so that per capita income y is zero) no environmental degradation will take place.

Recalling that d_p and y are respectively equal to D/P and Y/P, the previous expression can be rewritten as follows:

(7) $$D/P = a(Y/P) + b(Y/P)^2$$

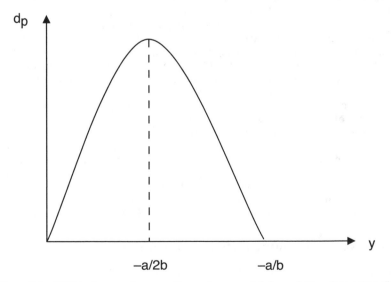

Figure 3.5   EKC in terms of per capita environmental degradation (equation 6)

Multiplying the right-hand side and the left-hand side of (7) by $1/y$ $(=P/Y)$, one gets:

$$D/Y = a + b(Y/P)$$

or equivalently:

(8) $$d_y = a + by$$

From the assumptions on the signs of the parameters a and b seen above, it follows that the latter relationship is represented by a downward sloping line with positive vertical intercept (Figure 3.6). Hence, if per capita degradation d_p has an EKC relationship with per capita income, degradation intensity d_y must be a decreasing function of per capita income for the whole set of income values that are consistent with an EKC above the horizontal axis (i.e., $0 < y < -a/b$).

A similar result emerges if we apply the same reasoning in the opposite direction, namely, if we assume that there exists an EKC in terms of degradation intensity d_y and derive the correspondent relationship between per capita

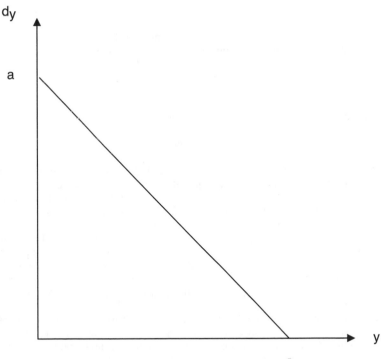

Figure 3.6   Diagram of equation (8)

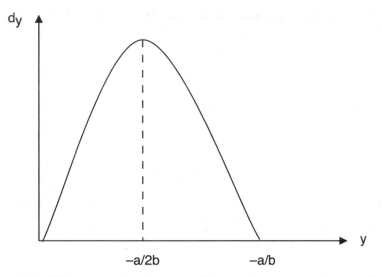

Figure 3.7   EKC in terms of environmental degradation intensity (equation 9)

environmental degradation and per capita income. In this case, the EKC in terms of degradation intensity (Figure 3.7) can be written as follows:

$$(9) \qquad\qquad d_y = ay + by^2$$

where $a > 0, b < 0$.

Multiplying both sides of (9) by y (i.e. Y/P), it yields:

$$(10) \qquad\qquad d_p = ay^2 + by^3$$

Therefore, if degradation intensity shows an EKC-relationship with per capita income, per capita environmental degradation must be a cubic function of per capita income. Figure 3.8 shows the diagram corresponding to equation (10). As the figure shows, per capita degradation d_p first increases and then decreases like the EKC in d_y. However, at low income levels $(0 < y < -a/3b)$, per capita degradation grows at an increasing rate, and thus much faster than degradation intensity. Also observe that $-a/2b < -2a/3b$, therefore, the curve in d_y reaches a peak at lower income levels than the correspondent curve in d_p. It follows that at intermediate per capita income levels $(-a/2b < y < -2a/3b)$ per capita environmental degradation keeps on growing although degradation intensity is on the decreasing portion of the EKC.

Moreover, each of the three variants of the EKC can have very different implications. This is evident if we look at a potentially different shape of the EKC. In fact, as Common (1995) has noticed, the Kuznets-type story that pollution first increases and then decreases with income is consistent with two possible cases: (a) at sufficiently high income levels, the quadratic curve falls to zero (Figure 1.5), (b) at sufficiently high income levels, the curve tends to a lower bound k (Figure 3.9).

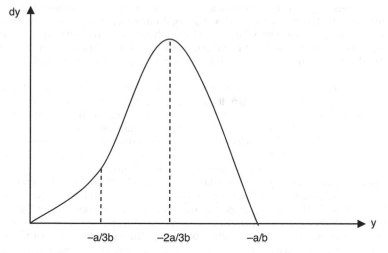

Figure 3.8   Diagram of equation (10)

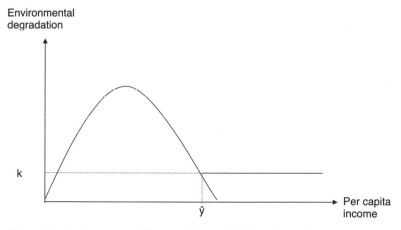

Figure 3.9   Environmental Kuznets Curve with lower bound

We already discussed case (a). As to case (b), if the vertical axis measures total emissions D the shape of the curve implies that emissions will become constant at a sufficiently high per capita income level $\hat{y}$. In other words, indicating with $\dot{D}$ the growth rate of total emissions, we have: $\dot{D} = 0$ when $y > \hat{y}$. However, if we measure d_p on the vertical axis, then *per capita* emissions will stabilize when per capita income y is high enough. In this case the growth rate of *total* emissions will not be zero, but equal to the growth rate of the population, namely:

$\dot{D} = \dot{P}$ when $y > \hat{y}$. Finally, if the vertical axis measures emissions intensity d_y, the existence of a lower bound implies that total emissions will grow at the same rate as total income beyond $\hat{y}$ so that: $\dot{D} = \dot{Y}$ when $y > \hat{y}$. Since total income can grow very fast in the most industrialized countries (that lie beyond $\hat{y}$ on the horizontal axis), this means that also total emissions can keep on growing very fast for ever.

In general, the choice of the correct version of the EKC to be used should depend on the environmental indicator that is taken into account. For instance, the EKC in terms of per capita emission is probably more suitable than the other two versions when the main source of environmental depreciation is the overexploitation of natural resources caused by population growth. However, the emission intensity version can provide a deeper understanding of the issue when pollution is mainly linked to heavy industrial production.

Some studies (Shafik, 1994; Kaufman *et al.*, 1998) have proposed the concentration of pollutants as an alternative indicator of environmental degradation. This is probably the most appropriate indicator when one examines global pollutants since their stock contributes to global warming more than their emissions (the so-called "stock externality" problem). This consideration cast further doubts on the evidence in favor of the EKC. In fact, a convex relationship often emerges in those studies that measure concentration rather than emissions of global pollutants (Kaufman *et al.*, 1998 for SO_2; Shafik, 1994 for CO_2).

4
Sustainable Development, Global Warming and Energy Trends

1   The current energy system

The current system of energy production, distribution and consumption (henceforth energy system) has many serious weaknesses: on the one hand, it is a crucial determinant of the undergoing process of global warming, on the other hand, it is very vulnerable from the security and economic point of view as the effective availability of its main energy sources and their expected prices are highly uncertain. There is wide agreement on the fact that the age of fossil fuels is bound to decline during this century, progressively giving way to a different energy system based on alternative energy sources. Opinion, however, is quite divided on the amount of fossil fuels reserves, on the characteristics that the new energy system should have as well as on which economic, environmental and energy policies should guide the pace of the transition process.

The current energy system contributes to climate change in a crucial way. There is compelling evidence that the rising concentration of GHGs due to anthropogenic factors causes global warming by increasing the amount of infrared radiation (heat energy) trapped in it (IPCC, 2007). The concentration of GHGs in the atmosphere is currently estimated to be equivalent to 430 parts per million (ppm) of CO_2, a value already much higher than that existing before the Industrial Revolution (280 ppm on average in the period 1750–1850). Climatologists maintain that this level of concentration has already brought about an increase of 0.74°C in the average world temperature (IPCC, 2007). According to the best available estimates, the concentration of GHGs in the atmosphere is rising at around 2.3 ppm per year and is expected to reach a level double to that of the pre-industrial period within a few decades. At this level of concentration there is serious risk that the global average temperature may rise beyond 2°C as compared to that of the pre-industrial era by the middle of the century, virtually committing us by inertia to a much superior global average temperature that might exceed 4°C by the end of the century (IPCC, 2007).[34]

Global warming is expected to have many severe impacts on the biosphere and on the wealth and health of the world population. Among its negative consequences, we recall the systematic melting of glaciers that reduces the fresh water available and increases the sea level, declining crop yields, increase in vector-borne diseases such as malaria and dengue fever, ocean acidification and reduction of fish stocks, collapse of tropical rainforests, biodiversity loss, desertification, increasing damage costs from extreme weather events (storms, hurricanes, typhoons, heat waves, floods, droughts), etc. The growing diffusion of these phenomena is likely to increase much further in the future along with the increase in the temperature. What is worse, poor countries are expected to suffer most of the negative effects brought about by climate change (Stern, 2006).

Today's energy system, however, is not only hazardous for the safety and health of the world population, but is also vulnerable from the economic and security points of view. This depends on the fact that the reserves of fossil fuels are limited and it is very difficult to predict the timing and economic consequences of the exhaustion process. In addition, the predictions on the effective availability of oil and gas are particularly difficult and unreliable since their reserves are remarkably concentrated in terms of both location and ownership.[35] This exposes energy production and distribution to considerable geopolitical dangers which became evident in the 1970s when the two oil shocks of 1973 and 1979 provoked a serious economic turmoil in the world economy due to the simultaneous increase of inflation and unemployment (stagflation).

Furthermore, the territorial concentration of fossil fuels reserves favored the consolidation of centralized and hierarchical energy infrastructures which accentuated the vulnerability of the energy model. World energy supplies depend on a network of oil and gas pipelines and petrol tankers routes – a network which has its "pumping heart" in the Middle East. Any problem occurring at the circulatory system which animates the world economy would have devastating repercussions on people's welfare. This has contributed to the dangerous conflicts for economic and political leadership over the area of the Middle East with serious consequences which could become even worse in the future.

Lastly, the very high costs linked to prospecting, extracting, refining and distributing oil and other fossil fuels require colossal investments which only mega-enterprises can manage. This has created an oligopolistic market dominated by a few multinational giants on whose strategies depend the world energy supply and the oil price. This in turn has strongly affected the performance of the world economy.

For all these reasons, the current energy system may seriously undermine the continuation of the world economic development. To get a deeper understanding on these issues, in this chapter we discuss to what extent the recent trends in the energy system are compatible with the requirements of sustainable development. For this purpose, we will adopt in this chapter a particular version of the decomposition approach introduced in Chapter 3, that will be applied here more specifically to the energy sector. By applying this method to the existing empirical evidence we will draw some indications on the desirable characteristics of the future energy system and on the most opportune policies to make the transition process consistent with the sustainability requirements.

2   The conventional position and its shortcomings

First of all, we intend to discuss the mainstream position concerning the production and consumption of energy – a position held by the most energy producers and agencies, although with different nuances, and often endorsed by the mass media. For ease of reference, we will call this dominant view as the "conventional position".

Despite a growing anxiety looming in the official and governmental documents, the conventional position is characterized by prevalent optimism on the capacity of unfettered markets, assisted by market-oriented technical progress, to resolve the problems raised by the current energy system. Although fossil fuels are non-renewable energy sources, the limits of their reserves are not considered stringent, at least in the next decades. This position is often corroborated by tables and figures showing that proven reserves of oil and natural gas have gradually increased in the last few decades (see, Figure 4.1).[36] Therefore, the expected lifespan, T, of many exhaustible resources, including fossil fuels, has been upwardly revised over time (Table 4.1), contradicting the forecasts of the Club of Rome (Meadows *et al.*, 1972) according to which oil supply would already have run out by the early 1990s.

The apparent paradox of an increase over time of the available stock of these exhaustible resources is normally explained by referring to technical progress that permitted the discovery of new reserves as a

Figure 4.1   Proven reserves of oil and natural gas

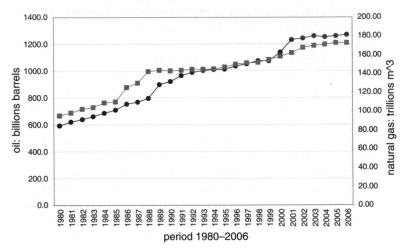

Source: Authors' elaboration on British Petroleum data (British Petroleum, 2007).

Table 4.1   Expected lifespan of fossil fuel reserves measured in number of years (T) starting from different base years (1970, 1994 and 2006)[37]

Fossil fuels	T_{1970} (*Source*: Meadows et al., 1972)	T_{1994} (*Source*: British Petroleum, 1995)	T_{2006} (*Source*: British Petroleum, 2007)
Coal	111	139	147
Natural gas	22	42	63,3
Oil	20	35	40,5

result of increasingly sophisticated methods of prospecting. Furthermore, the conventional view claims that technical progress will soon allow the exploitation – at competitive costs – of reserves that are not currently viable for reasons of location (e.g. under the sea), depth, and quality of the raw material. The observed increase over time of fossil fuels reserves and the underlying explanation have generated the widespread conviction that the age of fossil fuels is not due to end before the middle of this century and that the transition towards an alternative energy model may be managed in due course by market forces and market-led technical progress. Sheikh Yamani, the powerful Organization of Petroleum Exporting Countries (OPEC) leader of the past, used to say that the Stone Age did not end for a lack of stones and that the Age of Oil will not end for a lack of oil. From this standpoint, the transition will come about as soon as the cost of one kilowatt-hour (kWh) produced from fossil fuels will exceed the cost of one kWh produced by alternative energy sources. In this view the transition towards an alternative energy model based on the so-called "backstop technology" is not expected to occur before the middle of this century.

The conventional position does not deny the risk of recurrent shortages of fossil fuels, but they are interpreted as episodic instances that can be confined either to "cyclical" causes, when demand exceeds planned supply following a cyclical boom in national income, or to "extra-economic" causes, as in the case of the two oil shocks of the 1970s. The recurrent shortages of fossil fuels are thus seen as temporary phenomena to which the market is expected to respond spontaneously with a prompt and congruent price increase. The latter is expected to stimulate supply and technological progress. In particular, an increase in the fuel price is bound to shift the demand towards suppliers or reserves which, in consequence of such a price increase, become economically convenient. So, for example, the rapid increase in the oil price provoked by the two shocks in the 1970s, made it worthwhile to extract oil in other geographical areas, such as the North Sea, Russia and Mexico, where average production costs were considerably higher than in the OPEC countries. This determined a reduction over time in the OPEC's share of world oil production which led the member countries to reduce the price in order to gain back the share they had lost.[38]

As regards climate change, the conventional position maintained a rather optimistic attitude in the 1990s, one which is still basically held today. On the basis of the observed reduction in energy intensity and in the carbon content per unit of GDP, the conviction grew that the GHGs emissions generated by the energy system had started to stabilize. In this spirit, from the EKC applied to the energy sector, some have drawn the hurried conclusion that in order to resolve the environmental problems raised by energy consumption and production, it would suffice to promote economic growth.[39]

The conventional assessment of the qualitative features of the current energy system is reassuring but not convincing. First of all, it risks underestimating the physical scarcity of oil and natural gas. There are many indications that the residual reserves may have been over-estimated by "creative" geological accounting. The proponents of these estimates, in fact, may have an interest in inflating them. The producer countries might do so in order to obtain higher production quotas and better conditions for the large loans they contract with the banks and international organizations. Analogously, the oil multinationals which participate in the data-gathering process and in the estimates of the residual reserves, have an interest in over-estimating the reserves under their control in order to improve the performance of their shares on the stock exchange and to increase their bargaining power. A case in point is that of the Royal Dutch Shell that overestimated by about 20% the reserves of oil under its control in the period 1997–2003. This scandal, exploded in January 2004, provoked the resignation of its top management and the payment of huge fees to the UK and USA financial authorities. Similarly, other oil companies have substantially reduced their estimated reserves in the last few years (El Paso by 11% in 2004, Repsol-Ypf by 25% in 2006). While reserves revision is not a new phenomenon, its scope and magnitude have recently induced the United Nations to set forth a new methodology for assessing the world energy reserves and harmonize the existing terminology across different classifications (UNECE, 2004). Some countries (e.g. Canada), moreover, have introduced new disclosure systems compelling oil companies to rely on independent evaluators to certify their proven reserves (CSA, 2003).

Some recent contributions (cf. Porter, 2006, and the literature there cited) have started to question the growing availability of fossil fuels. In their opinion, the annual production of oil, and similarly of natural gas, is bound to follow an inverse-U pattern, generally called "Hubbert curve" from the name of the petrol geophysicist who first advanced the hypothesis in 1956. This hypothesis is fairly robust for each oil field. At the beginning productivity increases as the specific problems of recovery of the fossil fuel from a given field are progressively solved. When about half of the reserve has been exploited, productivity starts declining and keeps on falling until production has to stop, much before physical exhaustion, when the cost of production becomes too high to guarantee a profit.[40] The pattern of cumulated production thus follows a logistic curve, the derivative of which is described by a bell-shaped curve representing the annual production of the fossil fuel. Hubbert (1956) not only clarified the nature and causes of this pattern, but extended the hypotheses from a given field to the aggregate level, forecasting that the peak of the USA oil production would have occurred in the year 1970 and at the world level in the year 2000. His prediction for the USA proved to be remarkably accurate and this increased the prestige of his theory, while his prediction at the world level proved to be premature. The followers of Hubbert argue that the oil shocks of the 1970s and the ensuing widespread reactions have slowed down for at least two decades the consumption of oil postponing the peak for a few years, but that in any case we should expect the peak to be reached very soon (e.g. Deffeyes, 2001; Campbell, 2004; Goodstein, 2004). The critics observe that at the aggregate level oil supply is not given as it depends on its price. A rise in the latter increases oil supply as it stimulates more investment in prospecting new reserves, substitution with new sources of oil (tar sands, oil shales, ultra-heavy oil, etc.), and implementation of new technologies to exploit them.[41] Moreover, while the world supply of oil and gas might decrease in the next few decades, this does not apply to coal that is largely available at relatively low costs in some of the most energy consuming countries such as Russia, China and the USA.

The authoritative Hirsch Report (2005), written for the US Department of Energy by a team of high-level experts, shows that most projections estimate that oil production will peak before the year 2020. According to the Report, moreover, after the peak we should expect a severe and persistent shortage of liquid fuel with serious repercussions on the world economy such as cost-inflation, stagnation, structural unemployment. Taking action after the peak would involve a significant liquid fuel shortage for more than two decades, while starting a mitigation crash program 10 years before the peak would greatly reduce the costs of adaptation. The latter, however, would still be serious since even a mitigation crash program could not avoid a significant liquid fuel shortage for about a decade after the peak. Therefore, the risks of a late adoption of an emergency mitigation program are very high. On the contrary, a premature adoption of a severe mitigation program would involve only very modest costs. Basic risk-management considerations should thus induce policy-makers to act immediately with the necessary determination (Hirsch, 2005).

We will not discuss here the different viewpoints on the Hubbert curve as this goes beyond the scope of the present work. In any case, whether the Hubbert hypothesis is adequate or not at the aggregate level, it suggests that in the era of fossil fuels the world economy might progress on a knife edge, facing a trade-off between the scarcity of fossil fuels on the one hand and global warming on the other hand. If the physical scarcity of oil (and gas) is becoming seriously binding at the global level, as the supporters of the Hubbert curve maintain, this is likely to have an adverse effect on energy prices but a positive effect on the reduction of GHGs emissions. After the peak, oil production will bend downwards while energy demand is expected to continue at a sustained pace according to all most qualified projections (e.g. IEA, 2006). In the absence of easily accessible alternative fuels, the growing tendential gap between demand and supply might be bridged by a sharp increase in the price of oil that would lower its demand. The rise in the oil price could promote more effective energy conservation policies that have been insufficiently pursued in the past during periods of low energy prices, thus partially reducing the pressure towards higher prices. But without policy measures meant to accelerate and smooth the transition to a more sustainable energy system, the economic effects might be similar to those already experienced in the 1970s, cost inflation and stagnation, and in the 1980s, a persisting world depression. If, on the contrary, the physical scarcity of oil and gas will become binding only after a few decades, as the critics of the global Hubbert curve maintain, the persisting cheap price of fossil fuels will leave unchecked the dangerous progression of GHGs emissions that could reach a level inconsistent with the stabilization of the world average temperature. The same applies if the growing scarcity of oil and gas should increase the share of energy consumption met by coal that is more largely available, but also more polluting than the other fossil fuels.[42]

In order to exit from this dilemma we need policy measures that succeed in internalizing, rapidly but progressively, the externalities of the current energy system. The ensuing sizeable and progressive increase in the price of fossil fuels would slow down GHGs emissions and accelerate the transition to a different energy system without disrupting the process of world development. The speed and the nature of this transition crucially depend on the evolution of the cost of production per kWh for each energy source. A correct assessment of the intertemporal evolution of such a cost, which is crucial for steering the correct energy choices, is not only a question of fairly accurate forecasting but also of energy policy. If the large public subsidies granted to the production and distribution of energy from fossil fuel were abolished, this could considerably accelerate the transition to the use of renewable energy sources. Further acceleration could be achieved by channeling the above-mentioned subsidies to the renewable resources to encourage the immediate utilization of the potential economies of scale.[43]

Some powerful economic, financial and political interests, however, tend to slow down the transition process. All states and enterprises with big stakes in the fossil fuel sector would like to exploit the economic opportunities it offers for as long as possible. Furthermore, even the States that import most of the available fossil fuels are reluctant to take direct steps to reduce their consumption because of the sizeable tax revenues they earn from fossil fuel consumption.

Therefore, as to the market optimism characterizing the conventional position, it could be claimed that in the energy field the myth of the invisible hand in the competitive market appears particularly groundless. The allocation of energy resources and the prices for their use are moved by hands that are both visible and easy to identify, such as multinational oil companies, OPEC and the energy policies of the developed countries.

3   The current energy system, global warming and the sustainability gap

As mentioned above, the current trends of the energy system raise not only a problem of structural shortage, but also of polluting GHG emissions deriving from production and consumption of fossil fuels. Such emissions cause severe health damages and tend to alter the climate at the world level. Their health effects will be discussed in details in Chapter 5. In this section we intend to focus on the climate effects in order to examine whether the current energy trends are compatible with sustainable development, as far as global warming is concerned. As pointed out in the previous chapter, for economic development to be environmentally sustainable at the world level, the global environmental degradation should not increase over time. By sustainable development, therefore, in this chapter we mean development that does not increase GHG emissions, what will be defined for ease of reference as "GHG-sustainability". While this requirement is clearly insufficient to stop global warming (as will be pointed out below), it can be considered as an important first step to deal with climate change problems. Moreover, it provides a useful benchmark that allows comparing the simple stabilization of GHG emissions with more stringent reduction requirements such as those set by the Kyoto Protocol, or those required to stabilize the world temperature to a certain level.

We start the analysis by decomposing the impact on GHGs emissions of a few crucial socio-economic determinants using the following identity:

(1) $$G = Pyefg$$

where G stands for the emissions of GHGs; Y is the GDP; P is the population; $y = Y/P$ is per capita income; $e = E/Y$ is energy intensity, namely, energy consumption (E) per unit of GDP; $f = F/E$ is the share of fossil fuels (F) on energy consumption and $g = G/F$ is the intensity of GHG emissions per unit of fossil fuel consumed.

Identity (1) may be interpreted as a specific application to the energy sector of the decomposition approach discussed in Chapter 3 and is a straightforward generalization of the "Kaya identity", from the name of the Japanese scholar who first suggested an analogous identity to study the dynamics of CO_2 emissions (Kaya, 1990; Yamaji *et al.*, 1991; IPCC, 2001). Similar identities have been used so far mainly to give rigorous quantitative foundations to scenario analysis. We use identity (1) in this chapter in a different way and for different purposes. We intend to clarify a few crucial conditions of sustainability of the energy system from the point of view of global warming in order to evaluate to what extent the current energy system complied with these conditions and is going to deviate from them in the next decades in the assumption that the policy strategy is not going to change (the so-called "business-as-usual" scenario).

By taking the time derivative of the logarithms of the variables, from (1) we derive an identity that connects additively the growth rate of the variables (indicated with an asterisk):

(2) $$G^* = P^* + y^* + e^* + f^* + g^*$$

In the following analysis we will mainly refer to this second version of the identity since the growth rate of the relevant variables is intuitively appealing and easily calculable from available data, thus facilitating the analysis of the causes and consequences of global warming.

Identities (1) and (2) may be applied both at the global and at the local level. In this paper we focus mainly on the global process from the policy viewpoint in the light of the historical records, their projections, and comparative insights within a medium-run time horizon (from 10 to 30 years). We may distinguish within these identities between target variables, to which policy-makers assign desired values, and instrumental variables, that have to be controlled in order to reach these targets. The choice of policy interventions may be based on the analysis of cost trade-offs between the interventions on different instrumental variables in order to minimize policy costs given the objectives (Nordhaus, 2005). The over-arching target of our policy analysis is assumed to be the sustainable growth of per capita GDP, that is a growth rate of y that is consistent with a non-increasing path of GHG emissions ($G^* \le 0$). As to the remaining variables, a discussion of the factors underlying the demographic dynamics goes beyond the scope of the present analysis. In this chapter, therefore, we will take population growth P^* as exogenously given, so that the set of instrumental variables in identity (2) is restricted to energy intensity e, GHG intensity g, and the share of fossil fuels f.

From (2) we derive the following GHG-sustainability condition, namely, the condition that the growth rate of per capita income should satisfy to be consistent with a non-increasing path of GHG emissions ($G^* \leq 0$):

$$(3) \qquad y^* \leq - (P^* + e^* + f^* + g^*)$$

which can also be expressed a follows:

$$(4) \qquad Y^* \leq (e^* + f^* + g^*)$$

On the basis of these identities, it is possible to analyze what has happened in the world over the last three decades of the previous century and the forecasts of the Energy Information Administration (EIA) for the first three decades of the new century (EIA, 2006). The basic data are summarized in Table 4.2. The rate of growth of GHGs G^* is measured in the table, as a first approximation, with the rate of growth of CO_2 emissions. In fact, though CO_2 is just one of the many GHGs that contribute to climate change,[44] it is considered as the main cause of global warming since its emissions contribute for about three-quarter to total GHGs emissions. In addition, it has a particularly long estimated atmospheric lifetime (50 to 200 years). The concentration of CO_2 emissions in the atmosphere, moreover, plays a crucial role

Table 4.2   EIA scenario

World	G^*	Y^*	P^*	y^*	E^*	e^*	F^*	g^*	f^*
1971–1980	2,8	4,1	1,9	2,2	3,0	–1,1	2,5	0,3	–0,5
1981–1990	1,6	3,2	1,9	1,3	2,1	–1,1	1,7	–0,1	–0,4
1991–2000	1,4	3,4	1,6	1,8	1,6	–1,8	1,2	0,2	–0,4
1971–2000	1,8	3,3	1,7	1,6	2,1	–1,2	1,8	0	–0,3
2003–2030	2,1	3,8	1,0	2,8	2,0	–1,8	2,1	0	0,1

Source: Authors' elaboration on EIA (2006) and British Petroleum (2006) data.
Legend: G = CO_2 emissions, Y = income, P = population, y = per capita income, E = primary energy demand, e = E/Y = energy intensity, F = total consumption of fossil fuels, g = G/F = CO_2 intensity per unit of fossil fuel, f = F/E = share of fossil fuels on energy consumption. The star above each variable indicates the growth rate of the variable.

in the preservation of the equilibria of the biosphere also for reasons independent of global warming. In particular, a further increase in its concentration would increase the acidification of oceans jeopardizing their biological equilibria (see, e.g., Stern, 2006).

According to the EIA's forecasts based on the "business-as-usual" (BAU) scenario, global energy demand E is destined to increase until 2030 at an average rate of 2%. In the same period global energy intensity e is destined to fall by 1.8% as a result of technical progress but this is not enough to reduce CO_2 emissions that will increase on average by 2.1% (EIA, 2006).[45] Therefore, the estimated trends do not comply with the requirements of GHG-sustainability.

In addition, the energy trends are unlikely to comply with the requirements of social sustainability. Inequality in terms of per capita energy distribution is expected to remain very marked; this will strongly influence access to economic opportunities on the part of the most disadvantaged people, further increasing income inequality and poverty. The International Energy Agency (IEA, 2004) forecasts that in 2030 there will still be 1.4 billion people without electricity. Furthermore, in the developing countries 2/5 of energy consumption will still be based on traditional biomass which is a particularly inefficient and polluting source of energy.

Energy trends have been incompatible with sustainable development in the latter decades. Nevertheless, as can be seen in Table 4.2, the trends have been gradually improving over the last three decades of the 20th century, while they are expected to worsen in the first three decades of the 21st century. In particular, energy intensity e has fallen more and more rapidly from 1.1% in the 1970s and 1980s to 1.8% in the 1990s. This was the result of greater attention being paid to energy-saving following the oil shocks of the 1970s. In the 1990s, a significant contribution to this virtuous trend was provided by the systematic introduction of information and communication technologies (see Chapter 6). The progressive reduction in energy intensity, however, might be unable to continue in the next decades with respect to the 1990s, due to the more rapid growth of developing economies such as India and China. These economies are generally characterized by high energy intensity (and thus also high carbon intensity) which may cause high growth rates of CO_2 emissions in the future as their GDP grows.

The expected increase in total CO_2 emissions, however, is largely due to the incapacity of achieving significant improvements in g and f. The GHG intensity g is destined to remain constant over the next three decades, while the share of fossil fuels f, which had fallen (though at declining rates) in the past, is expected to revert its trend and grow in the future, although at a very low rate (0.1%). This suggests a worsening of the sustainable development scenario despite the expected reduction in the rate of demographic growth.

Behind these negative trends there is an overly slow transition process towards an alternative model based on the massive use of renewable resources: the International Energy Agency (IEA, 2004) forecasts that the percentage of world energy consumption met by all renewable sources will remain unchanged (around 14%) between 2002 and 2030.[46] Similarly, the total share of renewable energy sources in world electricity generation is expected to increase by only 1% (from 18% to 19%) in the same period. The explanation set forth for such a slow transition process is generally that energy produced from fossil fuels costs less and will continue to be cheaper for the whole period. This explanation, however, seems only partly valid. Indeed, this assertion is based on an unsatisfactory way of calculating the cost of kWh for each source of energy. First of all, no account is taken of external costs which in the case of fossil fuels are particularly high. The increase in CO_2 is bound to worsen considerably global warming with all its dire consequences. In addition, the production of fossil fuels can be just as dangerous in itself. It has been calculated, for example, that coal-mining alone involves many casualties each year. Finally, fossil fuels are very concentrated in a few regions of the world, thus creating strong tensions for the economic and political control of these areas that could lead in the future to a much higher cost of energy production with fossil fuels than that being forecast today.

4 Constant emissions and the Kyoto target: the income sustainability gap

The deterioration of sustainability that emerges from the previous analysis can be expressed by defining an income sustainability gap that measures how distant the income growth rate is from a given environmental target chosen by the policy-maker. Let us first assume that policy-makers aim at stabilizing current emissions, i.e. $G^* = 0$. While this target is insufficient to stop global warming (see below), it represents a minimum requirement to make sure that the pollution trend is not going to worsen. Replacing $G^* = 0$ in identity (2) and solving with respect to y^* we obtain the per capita income growth rate corresponding to constant CO_2 emissions. We indicate it with y^*_{max} since it is also the maximum growth rate of per capita income that complies with the GHG-sustainability requirement:

(5) $y^*_{max} = - (e^* + g^* + f^*) - P^*$

In the last 30 years the actual value of the rate of growth systematically exceeded the maximum sustainable value as defined above. We may define the income sustainability gap as the difference between the actual growth rate of per capita (total) income and its maximum sustainable value:

(6) $y^* - y^*_{max} = Y^* - Y^*_{max} = Y^* + e^* + g^* + f^*$

The empirical evidence reported in Table 4.2 suggests that the income sustainability gap diminished in the last three decades of the previous century although at a decreasing rate (from 2.8% in the 1970s to 1.6% in the '80s and to 1.4% in the '90s), but is expected to increase again to 2.1% in the next decades on the basis of the BAU scenario (EIA, 2006). This suggests that existing policies are inadequate not only to reach, but also to approach, the stabilization of current emissions. As mentioned above, moreover, this minimum target is by no means sufficient to stabilize global warming since the current flow of GHGs in the atmosphere (42 $GtCO_2$.e) is much higher than the flow that the biosphere is able to absorb (that it is estimated to be 5 $GtCO_2$.e per year). Because of the strong inertia inbuilt in the natural processes underlying global warming, it is calculated that, even if we succeeded in stopping now the GHGs emissions, the world average temperature would increase by another 1.5% before starting to diminish (Stern, 2006).

The maximum tolerable stock of GHGs in the atmosphere depends on the maximum increase of temperature we are willing to accept. According to many scholars, a rise in temperature of 2°C is the maximum tolerable threshold beyond which the damages provoked by global warming could rapidly become unbearable. This target has inspired the text of the Kyoto Protocol that has been negotiated in 1997 and came into force since February 2005. As is well-known, the Kyoto Protocol is an agreement under which industrialized countries commit themselves to reduce total GHG emissions by 5.2% at the world level as measured in the period 2008–2012 with respect to the 1990 level. More precisely, the goal is to lower by this percentage the overall average emissions calculated over the period 2008–2012 of six GHGs: CO_2, methane (CH_4), N_2O, sulfur hexafluoride (SF_6), hydrofluorocarbons (HFCs) and perfluorocarbons

(PFCs). This target represents about a 30% cut compared to the emissions level expected by 2010 without the Protocol. The national targets have been differentiated according to different parameters and negotiations. As to the developed countries listed in the Annex 1 of the Protocol, national targets range from emissions cut (by 8% on average for the European Union [EU], 7% for the US, 6% for Japan and Canada), to constant emissions (in Russia and New Zealand) to maximum allowed increases in the emissions level (by 8% in Australia and 10% in Iceland). Any Annex 1 country that fails to meet the Kyoto target will be penalized by having its reduction targets enhanced by 30% in the next period. On the contrary, the developing countries, generally referred to as "Non-Annex 1 countries", have neither emission reduction obligations nor a maximum emissions growth rate to comply with.

The effort to comply with the provisions is quite demanding. This can be easily seen by applying the decomposition approach presented above in the light of the Kyoto Protocol. As mentioned before, in order to stabilize the average increase of temperature within 2°C, the Protocol requires an average reduction of GHG emissions of 5.2% at the world level, so that G^* should be equal to -5.2 in identity (2). This implies that the sustainability gap with respect to the Kyoto target would be about 5% higher than according to the baseline of zero emissions growth, which makes it even more difficult to stabilize the temperature in the future at the current level even through a very tough policy strategy. Since in the meantime world CO_2 emissions increased by an additional 18% with respect to the 1990 level (EIA, 2006), to comply with the Kyoto targets the decrease of emissions in the last years of its application should be about 23%.[47] A similar increasing trend in CO_2 emissions has characterized many Annex I countries whose distance from the target has further increased rather than decreased since 1990. It is easy to conceive that the Kyoto objectives will not be easily obtained by most signatory countries and that the next years will be characterized by intense negotiations about the application of the sanctions and how to conceive the after-Kyoto global strategy against global warming. The current trends, however, are quite distant from the target. We have to conclude that from the point of view of global warming the rate of economic growth is at present highly unsustainable at the world level.

5   Implications for policy design

The decomposition approach as developed in this chapter can provide a useful tool not only to verify the sustainability of the current energy trends, but also to orientate the best policy strategy to control the global warming process.

Let us assume that $G^{*\prime}$ is the rate of reduction of GHGs emissions that a policy-maker aims at. Thus, for instance, we can think of $G^{*\prime}$ as the emission cut that is required to avoid a further increase in the world average temperature or to ensure at least that global warming does not increase too much (like in the case of the Kyoto Protocol).

For policy purposes we have to distinguish between artificial emissions G_1 and natural emissions G_2, net of the natural absorption capacity A. While the former emissions are produced by human activity, the latter depend on physical, chemical and biological processes that would be active also in the absence of any human impact. When we design a policy mix we have to take account also of the natural component G_2, because policy interventions may affect not only artificial emissions, but also natural emissions and their natural absorption rate. As a matter of fact, in a warmer climate plants and soils absorb less carbon from the atmosphere, the atmosphere absorbs more water, while permafrost thaws releasing a large quantity of CH_4, and the sunlight reflected by the ice cover of earth sharply diminishes. However, the impact of policy interventions on natural emissions and absorption capacity may sometimes be difficult to forecast because of the scientific uncertainty on the ways in which human action may alter natural dynamics and ecological equilibria.

As pointed out before, in order to reach a given target $G^* = G^{*\prime}$, we can mainly rely on three instrumental variables: the share of fossil fuels (f), GHG intensity (g) and energy intensity (e).

As for the share of fossil fuels f we have to reduce it by increasing the share of alternative energies. The BAU scenario, however, expects a further slight increase of f by 2030. A sizeable reduction of f in the next years is possible in the light of the recent technological advances that have been already successfully exploited by a few leading countries. At the world level, however, we cannot expect a significant rate of negative growth of the fossil fuels share unless their price will have a sizeable and persistent increase. Any reduction of f would have a great strategic value but we have to consider the future evolution of f as very slow in the near future. The burden of a medium run policy adjustment has presumably to fall on other instrumental variables.

As for the carbon intensity of fossil fuels g the obvious way to reduce it relies on a systematic shift towards fossil fuels with a lower carbon content taking account that, in the absence of an effective process of capture and sequestration of CO_2, natural gas emissions are about 60% less than those of coal and about 30% less than oil. However, this process of substitution is checked by a few serious obstacles. Cheaply accessible coal reserves are much greater than those of oil and natural gas. In particular, many important countries such as India and China have very limited reserves of oil and natural gas and huge reserves of coal so that the substitution of the latter with less polluting fossil fuels would run against their economic and security targets. Recent technological advances promise to allow a sizeable abatement of emissions also in the case of coal. In particular, the carbon intensity of fossil fuels g may be reduced also through carbon capture and storage (CCS). Technology for capturing CO_2 is already commercially available for large CO_2 emitters, such as power plants. CCS may reduce CO_2 emissions up to 80–90%, but increases the fuel needs by about 10–40% and the cost of energy by 30–60%. However, if CO_2 is injected and stored in exhausted oil and gas fields, this allows enhanced oil recovery that may cover the extra costs of CCS. A long-term option is carbon capture directly from the air using hydroxides. This technology, however, is not yet fully developed and it is difficult to forecast when it will become really operational. In any case, we have to act with determination to curb rapidly the value of carbon intensity of fossil fuels, but we cannot expect that this will soon translate in a significant negative growth rate of g at the world level.

Much of the burden of short- and medium-term policy adjustment thus falls on energy intensity. In this case we may figure out significant rates of reduction provided that we use all available policy instruments with great determination. The dramatic increase of oil price in the 1970s triggered by the two oil shocks shows that on this front it is possible to obtain rapid improvements provided that the price of fossil fuels increases enough to motivate systematic market and policy interventions.

The decomposition approach developed in this chapter may also help us to solve the awkward distributive problems concerning the costs of the policy interventions meant to cope with global warming. If we define net atmospheric pollution as GHGs emissions in excess of the natural level of absorption A, we can write:

(7) $$G - A = g_p P - A$$

where $g_p = G/P$

From (7) it follows that if total emissions equal the natural absorption capacity ($G = A$), per capita emissions g_p are given by A/P. On the basis of the "polluter pays principle", therefore, any state or group of individuals should pay the costs of pollution in proportion of its excess over A/P. This approach would be preferable to that adopted by the Kyoto Protocol that selected, quite arbitrarily, a base year (1990) that benefits some partners and hits others and assigns different objectives to single countries on the basis of complex and not always transparent criteria. Of course the value A/P is not constant over time, but changes very slowly: this allows a periodic revision of the baseline that could be based on a simple algorithm agreed by all parties. In particular, the natural absorption capacity could be increased by avoiding deforestation and promoting afforestation. The emissions from deforestation are estimated to amount to more than the 18% of global emissions, more than global transportation. Therefore, preserving forests by curbing deforestation and increasing afforestation would be a cost-effective way to reduce net atmospheric pollution (Stern, 2006).

6   Concluding remarks

In this chapter we aimed to analyze to what extent the current energy system based on fossil fuels is consistent with the requisites of sustainable development, focusing the analysis on global warming. The decomposition approach developed in this chapter may contribute to clarify the sustainability conditions required to cope with the risks of global warming and make explicit how far we currently are from the satisfaction of these conditions. Moreover, it may give us a few useful insights from the descriptive point of view as well as from the policy point of view and may contribute to orientate the general strategy of revision of the Kyoto Protocol.

This approach is certainly too simple to account for many important details of the interaction between socioeconomic processes and global warming. In addition, the identities on which it is based cannot be utilized for empirical estimations of correlations and causal relations between variables or to evaluate the costs and benefits of alternative policies. However, these identities help us to make explicit logical constraints on empirical and causal analysis favoring a correct use of economic and policy reasoning. Therefore, this approach may play a useful role as a bridge between ordinary language discussion of the issues, insufficiently rigorous but rich of semantic understanding, and fully fledged rigorous analytical and simulation models. Within the limited scope of the identities here discussed, their quantitative implications are correct by definition so that the uncertainty is restricted to their interpretation. Therefore, we believe that the decomposition approach, as developed in this chapter, may play a role to set a common ground between researchers having different disciplinary backgrounds, policy-makers and public opinion, helping to orientate the general outlines of the policy strategies aimed at controlling the process of global warming.

In particular, the use of the decomposition method as developed in this chapter contributed to clarify that the current energy system is trapped on a dangerous knife edge between scarcity of fossil fuels and global warming. If the peak of production of oil and gas is round the corner, as many supporters of the global Hubbert curve maintain, their price is due to increase significantly in the near future and this may accelerate the shift towards the systematic use of non-fossil fuels reducing the risks involved by the continuation of the process of global warming. On the contrary, if the physical scarcity of traditional fossil fuels (oil and gas) proves to be only weakly constraining in the next decades, as most critics of the global Hubbert curve contend, the increase of GHGs emissions would remain unchecked so that the process of global warming would accelerate with all its dire consequences. In both cases the growth of world GDP risks to be deeply disturbed, although for different reasons and with a different timing. If the scarcity of fossil fuels will be constraining in the next decades, the sharp increase of energy prices, in the absence of the alternative infrastructures and facilities necessary to shift smoothly to a different energy system, is likely to disrupt the process of economic growth because of a surge of cost inflation and/or stagnation of the kind already experienced in the 1970s and early 1980s as a consequence of the two oil shocks. On the other hand, if the physical scarcity of traditional fossil fuels will not be seriously constraining in the next decades, the process of global warming could rapidly overcome a threshold beyond which the continuation of world GDP growth would become severely constrained since the necessary defensive and adaptation expenses would become huge (Stern, 2006).

The current energy system is mainly orientated towards the production, distribution and consumption of fossil fuels. This locks the energy system within its current emphasis on fossil fuels because of huge sunk costs and weak alternative infrastructures, facilities and supporting policies. In this situation the sudden emergence of a persistent scarcity of oil or gas would most likely shift the energy system towards increasing use of coal and other fossil fuels much more polluting than oil and gas rather than towards alternative cleaner non-fossil sources of energy. To avoid this risk we should adopt a far-sighted policy strategy that accelerates the transition towards a different energy system in a smooth way. In the situation that we have tried to depict in this chapter the cost of inaction, or of inertial collective action, would be very high.

5
Inequality, Health and the Environment

The process of globalization affects more and more the life quality of people around the world. In particular, it impinges in different ways upon their health that is the most revealing single proxy of life quality. The health of people affects in its turn the demographic and economic growth of nations as well as their sustainability. Notwithstanding the fundamental importance of this complex network of interactions, however, the nexus between globalization, sustainable development and health has been so far insufficiently analyzed.[48]

This chapter aims at exploring the main channels of influence through which the recent process of globalization has affected the population health in different countries. This crucial influence has impinged on the sustainability of world development not only by affecting income growth but also income inequality and environmental deterioration. In order to explore the causal factors underlying the feedback between globalization and health, we try to identify the principal, both direct and indirect, empirical correlations between the main features of globalization and different indices of health; we then proceed to a preliminary discussion of their causal significance taking into account that the influence often runs in both directions.

We have to emphasize at the very outset of this inquiry, that the nexus between globalization and health is blurred by a partly spurious correlation between the indices that measure them. While globalization spread and intensified since the early 19th century (with the only exception of the period 1915–1945 encompassing the two world wars and the inter-war times), in the same period also the indices of health improved, mainly for the increasing prosperity of nations and the continuous progress of theoretical and applied medicine, pharmacology and hygiene. No doubt, globalization has given a contribution of its own to the strengthening of this positive correlation by promoting the growth of per capita income as well as by spreading updated medical knowledge, know-how, medicines and therapeutic instruments around the world. It is very difficult, however, to disentangle the specific contribution of globalization to health from that of scientific and technological progress, and of other economic, social, institutional factors that are in principle quite independent of, though correlated with, globalization.

The empirical evidence shows that the process of world development, as represented by the growth of per capita income, is correlated not only with income inequality within countries but also with health inequality across countries (see Figure 5.1). In the latter case we find a Kuznets-like pattern with a maximum around the early 20th century.[49] To the best of our knowledge this particular version of the KC concerning health inequality has been completely ignored in the economic literature, notwithstanding its optimistic implications for the positive role of globalization. In fact the latter improved dramatically per capita

Figure 5.1　Health inequality across countries

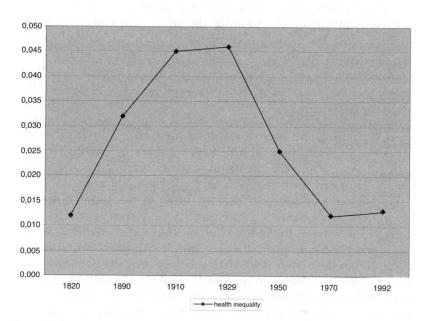

Source: Authors' elaboration on Bourguignon and Morisson (2002).

income in the globalizing countries, reducing the percentage of poor people and improving the average indexes of population health. The marked and progressive reduction of health inequality in the 20th century may be explained in part with the stabilization of between-country income inequality and in part with the beneficial transmission across countries of superior knowledge and know-how. Unfortunately, also in this case, the optimist message springing from the curve is questioned by the inversion of the trend observed since the early 1980s. We may speculate that this inversion is related to specific episodes such as the epidemics of AIDS (Acquired Immune Deficiency Syndrome) that hit particularly the poor countries especially in Africa, and the breakdown of health indexes induced by the poorly managed transition in Eastern European countries. These episodes point to shortcomings in the recent process of globalization due to deficient transmission of medical knowledge or institutional deficiencies in the transition to an open market economy. In any case, this example suggests that we need a detailed analysis of the causal links between globalization and health in order to be able to filter the beneficial influences of globalization from its potentially negative effects on population health.

In this chapter we focus in particular on a few specific causal links between globalization and health that may explain the observed deviations from the long-run positive correlation between them. The study of these socioeconomic factors of health is important for policy because the elimination, or at least the mitigation, of the negative influences of globalization and the corroboration of its positive influences could significantly improve global health.

1 The evolution of health factors in the last two centuries and the epidemiological transitions of the 20th century

Epidemiologists classify the factors that influence population health in five main categories: (i) genetic factors (genes inheritance and mutation); (ii) diffusion of health-damaging behaviors (such as diet, tobacco and alcohol use, drug addiction, physical fitness); (iii) quality of medical care and public health infrastructures (efficient diagnosis and therapy, sanitation, quality and availability of drinking water, etc.); (iv) ecological factors (pollution, exhaustion of natural resources); and (v) socio-economic factors (poverty, malnutrition, income inequality, depletion of social capital).[50] The relative importance of these categories of factors changed through time. In the early history of humanity, population health was mainly influenced by the all-absorbing struggle with natural phenomena (primarily atmospheric events such as flooding, drought, famine, etc.). Since the bronze age, beginning around the 2500 B.C., the human kind learned how to cope with most natural threats by developing better housing, more efficient and specialized economic activity (agriculture, animal husbandry, metallurgy, manufacturing and trade), and a more stable social organization aimed to ensure security, justice, and education. These advances led to the concentration of population in restricted spaces (towns and villages) and nurtured continuous wars between competing towns and tribes. This produced the conditions for widespread bacterial and viral infections (epidemics, pandemics and plagues) that became the principal threat to population health for more than 4000 years.

In the 19th century bacterial and viral infections were still the main threat to individual and population health. During the 20th century two major epidemiological changes occurred in developed countries.[51] The first one started at the turn of 19th century. The relative impact of infectious diseases on population health began to decline quite rapidly in consequence of more wealth, better nutrition,[52] advances in medical care, improvements of public health infrastructures such as quality of (and accessibility to) drinking water as well as modern sanitation. The steady increase of per capita income progressively removed the material constraints to the spreading of risky behaviors (sedentary life, high-fat diet, abuse of tobacco, alcohol and drugs, and so on). In consequence of these opposite trends, the main cause of death shifted from infectious diseases to chronic diseases:

> Tuberculosis, pneumonia, and sepsis have been replaced in population significance by coronary hart disease, high blood pressure, stroke, diabetes, cancer, emphysema, cirrhosis, and so forth (Tarlov and Peter, 2000, p.xiv).

The second epidemiological change started to spread since the middle of the 20th century but it enhanced its impact since the 1970s when, in consequence of the gradual diffusion of healthier life styles and increasing income inequality in many OECD countries, the main cause of chronic diseases shifted from risky behaviors to socio-economic factors. This shift occurred notwithstanding the increasing impact on health of ecological factors through natural alterations (global warming, increasing scarcity of drinking water and non-renewable energy sources, desertification, deforestation), genetic modifications (due to the thinning of the ozone layer and radioactive emissions from nuclear power plants and waste) and infectious diseases (spread by increasing pollution of water, air and soil).

In consequence of the second epidemiological change, the main socio-economic factors of health shifted progressively from absolute income (per capita GDP) to relative income (inequality in the distribution of income). Wilkinson, the well-known epidemiologist, called "epidemiological transition" the overall evolution process characterized by the two successive structural changes mentioned above. In his words, the epidemiological transition marks a fundamental change in the main determinants of health and seems to indicate the point in economic development at which the vast majority of the population gained reliable access to the basic material necessities of life (Wilkinson, 1994, p.64). When the individual income is very low, the access to medical care (diagnosis and therapy) is severely limited by absolute income, necessary to buy medicines, medical services and assistance. Epidemiological research, however, found that beyond a threshold of about $5000 of income per year, a further increase in individual income would improve health only quite marginally.

Epidemiologists estimated the relative importance of health factors in developed countries in consequence of the epidemiological transition.

As for the genetic causes, we have to distinguish two main factors: mutation of genes and polygenic inheritance, i.e. the specific combination of normal genes that confers a bias towards specific chronic diseases, such as high pressure, diabetes, and cancer. Research has found about 4000 mutant genes that may cause diseases such as sickle-cell anemia, cystic fibrosis, and Huntington's disease (Tarlov and St. Peter, 2000, p.x). Epidemiologists maintain that the relative incidence of these diseases is very low as it did not exceed a value around 5% of the total (*ibidem*). In the case of polygenic inheritance, for a chronic disease actually to manifest itself, concomitant circumstances have to concur, such as health-damaging behaviors or socio-economic factors. We may thus consider its impact important but only in the distribution of chronic diseases rather than in their aggregate incidence on population health.

As for health-damaging behaviors, epidemiologists estimate that their incidence does not exceed one fifth of the aggregate disease burden (Drever *et al.*, 1996). Moreover, they estimate that the impact of improved medical care on population health is surprisingly small as different studies attribute to it no more than a fifth of the overall influences during the last decades (see Tarlov and St. Peter, 2000, on the basis of studies by McKeown, 1976; Bunker *et al.*, 1994, and Bunker, 1995).[53]

According to these estimates we have to conclude that in developed countries, in consequence of the epidemiological transition of the 20th century, the main impact on health has by now to be attributed to social characteristics (in particular poverty, inequality in the distribution of income, depletion of social capital) and environmental factors (pollution, depletion of natural capital). In other words, we may say that the social and environmental conditions of sustainability have been playing an increasing role in determining population health. In addition, we notice that sustainability conditions also play an increasing, indirect role in enhancing the impact of the other health factors. The genes mutation was accelerated by environmental manipulations such as the thinning of the ozone layer (weakening the natural filter of cosmic rays), abuse of radiography, nuclear pollution and progressive introduction of genetically modified organisms (GMOs). Analogously, health-damaging behaviors are nowadays often triggered by social factors. A feeling of relative deprivation or stress nurtured by social factors may induce use of alcohol, tobacco or drugs, and encourage excessive food consumption. Finally, the availability of medical care and public health facilities, such as access to safe drinking water, adequate sanitation and medical care, obviously depends on socio-economic conditions and is currently jeopardized by severe cuts in public expenditure, motivated by budget strictures and privatization.

We may conclude that a study of the environmental and social conditions of sustainable development is becoming an increasingly crucial factor in the study and promotion of public health.

2   Influence channels between globalization, health and sustainable development

In the preceding section we have seen that, in consequence of the epidemiological transition, the sustainability conditions have become a crucial determinant of public health and of its cross-country variations. We know from the preceding chapters that the process of globalization has exerted a crucial impact on these conditions, and therefore indirectly also on public health. In addition, we have seen that the process of globalization has affected, and continues to affect, the evolution of per capita income that, in its turn, had a crucial role in the epidemiological transition of the 20th century.

In this section we intend to suggest a fairly comprehensive map of the main channels of influence connecting globalization, sustainable development and health. This map is summarized through a block-

Figure 5.2 Block diagram of the main correlations between globalization and health

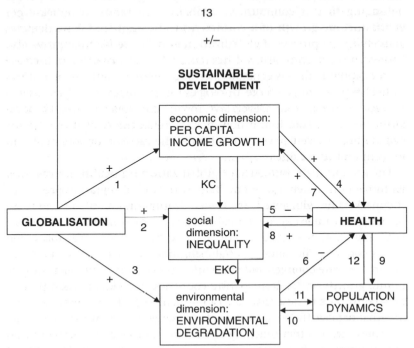

Note: The sign + indicates a positive correlation, the sign – indicates a negative correlation

diagram where the arrows express the direction of the influence between the key variables examined (see Figure. 5.2).

As we have seen in Chapter 1, the process of globalization affects the sustainability of development mainly through three pathways that we may label respectively as economic, social and environmental channels. The economic channel represents the effects of globalization on per capita income growth, the environmental channel its effects on a variety of environmental deterioration indices, while the social channel includes the consequences of globalization on income inequality and poverty.[54] This conceptual framework may help to understand the influence of globalization on health since per capita income, environmental degradation and income inequality are affected by globalization and have a remarkable impact on health.

As to the economic channel, the average per capita income of a community (at a local, national or international level) is generally considered as a fairly good proxy of its average standard of living and thus also a major determinant of the average health of the people belonging to this community. Globalization tends to increase per capita income growth of a country to the extent that it participates actively in the process of globalization and this tends to improve also its health conditions (arrow 4 in Figure 5.2). For instance, an increase in per capita income is generally accompanied by higher expenditures in health programs, better technologies improving the therapeutic facilities and higher education levels favoring the diffusion of updated medical know-how.[55] In addition, it may help to relax the budget constraints originating in severe poverty that hinder the capacity of poor people to prevent and cure a disease.

The second main influence of globalization on health derives from its impact on the environment. The worldwide integration process of the markets has globalized also the environmental problems and these have by now huge effects on health (such as the thinning of the ozone layer, pollution, the exhaustion of vital resources such as drinkable water: see section 3.1). The influence of globalization on environmental deterioration is a quite complex and ambiguous process. By increasing the economic growth of the participating countries, the globalization process may contribute to raise the scale of production and consumption activities that damage the environment. At the same time, however, the higher economic growth that generally characterizes more globalized countries may promote technological progress and thus reduce the intensity of environmental degradation. The health effect of globalization through the environmental channel thus depends on which of these two opposite influences tends to prevail. The increasing levels of air, water and soil pollution that have characterized most of the countries in the last decades seem to suggest that the negative effect has tended to prevail in this recent period. Globalization, therefore, may have indirectly contributed to deteriorate health through environmental degradation.

As for the social channel, it is well-known that the health of the poor has higher income elasticity than that of the rich. Cross-country evidence suggests that life expectancy increases with average per capita income in relatively poor countries, whereas this relationship tends to vanish for relatively rich countries (Preston, 1975). This can be clearly seen by looking at Figure 5.3 that shows the relationship between life expectancy and per capita GDP in year 2005 based on WB data referring to 175 countries.[56]

Similar results emerge also in single-country studies. Using a survey on health and income in Britain, Wilkinson (1992) finds that several

Figure 5.3 Life expectancy and per capita GDP in 175 countries in 2005

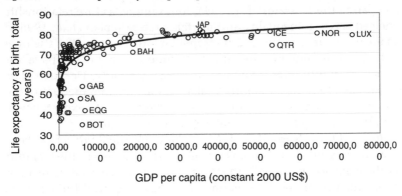

Legend: BAH = Bahamas; BOT = Botswana; EQG = Equatorial Guinea; GAB = Gabon; ICE = Iceland; JAP = Japan; LUX = Luxembourg; NOR = Norway; QTR = Qatar; SA = South Africa.

Source: Authors' elaboration on World Bank data (World Development Indicators, 2007b).

health indicators increase rapidly as income rises from the lowest to the middle classes of the income distribution, while no further health improvements occur at high income levels. Similarly, using data from the National Longitudinal Mortality Survey in the USA, Deaton (2002) observes that the male (age adjusted) probability of death decreases rapidly as income grows at low family income levels, while it flattens out at high family income levels.

What we have reported so far is consistent with the traditional view that health is mainly affected by absolute income. If so, a reduction in income inequality would improve population health only because individual health indicators increase at a decreasing rate with income. In recent years, however, several studies have argued that socioeconomic inequality has also an independent impact on individuals' health (arrow 5 in Figure 5.2), particularly in developed countries. A host of new evidence in different disciplinary fields clarified that, after a threshold of minimum income is reached (of about US$5000), income inequality becomes a crucial determinant of health. Using data on nine OECD countries, Wilkinson (1992) finds evidence of a strong correlation between life expectancy and income distribution that is independent of absolute income.[57] Similar results emerge in several other studies that focused on different groups of countries and periods of time (e.g. Kennedy *et al.*, 1996; Cantarero *et al.*, 2005; De Vogli *et al.*, 2005; Leigh and Jencks, 2007).

The same relationship, moreover, may also apply at the local level. Comparing the 50 states of the USA, for example, a close relationship emerged between inequality and mortality rates (Kaplan *et al.*, 1996).[58] Analogously, among the 282 metropolitan areas of the USA the ones with the most unequal income distribution turn out to have the highest mortality rates (Lynch *et al.*, 1998). Similarly, De Vogli *et al.* (2005) have found that among Italian regions income inequality has had an independent and more powerful effect on life expectancy at birth than per capita income and educational attainment.

Although these regressions did not control for some further explanatory variables and there is not yet unanimous consensus in the literature on the evidence available,[59] these results suggest that relative income, independently of absolute income, may have a crucial influence on health. More generally, the relative deprivation suffered by people in the lowest deciles of the income distribution may determine their exclusion from the social activities that promote or preserve health. Moreover, as several empirical papers have pointed out (see section 3), relative deprivation may be a source of psychosocial stress, loss of self-esteem and chronic depression which tend to damage the individuals' health. People compare themselves with reference groups around them (neighbors, co-workers, friends, relatives, TV stars, and so on) and may suffer from chronic psychological stress when comparison with these benchmarks is unfavorable.[60] These psychological mechanisms, which are at work mainly within the part of population not affected by material deprivation, can adversely affect people's health (see, e.g., Sapolsky, 1998; Brunner and Marmot, 1999; Wilkinson, 2002). The assertion that relative income has a crucial independent impact on population health came to be called "Relative Income Hypothesis" (from now on RIH).

Since the RIH implies that increasing inequality damages the health of a population, we may say that globalization indirectly contributes to deteriorate health through an increase of income inequality, as observed in many OECD countries in the last thirty years or so (see retro Chapter 1).

To get a deeper understanding of the complex link between globalization and health, in what follows we will take a closer look to the way inequality may affect health.

3   The influence of inequality on health

Though the relevance of psycho-social factors on health has been occasionally recognized since long,[61] until very recently only very few scholars claimed that they are an important cause of global health.[62]

In addition, only lately the underlying physiological mechanism began to be understood. As a reserve of (relatively liquid) financial capital is crucial to absorb economic shocks, and a reserve of natural capital to absorb environmental shocks, analogously it has been argued that, in order to withstand physio-psychological shocks, a crucial role may be played by the intensity and quality of social relations, or what is often called "social capital". In particular, the lack of social trust was shown to be positively and significantly correlated with mortality in the USA (Kawachi *et al.*, 1997), with a correlation coefficient that ranges between 0.71 and 0.79 depending on the kind of social trust indicators used for the analysis.[63] Analogously hostility was found positively correlated with mortality. For example, Williams *et al.* (1995) estimated that mean hostility scores of ten cities in the USA were strongly and significantly correlated with their mortality rates after adjusting for race, age, gender, income and education level of the individuals.[64] On the other hand, trust and hostility appear to be strictly correlated to inequality. Two commonly used indicators of social capital (civic engagement as measured by membership in groups and associations, and social trust) were significantly associated to inequality in the USA (Kawachi *et al.*, 1997). Similar results were obtained by Uslaner (2001), who found a high correlation coefficient ($r = -0.684$) between inequality and trust in a cross-country analysis.[65] As the author has showed, this connection between the two variables holds true also in multivariate tests that take into account economic, cultural and religious aspects that might affect the observed levels of trust and inequality in the selected countries. In particular, by estimating a simultaneous equation model to test the direction of causality between trust and inequality, he found that trust has no effect on economic inequality, whereas the latter turns out to be the strongest determinant of trust among the explanatory variables. Analogously, many studies (see, e.g., Hsieh and Pugh, 1993; Kaplan *et al.*, 1996; Leigh and Jencks, 2007) have confirmed the existence of a close relationship between income inequality and violent crime indicators that can be interpreted as indirect measures of hostility and depleted social capital.[66]

Summing up, the empirical evidence suggests that inequality acts as a wedge between people that engenders mistrust and hostility with negative effects on people's health, the more so the more incomes are unrelated or non-proportional to individual effort and merit. This may explain why the most egalitarian developed countries, not the richest, tend to have the highest life expectancy.[67] The close relationship between income inequality and mortality rates that is observed in cross-country studies emerges also in time series referring to single countries including Russia, United Kingdom and Taiwan.[68]

We may interpret income inequality as a measure of the intensity of relative deprivation affecting individuals in a society. Several studies found that in human and non-human primates (such as baboons and macaques) the experience of a low status severely damages health producing "obesity, glucose intolerance, increased atherosclerosis, raised basal cortisol levels and attenuated cortisol responses to experimental stressors" (Wilkinson, 2002, p.15 and literature there cited). The physiological mechanism is based "on the effects of sustained activation of the hypothalamus-pituitary-adrenal axis and the sympathetic nervous system. The stress response activates a cascade of stress hormones that affect the cardiovascular and immune systems" (*ibidem*, pp.15–16).

The mechanism through which chronic stress jeopardizes the health of individuals is very similar to economic "short-termism", i.e. the myopic emphasis on short-term objectives to the cost of jeopardizing the achievement of longer-run objectives. In both cases all the available resources are mobilized to obtain a desired short-term goal even at the cost of jeopardizing the sustainability of good performance in the longer term. In fact, whenever a human being has to face an emergency, the body mobilizes all the physiological resources that may be useful to face the exceptional threat preparing muscular activity for fight or flight and/or alerting the nervous system for devising a quick solution to the challenge. The energy mobilized to face the immediate task, however, is subtracted from the physiological resources available for routine functions such as tissue maintenance and repair, growth, digestion and depuration of liquids and food through liver and kidneys, reproductive and immunity functions. This mechanism may be very efficient when the emergencies are brief and rare because in this case the suspension of routine functions does not produce serious damages. On the other hand, this emergency response is bound to affect health in an irreversible way when the shocks are frequent or permanent, like in the case of a worsening social status or relative deprivation. An increase in income inequality involves for the less advantaged people a reduction in social status and an increasing feeling of relative deprivation.

We have to stress the link between the physiological mechanism that explains how inequality deteriorates health and the economic mechanism that explains how certain aspects of globalization may deteriorate the economic "health", i.e. the stability and sustainability, of the economic performance. In both cases, the pathology originates from short-termism. In the last three decades globalization, driven by the principles of privatization and deregulation, progressively shortened the time horizon within which DMs optimize their strategies. We can examine this mechanism in some more detail by focusing on five of its salient factors.

The first one is the growing importance of the financial side in the balance sheets of corporations and households. Financial decisions are liable to big, often unexpected, gains and losses and have to be revised almost continuously in the light of the latest available information, thus greatly contributing to the shortening of the time horizon of economic decisions. Globalization accelerated this trend by unifying financial markets and increasing the size and velocity of "hot money" transferred at very short notice from one sector or country to the other for speculative purposes. This greatly enhanced the instability of financial markets and the size of potential losses and gains of financial decisions, focusing the attention of operators on the speculative factors rather than on the long-run trends of economic fundamentals (see Chapter 6).

A second important factor of short-termism is the growing flexibility of labor markets and industrial relations. Workers are compelled to shorten the time horizon of their decisions while the employers have the opportunity of revising their choices concerning the size and use of the labor force almost continuously on the basis of speculative considerations.

A third significant factor may be found in the field of corporate governance. Managers are evaluated and rewarded according to indices of performance calculated over increasingly short time horizon. This trend has negative implications on the sustainability of the economic performance of the firm and on its compliance with the tenets of business ethics and is a source of greater stress for the top managers and all the people affected by their decisions (see Chapter 7).

The fourth factor that we want to stress, the growing role of the mass media, is more general and progressively became a crucial determinant of economic, political and cultural processes in modern societies, including the socio-economic and physio-psychological processes mentioned above. The growing diffusion of the mass media, in particular television, flooded free time with information flows strongly biased towards negative events and risks often unduly dramatized. This spread feelings of insecurity and fear that greatly contributed to reduced social interaction, depletion of social capital, increasing stress and enhanced short-termism.

Finally, the fifth factor is the "neoliberal" market ideology that justified the first three factors and was supported by large part of the mass media often prone to convince people that the negative effects of globalization are unavoidable "collateral effects" of modernization (see Chapters 6 and 9). This ideology coalesced in the 1970s and became rapidly hegemonic in many influential quarters in the 1980s, and influenced the choices of political elites. This point of view directed economic policy towards the systematic privatization of economic resources (including many public goods and global commons) and generalized deregulation of markets (even when regulation was justified by social and environmental externalities). This policy strategy greatly undermined in many countries the scope and efficiency of the welfare state and the underlying safety nets, contributing to the depletion of social capital, the growing stress of people, the rising impact of chronic diseases, and so on.

The recent phase of globalization has greatly reinforced the trends here briefly recalled. The increasing importance of financial capital was promoted by the radical liberalization of capital movements across countries. The growing flexibility of labor markets and industrial relations was enhanced by the increasing international competition based on the opportunity of shifting capital in the countries and sectors where the flexibility of labor is higher. In addition, the growing international mobility of capital and skilled labor encouraged the adoption of short-termist capital governance and reward systems. Globalized mass media made anyone aware in real time of catastrophes, crime episodes, wars and other negative events happening anywhere, also in distant countries. Finally, global cultural and political processes rapidly spread the values of the neoliberal ideology even among people greatly damaged by neoliberal policies.

Summing up, the growing short-termism progressively increased the stress of workers, entrepreneurs, shareholders and households and this nurtured an analogously short-termist physio-psychological response that undermined their health. Of course, this effect is particularly visible and sizeable in individuals affected by absolute and relative deprivation and weakly protected by a social security network and accessible social capital. This suggests a new strategy of policy intervention that it would be useful to explore in the future. We will come back on this issue in the last section of this chapter.

4 Critiques of the Relative Income Hypothesis and their soundness

As all scientific hypotheses, also the RIH raised criticisms of different nature (for a survey see the introduction to Kawachi *et al.*, 1999). We may classify the main criticisms to the RIH in three separate strands, none of which, however, seems to undermine in a decisive way the fundamental soundness of the RIH:

a)   Some critiques pointed out that the RIH is inconsistent with the positive correlation between increasing income inequality and the contemporaneous improvements in life expectancy observed in the last decades in most industrialized countries (see, e.g., Judge, 1995; Saunders, 1996). This criticism emerges from a misunderstanding of the scope of the RIH. The latter does not pretend to explain the long-run global trend of life expectancy that depends on a host of factors going beyond that of income inequality. The RIH only claims to explain the negative deviations from this positive long-run trend.

   b)   A second strand of criticism focused on the alleged methodological shortcomings of the studies that claimed empirical support to the RIH.

First, it was observed that these studies referred to different indexes of inequality without justifying the reasons of the specific choice. This may raise the suspicion of an ad hoc choice in order to corroborate the hypothesis. This criticism, however, is greatly weakened by the observation that most measures of income inequality are strictly correlated with each other (Kawachi and Kennedy, 1997).

Another criticism pointed out that most published studies did not adjust the estimates of the impact of income inequality by taking account of other relevant variables such as taxes, transfer payments, and household size. On the other hand, more sophisticated replications of the above studies adjusting for the missing variables did not change the substance of the results obtained by earlier studies (Kawachi and Kennedy, 1997).

   c)   The main challenge to the RIH came, however, from the third strand of criticism. Since a concave relationship has been observed between absolute income (that is, per capita GDP measured on the horizontal axis) and life expectancy (measured on the vertical axis), it is obvious that transferring income from the poor to the rich must result in a greater improvement of the health of the poor as compared to the smaller reduction in the life expectancy of the rich. According to the opponents of the RIH, this observation is consistent with the hypothesis that only absolute income is a genuine cause of health, while the relative income turns out to be a spurious cause (see, e.g., Fiscella and Franks, 1997; Gravelle, 1998).[69]

Compelling as it seems at first sight, this argument is in fact inconclusive. In order to understand the real implications of the above observation, we have to distinguish between ontologic causality, that occurs when we detect in the empirical evidence an effective mechanism of production of the effect, and pragmatic causality, when we are able to control the effect by manipulating the cause, whatever its ontological reasons (Woodward, 1997; Hoover, 2001). The observation raised by the critics of the RIH, as a matter of fact, greatly corroborates it from the pragmatic point of view: even if we believe, and can prove, that only absolute income – and not relative income – is a genuine ontological cause of health at the individual level, we may considerably improve the health of a population by reducing the inequality in the distribution of income. From the policy point of view this is what really matters, therefore we can conclude that from the pragmatic point of view the RIH is not falsified.

We may then discuss whether relative income should be considered also an ontologic cause of health. From this point of view the observation that the relationship between absolute income and health is non-linear only proves that absolute income is in principle an ontologic cause sufficient to explain the correlations observed in the empirical evidence between income inequality and health but it does not exclude a possible role also for the latter variable. We may say, however, that the existence of plausible pathways explaining the influence of inequality on health, discussed in the preceding section, suggests that in many cases we should expect to find an independent causal effect also from the ontological point of view. Bad health of poor people due to infectious diseases may be transmitted to other people, even those belonging to the top levels of social stratification. In addition, relative deprivation, the burden of which may be felt virtually by anyone but the restricted elite at the top of social stratification, increases with income inequality adding a new independent influence path of the latter on population health. The consequences of an acute feeling of relative deprivation may nurture chronic diseases, crime, and health-damaging behaviors. This may damage other individuals including those at the top of social stratification who may become victims of crime, absenteeism, poor services, myopic and antisocial behaviors, even infectious diseases induced by a fall in the immune defenses of stressed individuals, and so on.

The criticisms briefly surveyed above warn the analyst and the policymaker that, although we do not know yet how and to what extent inequality affects health, the knowledge accumulated so far suggests that more equality in income distribution would improve population health.

5   The influence of environmental degradation on health

In recent years numerous scientific studies have analyzed the effects that individual forms of environmental degradation can have on a person's health. Some of these analyses, such as the United Nations study on the so-called "Asian cloud" (UNEP, 2002), have recently received increasing attention in the mass media and on the part of public opinion for their interesting results. The World Health Organization (WHO) has estimated that bad environmental conditions are directly responsible for about 25% of all cases of preventable illness all over the world (WHO, 1997). In order to analyze the direct causal links between environment and health (summarized by arrow 6 in Figure 5.2), it may be useful to classify the health impacts of environmental degradation by distinguishing between atmospheric, water and soil pollution.[70]

5.1   Effects of atmospheric pollution

Atmospheric pollution is considered the main cause of the large increase in cases of respiratory diseases observed in recent years. Some particularly volatile pollutants such as particulate matters (PM_{10}), nitrogen oxide (NO_x) and SO_2 – discharged by cars traffic, heating, and manufacturing – can penetrate as far as into the bronchioles, provoking asthma, bronchitis and emphysema (Worldwatch Institute, 1990).[71] In Italy, it has been calculated (Galassi, 2002) that the number of patients with smog-related chronic coughs has doubled in the last ten years and about 20% of otherwise healthy non-smoking Italians suffer from this disease. This is all the more worrying because it affects especially individuals in the younger age groups thus damaging the average health conditions of future generations. Children living in Italian cities, for example, have a 20% higher likelihood of suffering from asthma than those living in rural or mountain areas where polluting emissions are lower.[72] The data relating to the developing countries are even more alarming. A recent study of some Latin American capital cities reported by *The Economist* (2002a), estimated that a 10% reduction in ozone and particulate emissions by 2020 could avoid 37,000 premature deaths among the inhabitants of Mexico City and 13,000 in San Paolo. Another study carried out in Bangladesh by the WB estimated that the high level of atmospheric pollution in this country's towns is responsible annually for 15,000 premature deaths and a million cases of disease, with an estimated overall cost between 200 and 800 million dollars a year (World Bank, 2000, p.3). Bangladesh is one of the countries worst hit by the effects of the so-called "Asian brown cloud", a thick cloud formed by carbon particles and carbon monoxide, sulfur and nitrogen gases that stretches for about 16 million square kilometers over a large part of Asia. The cloud – caused by continuous burning of forest areas, emissions from electrical power stations and road traffic, and dust from desertified land – constitutes a new global emergency that has recently come to the fore because it brings about serious respiratory problems and it could easily spread to other countries and continents, carried by the wind.

Some authors think that the impact of atmospheric pollution on individual health may be even greater than that estimated in the above-mentioned studies which restrict their attention to the increase in respiratory diseases among the populations under consideration. Besides respiratory conditions, atmospheric pollutants are often responsible for cardiovascular diseases since, once inhaled, pollutants are carried round the body in the blood. It was observed (WHO, 1997) that high concentration of carbon monoxide in the air reduces the blood's capacity to absorb oxygen and that an increase of PM_{10} levels in the blood of 10 grams per square meter raises the incidence of death by cardiovascular disease by about 1%.

GHGs also have other negative effects on health. As is well-known, the depletion of the atmosphere's ozone layer as a result of GHGs increases the population's exposure to ultraviolet rays which may account for the increasing cases of skin cancer and eyes damages. Lastly, atmospheric pollutants can also damage health because they are deposited on water and soil, thus adding to the contamination of the water we drink and the food we eat.

5.2   Effects of water pollution

One of the measures of water pollution often found in the literature is the concentration of faecal coliform bacteria in water where there is no efficient treatment in place. The concentration of these bacteria, which are found in human and animal faeces, is a good index of the quantity of pathogenic agents responsible for diarrhoea, cholera, hepatitis, typhoid and other illnesses of the digestive system. Recent studies (WHO, 1997) have estimated that these diseases can be ascribed in 90% of cases precisely to the lack of clean water and to inadequate sanitation. Those worst affected are children in developing countries (where 95% of water is untreated), thus creating a serious obstacle to the future growth of these countries and to a reduction of the gap between rich and poor countries.[73]

Another factor of water pollution that has serious consequences for human health is the presence in water of heavy metals (such as lead, cadmium, mercury, arsenic and nickel) and polluting chemical products (such as Poly-Chlorinated Biphenyls (PCB), Dichlorodiphenyltrichloroethane (DDT) and dioxins). People ingest these elements by drinking water since they are difficult to remove under normal treatment processes, or when they eat fish where metals can accumulate. Various studies demonstrated that some heavy metals, such as nickel, cause serious damage to the nervous system, others, such as lead, mercury and arsenic, harm liver and kidneys.[74] All heavy metals and many chemical pollutants are also thought to be responsible for tumor formation. In this respect, a study on Lake Michigan (Glenn *et al.*, 1989) found that a high level of consumption of fish from this lake, polluted with high concentrations of PCB, DDT and other toxic chemical substances, increased the risk of a tumor by about 1%.

A recent example of water pollution caused by heavy metals that is causing great concern is to be found in Bangladesh and the Indian region of Bengal. In well waters used for drinking by the local population since the 1980s, the quantity of arsenic found was fifty times greater than the permitted safety level (*The Economist*, 2001). A WHO study (Smith *et al.*, 2000) estimated that the contaminated population could number between 35 and 77 million people, underlining the fact that prolonged exposure to arsenic causes skin disease (already evident in the populations of the villages concerned) and the appearance of tumors of lungs, bladder, liver and kidneys.

Furthermore, water pollution in combination with atmospheric pollution can modify the habitat of some ecosystems (temperature, humidity, vegetation density, etc.). This can encourage the survival and spreading of insects that are particularly harmful because of the diseases they may carry. This is the case of mosquitoes which transmit various diseases including malaria. This serious disease is thought to be responsible every year for a million deaths among children under 5 years and is becoming an increasingly serious problem, especially in sub-Saharan Africa where 90% of the world's malaria cases are concentrated (WHO, 1997).

5.3   Effects of soil pollution

Many chemical, biological and radioactive pollutants tend to settle on the soil, contaminating both the crops planted there and the resultant agricultural products. This can cause serious harm to population health which can then be passed on to the next generation and last for many decades. One example is the pollution of food in Vietnam following the use by American troops, during the war, of an herbicide called "Agent Orange" which later proved to be carcinogenic.[75]

In addition, soil pollution damages the health not only of farmers who work contaminated land and of children playing there, but also of the surrounding population since dust from the polluted area can be carried elsewhere by the wind. Direct contact with contaminated soil and with the numerous microbes and parasites contained in it is particularly harmful for children who are extremely vulnerable.[76]

Not only pollution but also overworking the soil can damage the health of the population. This is particularly true for rural families in poor countries which are dependent on the food they produce. The attempt to achieve a minimum level of subsistence sometimes drives rural people to over-exploit land reducing its productivity. Lower productivity in turn reduces calorie and protein intake on the part of the farmers, reducing their productivity and making them more vulnerable to diseases. The loss of income resulting from illness and lower land and labor productivity increases the indigence of the farmers generating a vicious circle between poverty, environmental degradation and population health.

6   Reverse causation between health and sustainable development

The analysis developed so far has examined the consequences that globalization may have on health through three crucial dimensions of sustainable development, namely, income growth, inequality and environmental degradation. As many economists have underlined, however, there exists also a reverse causality going from health to the economic, social, and environmental conditions of sustainable development. We intend now to analyze these reversed causality channels in order to evaluate their strength and nature.

6.1   The impact of health on economic growth

Recent empirical studies have shown that a country's economic growth is closely correlated with the average health of its inhabitants. Countries with low infant mortality rates (assumed as a proxy for a country's health conditions), grew more rapidly between 1964–95 than those with higher mortality rates (WHO, 2001). Various empirical "cross-country" analyses seem to confirm that good health conditions can contribute to explain economic growth (as suggested by the positive sign on arrow 7 in Figure 5.2).[77] By introducing, besides health, some traditional explanatory variables of economic growth into the econometric model (initial income level, economic policies, and the structural characteristics of the countries), these studies found that the coefficient of the health variable is statistically significant and that a 10% increase in life expectancy at birth gives a 0.3–0.4% increase in a country's annual economic growth.[78]

It is possible to identify three main channels through which the health conditions prevailing in one country can influence its economic growth: (i) investment in the country; (ii) the average educational level of individuals; (iii) individuals' productivity. In the first place, a worsening of average health conditions discourages investment in the country. High incidence of a disease like malaria, for example, increases absenteeism and turnover in the labor market augmenting staff training costs for companies. This makes companies less likely to invest in the country and therefore the latter remains with lower growth capacity. In South Africa, for example, the incidence of AIDS among workers convinced many companies to cut their investment programs (WHO, 2001). An epidemic or a general worsening of population health can further reduce the rate of capital accumulation in a country since it reduces households' savings rate. This can happen either because the disease obliges families to face higher medical expenses, or because it shortens life expectancy and so also reduces the incentive to save for future consumption. Lastly, the accumulation of capital in a country hit by an epidemic falls also because the risk of contracting the disease discourages tourism and related investments in the area.

Secondly, as emphasized by a WHO report (WHO, 2001), the prevalence of bad health conditions in a population adversely affects not only investment in physical capital but also in human capital. When an adult member of a family is ill the sum of money that can be spent on children's education is curtailed both because the household spends more in order to treat the illness and because disposable income is reduced. Since the incidence of a disease is higher among poor families where there are already tight cash constraints, the children may be obliged to leave school prematurely to help support their family. The low level of investment in human capital seen in countries with poor average health conditions is also the result of low life expectancy which, by reducing the temporal horizon of an individual, makes the initial investment in education less profitable. Furthermore, high infant mortality drives poor families to have many children. This reduces the amount that the family can spend on each child, leading therefore – for a given level of disposable income – to investing less on their education. This may have repercussions on successive generations. As argued by WHO (2001), the less education received by girls, the lower their future earnings will be and therefore the lower the opportunity cost of staying at home to raise their children once they reach adulthood, which means they will also have many children. In addition, the high birth rates generated by this behavior tend to reduce the proportion of the population of working age which various studies find to be directly proportional to per capita income (see, e.g., Bloom *et al.*, 2001a). Lastly, the early death of many adults prevents the passing on of precious knowledge to the next generation, which also lowers the level of human capital. This aspect is particularly important in African countries hit by the epidemics of AIDS, where the techniques of working the land are mostly passed on from father to son (WHO, 2001).

A third way in which the health of a population influences economic growth is through individual productivity.[79] A poor state of health increases the number of sick days taken by workers and reduces both their physical and mental productivity. In addition, it reduces children's ability to learn, thus adversely affecting their future educational achievement. In this regard, many studies (see, for example, Pollitt, 2001) have found strong links between a lack of iron and vitamin A in the organism and reduced cognitive skills. An individual's poor state of health can also have a negative spillover effect on the productivity of other family members or of people close to them. If an individual is ill other family members may have to give assistance, reducing the number of hours they can dedicate to their own work and often also reducing their productivity at work. This productivity loss may be the result of the poor concentration and stress caused either by worrying about and/or giving assistance to the sick relative.[80]

Summing up, it can be said that the health of a population influences also the "health" of the economy. If a population is in good health this will generally encourage economic growth in the country, whereas the opposite occurs if the population is in bad health. In this light, health policies can promote economic growth, while the latter tends to improve health. The existence of circular relationships between health and economic growth can therefore give rise to vicious or virtuous circles according to the policies employed. Through its influence on economic growth, health can affect also inequality and environmental degradation. For those cases in which the KCs are empirically robust,[81] promoting health policies may help increase a country's per capita income (moving along the horizontal axis) and eventually reach the downward side of the two curves where inequality and environmental degradation tend to decrease.

Health, however, can also have other feedback effects on inequality and ecological degradation that are independent of income growth. We now turn to the analysis of these additional effects.

6.2   Feedback effects of health on inequality

There is a growing debate in the literature about the possible explanations underlying the observed correlation between health and inequality. In sections 4 and 5 we have discussed how and to what extent inequality can affect health, but it seems reasonable to argue that there exists a bi-directional link between these two variables. The health of the poor is generally worse than that of the rich since the rich enjoy higher living standards and easier access to the health care system than the poor. This fact tends to widen the gap in terms of present income and future income capacity, thus increasing the level of inequality in the country (Gwatkin, 2000). The children of poor families, in fact, generally have worse health than the children of rich families, and this adversely affects their future earning possibilities as adults. It has been observed, in fact, that even when the children of poor and rich families receive the same level of education, the former may suffer inferior cognitive capacities because of worse health conditions. For instance, several studies find a strong correlation between reduced cognitive capacity and low nutritional status, e.g., lack of iron and vitamin A in the organism (Bhargava and Yu, 1997; Pollitt, 2001). Health, therefore, as many other individual traits (e.g. wealth, race), may explain much of the intergenerational transmission of economic status (Bowles and Gintis, 2001).

Moreover, low health conditions can increase inequality not only within countries, but also across them (WHO, 2001). Developing countries, in fact, often have poor average health conditions that hinder their ability to grow and converge towards the developed economies. Countries with high rates of infant mortality have grown more slowly during the period 1964–1995 than countries with low levels of the same variable (WHO, 2001). Thus, inequality jeopardizes health and health in its turn strongly affects the earning capacity of individuals (arrow 8 in Figure 5.2). This feedback may trigger a vicious circle between bad health and inequality that risks to progressively reinforce both of them.

6.3   Feedback effects of health on the environment

The health of a population can indirectly influence the quality of its environment as a result of two factors which have an impact on environmental degradation: economic growth and population dynamics. We have already discussed how health can affect economic growth. As to the population dynamics, the growth of the population is influenced by its average health conditions that strongly affect the birth rate. In this respect, it has been observed that the countries with the highest fertility rates are those that also have the highest infant mortality rates.[82] This is because in countries with a high number of deaths in the first years of life, parents tend to have more children to ensure that at least some of them survive into adulthood. This trend is further reinforced by the fact that in many developing countries, having children is the only way parents can provide for their old age. As a result, the populations with the highest infant mortality rates are also those that grow most quickly, because the high rates of infant mortality are more than compensated by the high birth rates.[83] Reducing infant mortality in these countries would therefore tend to reduce population growth.

A lower population growth would have in turn a positive effect on the quality of the environment. Environmental degradation is so strongly influenced by the size of the resident population that the demographic issue holds center stage in the sustainable development debate, right from the first contributions in the literature (cf. Holdren and Ehrlich, 1974). The size of the population does, in fact, determine the amount of natural resources used to satisfy consumption needs and thus also the carrying capacity of an ecosystem. Demographic growth is likely to damage the environment since it is accompanied by both an increase in the demand for environmental goods and an increase in the waste coming from the growing production and consumption of a more numerous population. Therefore, the causal link we have just described starts with health, moves on to population dynamics and ends with the environment, as described by arrows 9 and 10 in Figure 5.2.

Alongside this link, we can nevertheless identify another one moving in the opposite direction, starting with environmental degradation and leading to average health conditions (indicated by arrows 11 and 12 in the block diagram), making the relationship between health and environment bi-directional, mediated by variations in the population. The high level of environmental degradation in some areas of the world has, in recent years, led to increasing migratory flows of "environmental refugees" (El-Hinnawi, 1985) who move on to escape from the pollution of their traditional habitat. There are so many cases of migration caused by environmental degradation that some authors (cf. Myers, 1997) argue that these refugees might become the largest group of involuntary migrants in the near future, while others (cf. Bates, 2002) have attempted to classify some typologies of environmental refugees to provide a theoretical framework to the fast-growing literature on the subject. Amongst the examples given is the migration of 7 million Vietnamese rural people to the cities during the war with the United States because of the destruction of the forests and harvests following the use of the previously mentioned herbicide "Agent Orange" (Glassman, 1992). Another example is that of the 15 million people who may well be forced to leave Bangladesh by 2050 as a result of a rise in sea level (Myers, 1993). Migration caused by environmental degradation tends to change the population's distribution over the territory which can in turn affect the health of the population. An increase in population density in the cities, for example, can facilitate the transmission of diseases such as tuberculosis, meningitis, poliomyelitis, and measles which spread rapidly, mainly in the overcrowded hinterlands of large urban centers which also suffer from poor sanitation.

Summing up, the existence of inverse causality is confirmed by our analysis but, contrary to a diffuse opinion among economists, this does not imply the spuriousness of the direct influence of globalization on health. This is emphasized by epidemiologists who argue that "although ill health can affect socioeconomic position, the bulk of the research evidence indicates that the predominant force is in the direction of socioeconomic position influencing population health" (Tarlov and St. Peter, 2000, p.xv). They "have tracked individuals from relatively early on their careers (when they were free of illness), and demonstrated that low incomes lead to the higher onset of morbidity and premature mortality" (Kawachi and Kennedy, 2002, p.61; see also Wilkinson, 1996 and Tarlov and St. Peter, 2000, p.xv). We believe that we have to take seriously the argument put forward by social epidemiologists. In any case the coexistence of direct and inverse causality produces a vicious circle between income inequality and health that is very difficult to reverse.

7 Further influences of globalization on health

After examining the effects of globalization on health through economic growth, inequality and environmental deterioration, and the bi-directional nature of these links, let us now move to the analysis of a few further health effects of the worldwide economic integration (arrow 13 in Figure 5.2).

Globalization may increase the cross-border transmission of infectious diseases by augmenting the movements of people and the consequent risk of contagion. People move from the North to the South and vice versa mainly for tourism and labor, although other causes can also contribute to this flow.[84]

These large multi-directional movements of people that characterize the globalization process can spread, therefore, transmissible diseases across countries, which raises the health interdependence between developed and developing countries. Thus, for instance, large migrations from the South to the North may increase human settlements in poor areas without adequate sanitation and access to safe water (e.g. suburban areas in large Northern towns), augmenting the consequent risks of contagion throughout the Northern population. The world-wide diffusion of AIDS (apparently originated in Western Africa in the 1930s) and the transmission of multi-drug resistant tuberculosis from poor to rich countries provide other important examples of how low health conditions of the poor can have negative spill-over effects on the health status of the rich. The outbreak of SARS and avian flu are other recent examples. As these examples show, inequality tends to strengthen the health interdependence between developed and developing countries. In a globalized world, in fact, the health of a country crucially depends on infectious diseases that are bred by poverty in some far-distant country (Sandler and Arce, 2002).[85]

Globalization has also a direct health effect through the consequences that international agreements can have on the health of the populations involved (Woodward *et al.*, 2001). The international agreements on food security standards and on the use of GMO, for instance, can have large positive as well as negative impacts on public health. These agreements pose important trade-offs between conflicting interests. The food security standards imposed by some developed countries, in fact, can protect the health of their inhabitants. The imposition of these standards, however, may come at the cost of reducing the exports of developing countries. If so, low-income countries might become even poorer, with a consequent negative impact on their average health and on inequality between countries. Similarly, the adoption of GMO poses a delicate trade-off between the need to feed an ever-increasing population in the developing countries (that have the highest rates of demographic growth) and the unknown consequences that GMO might cause to their population in terms of health risks and variability of the agricultural production.

The recent agreements on TRIPS provide another example of how the governance of globalization can directly affect public health. Even in this case, a trade-off arises between the need to promote research in health technologies (that generally takes place in developed countries) and the need to protect public health in developing countries that cannot afford high-costs medicaments. The "Declaration on the TRIPS agreements and public health" promulgated at the WTO meeting in Doha in November 2001 tried to find a compromise solution between the opposite interests of developed and developing countries in this field. While reaffirming the commitment of the WTO members to the TRIPS agreement, the Declaration recognized that each member has the right to grant compulsory pharmaceutical licenses in case of national public health crises, especially those resulting from Human Immunodeficiency Virus (HIV) or AIDS, tuberculosis, malaria and other epidemics that afflict many developing countries. Most of these countries, however, were unable to make effective use of this right since they had no manufacturing capacities in the pharmaceutical sector and wanted therefore to be allowed to import the necessary pharmaceutical medicaments from countries that can sell them at low costs. This request caused a lively debate between developed and developing countries that have reached an agreement on this issue only after several months in Geneva (August 2003). During this long bargaining process, Brazil has asked for WHO to be involved in the negotiations to safeguard its own interests, which further confirms that global governance and public health are strictly intertwined.

The international agreements on labor standards represent another important case of global governance that can affect public health, particularly in developing countries. The possible existence of "sweatshops" working for some multinational corporations in developing countries and the use of children in their production process have recently attracted much attention in public opinion. The actual extension of this phenomenon is still the object of debate.[86] Some legitimate concerns exist, however, on the potential impact that these labor conditions might have on population health in developing countries. The exploitation of adults and children in unhealthy labor conditions could breed diseases among the poor in the developing countries and thus deteriorate health in these countries. If so, this would tend to raise inequality both within developing countries and across countries. On the other hand, one must be aware that imposing in the South the same labor standards of the North might increase labor costs in developing countries and reduce the incentive of Northern enterprises to invest in these countries. As the other international agreements mentioned above, therefore, also those on labor standards might generate a trade-off in developing countries between better health from higher labor standards and lower income (thus possibly lower health) from a reduction in investments.

Another channel through which global governance can directly affect public health is given by the international environmental agreements. The reduction in CO_2 emissions promoted by the Kyoto agreements, for instance, would largely benefit the health of the world population, regardless of where this reduction occurs. However, if the environmental policies required by the Kyoto Protocol had recessive effects, cutting CO_2 emissions might come at the cost of a reduction in per capita income and thus also of the average health conditions. Moreover, if the implementation of the Kyoto Protocol increases the costs of production of the firms that operate in developed countries, these might shift their polluting activities from the North to the South with potential negative effects on the health conditions of the population living in developing countries. If so, like in the cases examined above, the adoption of the international environmental agreements in the North might generate a trade-off in the South between better health (from lower CO_2 emissions at the world level) and lower health (from higher concentration of polluting activities in developing countries). Although the "pollution haven hypothesis" has found little empirical support so far, one cannot deny that such a displacement of polluting activities has occurred in a few deplorable cases and could occur in the future, particularly if the environmental costs of production were to increase substantially.[87]

A deeper analysis of the economic and social implications of these international agreements goes beyond the scope of the present work.[88] These few examples, however, although largely incomplete, can help to clarify the strict linkage between globalization, health and inequality across countries. In all these examples, in fact, the governance of globalization and its direct impact on public health raises potential trade-offs and conflicts of interests between the North and South of the world that are likely to increase, the higher is the level of inequality across countries.

6
The "New" Globalization

Globalization is an evolutionary process that modifies its structural features with time. Although structural change is generally slow and steady, sometimes it undergoes sharp accelerations. These periods of structural break permit a conventional, but not altogether arbitrary, subdivision of the process of globalization in well-defined periods. Each period shares a few common features with the preceding periods but is characterized by distinctive features that mark a discontinuity with the past. Of course the subdivision in periods may be more or less fine according to the analytic and policy purposes.

In this book we have identified the third decade of the 19th century as the starting point of the era dominated by "modern" economic globalization that is based on the internationalization of markets. Within it we distinguished three broad periods: the "first" globalization until the First World War, the "de-globalization" in the period that encompasses the two World Wars, and the "second" globalization since 1945. Within the second globalization we distinguished three sub-periods: that of Bretton Woods between 1945 and 1971, a transition decade in the 1970s, and that of the "Washington consensus" until the end of the past Millennium (see Chapters 1 and 8). Within each of the sub-periods it is possible to introduce further distinctions in phases that allow more detailed analysis of the historical processes and causal relations that characterize each of them.

In this chapter we limit ourselves to focusing on the phase from 1995 to 2000 that we are going to call "new" globalization. This conventional terminology simply aims to evoke the two main elements characterizing it: the rapid rise of the "new economy" up to the year 2000 and the consolidation of new ways of regulating the international markets brought about by the activity of the WTO established on

January 1, 1995. While the traditional globalization was propelled by the growing mobility of goods, energy and capital, the "new" globalization was propelled specifically by the growing mobility of information through the Worldwide Web of the Internet. The reduction of costs and access time to global and local information brought about a transformation in the structure of production and distribution of goods and services deeply influencing the process of globalization itself. We focus in this chapter on the risks and opportunities deriving from the emerging features of the process of new globalization, assessing to what extent we may benefit from the new technologies in order to consolidate sustainable development at the world level.

1   The "new economy": a critical appraisal

At a first glance the process of globalization which started after World War II does not seem too different from that of the second half of the 19th century, as it was propelled by a rapid expansion of world trade made possible by the continuous improvement in transport and a progressive reduction of protectionist measures. However in the late 1990s a profound transformation in the organization of production and distribution of goods and services started in the most advanced economies (in particular in North America and Europe) rapidly spreading to the other developed economies and substantially affecting the process of globalization itself. The interaction of economic exchanges and relations typical of the traditional process of globalization has become increasingly entrenched in the elaboration of information, including that transmitted and processed through the Internet. This new way of organizing the economy was soon called the "new economy" by the mass media.[89] We adopt this terminology here whilst emphasizing that its meaning, features and implications still require a thorough appraisal. At the end of the 1990s the new economy was often exalted as the beginning of a new era of prosperity and economic progress, while after the burst of the speculative bubble in 2001 and the ensuing deep and prolonged depression, it was generally denigrated as a source of dangerous illusions if not of degenerative processes in the economic and social fabric. There have been only few attempts to make a comprehensive appraisal of its positive and negative implications.[90] In particular, a thorough analysis of its impact on the globalization process and on the sustainability of development is almost altogether absent. This deficiency of the literature is particularly remarkable also because the trend of penetration of Information and Communication Technology (ICT) in the economy did not decline in recent years and is deeply transforming the structure of the economy. In this section we offer a preliminary contribution to this end.

It is useful to distinguish four aspects of the new economy: technological, economic, financial and policy implications. For each of these aspects we are going to distinguish what we can call a "mythical" vision that is based upon a sanguine appraisal of its novelties, and a more "realistic" vision that sees the new economy as an evolutionary stage characterized by a sizeable but thoroughly circumscribed discontinuity with the past that may have both positive and negative implications.

As for the *technological* aspects, the "new economy" was nothing but a systematic application of ICTs to the process of production and distribution of goods and services, propelled by the epoch-making innovation of the Internet. In this sense the new economy was seen by its supporters as the fourth industrial revolution after the first at the end of 1700 brought about by the systematic introduction of steam machines, the second propelled by the construction of the railways network, and the third fueled at the turn of the 19th century by systematic electrification of industrialized economies. Each of these clusters of innovation played an epoch-making role because of their pervasive nature that was bound to affect in due course all the aspects of the economy. According to Metcalfe's well-known law, often mentioned in reference to the new economy, the value of a network is proportional to the square of the number of its nodes. Hence the railway network sizably reduced the cost of transporting goods and people, the electricity network sharply reduced the cost of transporting energy, while the Internet reduced that of information. Someone went so far to interpret the Internet as the ultimate meta-net able to connect directly each person with any other (*"one-to-one"*) without hierarchy and intermediation. In this view, each of these clusters of innovations made market relations both broader and deeper, thereby favoring their globalization.

This "mythical" point of view is not fully groundless but has to be downsized in the light of facts. The cluster of innovations triggered by the Internet may be interpreted as the third wave of innovations in the process of gradual introduction of ICT. At the end of the 1960s and early 1970s there was a first wave connected to the introduction of *mainframe* computers in bigger firms and public administrations. In the late 1980s there was a second wave of innovations triggered by the introduction of personal computers. These two waves were a necessary premise for the third in the late 1990s triggered by the introduction of the Internet.

Each of these innovation waves was characterized by a cycle of investments that accelerated in the phase of initial diffusion of the new cluster of innovations, stimulating the expansion of the entire economy, but decelerated as soon as the market became saturated after a few years, thereby triggering a phase of depression. In the case of investment in ICT, these cyclical fluctuations occurred around a growing trend that may be roughly fitted by an exponential curve and there is no reason to believe that this trend has to change in the near future.

These remarks may help us to place the new economy boom and the ensuing depression in a more realistic perspective. The boom triggered by the new economy was neither surprising nor new from the point of view of economics; analogously the ensuing cyclical fall in ICT investment was a physiological event. Moreover, there is no reason to believe that the first three waves of ICT investment will not be followed by new waves pushed by clusters of innovations that perhaps we cannot yet think of, confirming the growing trend. In any case, the boom of the new economy confirmed that knowledge is becoming the fundamental productive factor. Therefore, investments increasingly focus on the production, elaboration, and diffusion of knowledge exploiting more and more the potential of ICTs.

The preceding remarks aim to downsize both the excessive hopes raised by the boom of the new economy and the excessive pessimism raised by its crisis. Some might object that the cycle of the new economy was more marked than the other post-war cycles, with the only possible exception of the fluctuations of the 1970s that were greatly amplified by exogenous factors (the two oil shocks). However we are going to show in the next section that this did not depend so much on real factors but rather on financial factors. In any case the network of relationships between economic agents still seems to be quite hierarchical and highly intermediated by firms, public institutions and non-governmental organizations (NGOs).

Let us now shift to the *economic* aspects of the new economy. In this field, the mythological point of view was particularly misleading. It was even claimed that the economic laws were superseded, thus determining the end of the business cycle and the beginning of a more rapid, still sustainable, steady growth due to an acceleration of productivity resulting from the systematic introduction of the new ICTs. After the burst of the speculative bubble of the new economy it became clear to every one that there is no reason to expect a significant change in the economic laws. Admittedly, the new economy enhanced the importance of cognitive and financial factors, but in both cases it was climbed only a further step up a long staircase. This did not alter the basic laws of economics but only some of their concrete manifestations. In particular, it is erroneous to maintain that the market, modernized and globalized by the new economy, does not need regulation nor counter-cyclical policies, nor support to consolidate development and its sustainability.

As for the *financial* aspects, the financial intensity of the economy, firms and families increased, and the crucial role of the stock exchange increased (Chapter 1). The new, much higher, price/dividend ratio was considered sustainable on the basis of mistaken expectations of higher sustainable productivity and income growth coupled with the groundless prediction of a demise of the business cycle. In addition the fact that families hold a higher percentage of assets in shares induced a few experts to believe in the demise of the Phillips curve that is the tendency of wages to accelerate when unemployment falls beyond a certain threshold. However, the business cycle is there to stay not only for the usual real factors, but also for financial reasons that are increasingly important (see Vercelli, 2000). As for the price/dividend ratio the value reached at the end of the period was clearly unsustainable as was made clear by the ensuing fall.

Finally, as a general consideration, the utopian view of the new economy spread the unfounded opinion that the ideal market of perfect competition had been substantially realized, implying the demise of economic policy. As argued in the first chapter, however, the real markets are still quite distant from the ideal market and still require a system of policy rules aiming at their minimal but efficient regulation (see sections 5 and 6).

2   ICT and sustainability: opportunities

In order to understand the implications of the new economy for the sustainability of the world development we have to clarify to what extent real markets are actually able to approach the ideal model of perfect competition.

In principle, the new economy may push real markets closer to the abstract model of perfect competition. This may happen in particular because the systematic application of ICT may reduce: (i) the *information asymmetry* between potential traders by offering, in principle, cheap access to economic and financial information to every agent concerned;

(ii) the *transaction costs* necessary to realize the 'double coincidence of wants' among traders, i.e. the matching between demand and supply, in particular by reducing the searching costs; (iii) the *barriers to entry* in the market for new enterprises since it is much cheaper to set up a new business wholly or partially online than with a traditional brick-and-mortar shop or office, and because it is easier for the would-be entrepreneur to gather all the necessary technological, bureaucratic and commercial information for starting up the new business; it may be also easier to find the necessary start-up capital to the extent that the supply of venture capital has been stimulated by the spreading of the new economy.

In addition, according to a few observers, the new economy may reduce the existing *scale and scope economies* in the productive and distributive sectors. This depends in particular on the interaction between the points mentioned above. In particular, the reduction in information asymmetry and transaction costs was expected to remove the main reasons for vertical integration (Coase, 1960) and encouraged each firm to specialize in its core business by outsourcing the acquisition of all the required goods and services. The reduction of the barriers to entry coupled with the increasing velocity of technical change assured some degree of contestability also in the sectors more affected by tendencies towards natural monopoly. However, the ICTs also offered new occasions of scale and scope economies related to the growing role of virtual networks[91] and the increasing importance of the gate-keeper that regulates access to them.[92]

Finally, a few observers claim that the new economy may reduce the *average size of enterprises* since in many sectors small and medium enterprises have more chances of survival and growth (Storey, 1994). This depends not only on the points mentioned above but also on the reduction in the comparative disadvantage of small-medium enterprises (SMEs) *vis-à-vis* large enterprises, and on the contemporaneous increase in their comparative advantage. Among the reasons for diminishing comparative disadvantage we can mention the easier access to global information even about distant markets, easier access to technological information through the burgeoning societies of technological transfer and advice, and the new possibilities of distribution of goods and services through e-commerce. Among the factors enhancing the competitive advantage of SMEs we can mention the increasing value of the flexibility typical of small size firms in markets that evolve at increasing speed (see, e.g., Vercelli, 1989).

It was also claimed that for all the reasons mentioned above, the new economy increases the power of the final user of goods and services by increasing their customization and the transparency of their prices. The so-called 'sovereignty of the consumer' (or, more in general, of the final user of goods and services) long since stressed in the economics textbooks may now become more realistic than it was before.

Summing up, it is reasonable to suppose that, to the extent that the new economy actually approached real markets to the pure model of competitive markets, in principle it should also have improved the allocation of economic resources, i.e. economic efficiency. This is relevant for sustainability. More efficiency implies that the same amount of goods and services may be produced with fewer resources, including exhaustible natural resources, and with less pollution. Economic efficiency, however, is a necessary but not sufficient condition of *eco-efficiency* (see in particular Schmidheiny and Zorraquin, 1996) since we also have to consider environmental externalities. According to some observers, the diffusion of the new economy offered many opportunities for enhancing also the eco-efficiency of economic processes. The basic reason is that knowledge is increasingly becoming the principal factor of production and knowledge does not in itself pollute or waste natural resources.

In particular, the spread of the new economy provided new opportunities for reducing *energy consumption*. First of all, the systematic application of ICT to all the economic sectors may sizably increase the total factor productivity. For example, in the USA the ICT is believed to have been the key factor in the sizeable acceleration of productivity growth in the late 1990s, since two-thirds of it was due directly to ICT production and investment: nearly half of the acceleration in productivity growth was due to capital deepening produced by investment in ICT, while the other half was due to faster total factor productivity growth of which two-fifths depends on the growing inefficiency in the ICT sector itself.[93]

It was estimated that the spread of the new economy may accelerate the reduction in energy intensity, measured in energy consumed per dollar of gross domestic product. In the USA, the rate of reduction in energy intensity has increased from 1% in the early 1990s to 3% in the late 1990s, in part (about one-third) due to structural reasons (growing weight of the ICT sector that is relatively less energy intensive) and in part (almost two-thirds, taking account of a small statistical residual) because of gains in the energy efficiency of all sectors made possible by the systematic introduction of ICTs. This has produced in the same period a substantial stabilization in the emissions of GHGs notwithstanding the strong rate of growth of the economy (see Romm *et al.*, 1999, p.5, and Chapter 4).

The new economy may accelerate the *dematerialization* of the process of production and distribution of goods. This is due first of all to the process of substitution of electronic files for material goods and services (a process that has been called *e-materialization*). A case in point is the use of paper that is currently substituted by e-mail, electronic catalogues, e-books, etc. The *paperless office* has been already realized in a few high-tech firms, such as Microsoft (see Gates, 1999). Any reduction in the use of paper is welcome for improving sustainability because the manufacture of paper is one of the most environmentally critical industrial sectors as it puts pressure on a crucial scarce resource (forests) while greatly polluting at the same time water, soil and atmosphere. The reduction in warehouse and office space made possible by the ICTs could make another significant contribution to dematerialization (see, e.g., Romm *et al.*, 1999).

In addition, the new economy could promote *telework* that is assuming a prominent role in many high-tech enterprises. For example, about the half of AT&T employees work at least partly at home with a reported increase in productivity and job satisfaction.

Finally, the new economy may contribute to matching better and more rapidly demand and supply of goods and services, in particular through the progressive development of the *e-commerce*, reducing the costs of searching for the right supplier or for reaching potential customers, while increasing customer satisfaction. This virtually eliminates the risk of unsold goods, reducing the size of *inventories* and hence also the need of *warehouse space*, and allows huge savings in square meters, electricity, natural gas, and GHG emissions (for an estimate concerning the USA, see Romm *et al.*, 1999).

The new globalization of real markets may, *ceteris paribus*, accelerate the pace of growth at the world level to the extent that it improves the allocation of resources at the global scale. This in itself tends to deteriorate the quality of the environment because of the growing negative environmental externalities of economic activity at the world level since more natural resources are used and more pollution is released into the biosphere (for the evidential underpinnings of this stylized representation see, e.g., De Bruyn *et al.*, 1998). The nexus between economic growth and negative externalities, however, may be shifted in a favorable direction as new technologies and policy measures change the structure of the natural inputs and of the outputs emitted in the natural media. As a consequence of these shifts, the relationship between the stage of development (somehow measured by per capita income) and global natural externalities may well become positive after a certain threshold as environmental awareness and technological know-how improve. In particular, the globalization of information strongly accelerated by the spread of the new economy allows the introduction of the best environmental practices all over the world, thereby favorably shifting the trade-off between the rate of growth and sustainability.[94] The net effect may eventually become positive provided that the favorable shift of the trade-off mentioned above is vigorously driven by the growing environmental awareness of the final users of goods and services and by suitable environmental policies (see the next section). In addition, the transfer of technological knowledge and know-how from leader economies allows the followers to pursue a similar pattern of development in a more favorable position.

A case in point is that of energy intensity. In principle, more growth implies more energy consumption and therefore more rapid exhaustion of resources (such as oil) and more pollution. This problem has been aggravated by the increase in energy intensity observed in all the countries in the early stages of development. In the most developed countries, however, empirical evidence suggests that in the long run the growth of energy intensity tends to slow down and eventually reverse (see Chapter 4). In addition, the inverted-U curve of the follower countries typically shifted downwards as a consequence of the transmission of technological expertise and know-how from leaders to followers (*ibidem*). The exception represented by the ex-Soviet countries, China, and most developing countries suggests that in these cases, though for different reasons, the transfer of technologies and know-how was slow and inefficient. This observation suggests that the beneficial transfer of knowledge from the most advanced economies to the other economies may be much accelerated by the spread of the new economy in less developed countries and by appropriate transboundary policies aimed to exploit the new opportunities.[95]

3   ICT and sustainability: risks

The diffusion of ICTs may offer important opportunities for enhancing the sustainability of development. The impact of ICT on the globalization process, however, may have also dangerous implications for sustainability that we intend to consider in this section. We can classify these risks in two categories: those that impede the realization of the opportunities mentioned in the preceding section and further risks. Let us discuss at the very outset the first category of risks.

The reduction of information asymmetries is limited by the availability of efficient access to the Internet in the office, at home or at wireless points, as well as by the effective expertise of the user and her ability to filter and interpret the relevant information. First of all, generally speaking, the excess of information available in the Internet may seriously jeopardize the selection and fruition of the relevant information. Moreover, the meaning of information depends on the cognitive structures and the background knowledge of the users. Taking account of all these factors, the asymmetries in the effective capacity of fruition of the relevant information may well have actually increased due to the diffusion of the ICTs.

As for transaction costs, a sizeable reduction is possible only when the goods and services exchanged are highly standardized and their characteristics are well-known to clients (as in the case of books). In all other cases, the need to personally inspect and compare the goods and services offered sets a limit to the reduction of transaction costs that cannot be easily shifted even by further technological advances in the virtual markets.

Also the claim of a weakening of the barriers to entry in the markets does not seem to be well grounded. This assertion was inspired by a temporary phenomenon: the boom of new high-tech firms that mushroomed in the late 1990s in order to exploit the euphoric expectations of that time. Many of these new entries, however, had to face harsh realities and were swept away by competition. There is a long-term trend, which started in the 1970s, of a growing importance of small and medium enterprises originated by an increasing demand for flexibility (Storey, 1994). This slow growth does not seem to have accelerated in the late 1990s. On the contrary, the tendency to a reduction of the average firm size was to some extent countered by the emergence of new opportunities of scale and scope economies based on the size of virtual networks and of software standardization.

For all the preceding reasons the sovereignty of the final user of goods and services has not yet been achieved in practice as the gap between the real market and the ideal perfect-competition market is still quite sizeable (see Chapter 1). The growth in efficiency has occurred mainly in the most advanced technological sectors, in part for reasons independent of, or complementary to, the introduction of new technologies, being grounded in the growing flexibility of labor markets and industrial relations that jeopardizes the social sustainability of development. Eco-efficiency may improve with miniaturization and dematerialization, including the electronic version (also called e-materialization). For example, the process of dematerialization may contribute to the reduction of energy consumption. It has been estimated that the e-materialization of paper alone may cut energy consumption in the USA in four years by about 0.25% (see Romm *et al.*, 1999). However it must be stressed that the introduction of ICT devices does not necessarily imply e-materialization. For example, if the successive drafts of an electronic file are systematically printed (for correction, comments, record, etc.) the net use of paper may increase. In order to avoid that, it is necessary to intervene with active policies such as those already successfully pursued by the firms that have realized fully paperless offices (see Gates, 1999). So far, however, electronic dematerialization is far from having achieved its full potential.

Also the environmental benefits arising from the introduction of the new ICTs are by no means automatic. A case in point is the progressive diffusion of e-commerce. The individual packaging and shipping of goods from a perhaps distant country may increase the environmental costs of the distribution of goods (fuel, pollution, waste, etc.) In order to avoid this, consistent active policies must be implemented, such as those already successfully introduced in Germany and other countries for curbing the abuse of packaging.

The diffusion of ICTs of the new economy may also have negative effects on energy consumption since it encourages the systematic use of electronic devices at home and at the workplace. Therefore there is no guarantee that the positive net effect observed in the USA in the late 1990s is bound to persist there, or occur in other countries. In order to obtain these results, active policies must be pursued (see *retro* Chapter 4).[96]

As we have seen, there are still many serious obstacles to the realization of the opportunities promised by the spread of ICTs. They must be removed through suitable policy interventions that we are going to discuss in the next chapter. Besides these risks we have to allow for further risks introduced by the systematic adoption of the ICTs. In particular we should be aware of the risks arising from the new globalization of financial markets. In principle, anyone can gain prompt access to these markets via the Internet (connecting from home or elsewhere, even walking down a street, through a WAP portable telephone or wireless point) and may exchange stocks all over the world without interruption. This has fostered the emergence of a stock-exchange market virtually unified at the world level, greatly increasing the number of traders, including a soaring number of amateurs among them, and sharply reducing transaction costs. In addition, an increasing amount of information has been made available on the Web for anyone interested, thus virtually eliminating information asymmetry. As a consequence, we have more competitive global financial markets that may improve the allocation of financial capital with beneficial fallout on the real side (e.g., more efficient international arbitrage and availability of venture capital for new entrepreneurial ideas). However, the global financial markets also exhibit huge problems.

First of all globalized financial markets are liable to be more unstable. The main trouble so far is not with what we have called above *institutional* instability (see *retro* Chapter 1). A huge process of mergers and affiliations increased the size of the main global financial operators, but at same time the new economy offered new opportunities of growth also to the most dynamic small operators. However, if the process of concentration continues to be insufficiently regulated at the world level it could eventually jeopardize competition as soon as the contestability of financial markets begins to weaken. In any case the *dynamic* and *structural* instability of financial markets has greatly increased in recent decades as a result of the process of globalization and it has further accelerated due to the spread of the new economy. This has been clearly revealed by a sequence of dramatic financial crises with serious global repercussions (European Monetary System, 1992; Mexico, 1994; Far East Asia 1997–98; Russia, 1998; Brazil, 1999; Argentina, 2001 and so on). In addition, the volatility of stock prices has apparently increased in recent years (see Shiller, 2000). The main reason may lie in the growing impact of the so-called 'herd behavior' of traders on stock prices as the size of the herd progressively soared, and the impact of weakly regulated markets at the world level became increasingly evident.

Moreover, the increase in the volatility and instability of financial markets strengthens the tendency towards a rapid and marked shortening of the decision horizon. The size of potential returns or losses involved in speculation is becoming so large as compared to the returns or losses involved in long-run entrepreneurial decisions that too much capital, resources and energies are shifted towards short-term trading and speculation. This increasing short-termism is the crucial issue raised by the new globalization process; though this tendency started long ago,[97] it is now greatly strengthened by the current process of new globalization. Financial bubbles, financial crises, and many negative externalities of economic growth stem from it. In particular, there is strong empirical evidence suggesting that greater volatility in capital markets brings about greater volatility in GDP growth rates that is correlated in turn with slower average growth, increase in poverty, and negative externalities including environmental degradation (Vinod, *et al.*, 2000, p.12). In addition, short-termism brings about an irrational overvaluation of current values, costs and benefits and undervaluation of future values, costs and benefits, and this is clearly inconsistent with decisions compatible with sustainable development. In particular this attitude has strengthened the implementation of grow-now-clean-later policies that have disastrous effects for sustainability.[98]

A further crucial problem raised by the current process of new globalization is a weakening of business ethics.[99] This is strictly connected with the increasing short-termism of the economic agents. The prescriptions of ethics are often leading to the repression of behavior committed to short-term goals in favor of longer-term goals. For example, drugs, alcohol and smoking may give an immediate sense of satisfaction but only at the expense of "sustainable health". The same is true when the interests of other people are involved by a certain decision: it is possible to obtain immediate advantages by damaging other people but only by stimulating at the same time disruptive retaliation or breaking the basic structure of markets and society that requires trust (Sen, 1999).

Increasing short-termism and the weakening of business ethics affect both real and financial global markets and are undermining the social and environmental sustainability of growth at the world level (see Chapter 7). Since a complete evaluation of environmental costs and benefits requires a long-time horizon, economic decisions, in the absence of incisive environmental regulations, tend to be increasingly biased against sustainability.

4   The new regulation of international markets and the role of the WTO

The transformations of the structure and technology of the international economy that emerged with the new economy poses new challenges to the regulation of international markets. We want to examine here whether the evolution of international regulatory institutions may be considered an adequate response to the new challenges. As we have seen in the first chapter, the set of policy rules meant to regulate the international markets introduced by the peace conference of Bretton Woods in 1944 broke down in the early 1970s. After a brief transition phase during the 1970s, in the 1980s a new system of policy rules emerged that gave up the Keynesian inspiration of the Bretton Woods period. Focusing on the risks of state failures and playing down the risks of market failures the new policy paradigm aimed at the systematic deregulation of markets and at the privatization of all activities with a potential economic impact. The new regulation of international markets was managed by the same international organizations set up at Bretton Woods (*in primis* the IMF and the WB) that in the new circumstances changed quite radically their policy philosophy (see Chapters 1 and 8). It soon became clear that in the new regulatory regime the liberalization of international exchanges required a new organization with more power and operational facilities than the existing GATT rounds. After a long gestation the new organization started to operate on January 1, 1995 under the name of WTO.

The establishment of the WTO was favorably received by most countries, including the developing ones which expected it to act as an impartial referee with the authority to enforce free trade rules with all partners, including the most powerful countries. At the beginning almost no one realized that the charter of the organization concealed potential dangers that became evident only with experience. Though the adhesion of the international community to the WTO was almost unanimous, the effective participation of member states in the decision process proved to be wanting and asymmetrical. Only the most powerful countries could afford to keep consistent permanent delegations able to update information in real time and to exert a sizeable influence. The senior officials of the WTO received delicate responsibilities that may be likened to those of powerful judges, as they have to settle disputes over violations of free trade rules received by member countries. Whenever such violations are confirmed and result from a law approved by a member country, they condemned it to pay very hefty fines unless the law was repealed. This delicate decision process was delegated to the top officials of WTO without having previously secured the necessary transparency and accountability of their behavior.

The effective behavior of the WTO was soon considered questionable by many observers both in terms of procedures and merit. The first anomaly lies in the very low probability of a complaint being rejected, since this decision can be taken only if supported by the unanimous agreement of all the member countries, including the country that started the procedure. In addition, there is no chance for the country accused or other stakeholders to organize a defense. In particular, there is no possibility to bring witnesses or to produce scientific documents in defense of the contested law. As for merit, the tendency emerged to interpret environmental and social constraints as non-tariff barriers to trade, even when introduced by multilateral agreements signed by member-countries. According to the WTO charter, trade constraints could be admitted only if science unanimously demonstrated their necessity; this is extremely unlikely to happen since modern science is rarely unanimous, is generally reluctant to make definitive assertions and relies on probabilistic assertions (health hazards of smoking are a case in point). This is why the WTO has forced many countries to repeal laws imposing environmental, social and health barriers to international trade in order to assure sustainability of development. Let us briefly recall a few examples (for these and many other examples see Wallach and Sforza, 1999; Esty, 2001).

As for environmental pollution, on the initiative of Canada, the EU countries had to repeal the law imposing constraints on the import of building products containing asbestos; on the initiative of Venezuela, the USA had to repeal a law stipulating the maximum pollution from car exhausts, and on the initiative of the EU, a law imposing fuel economy standards in accordance with the Clean Air For Europe (CAFE) international treaty. Analogously, on the initiative of the USA, Japan had to repeal the law imposing constraints on CO_2 emissions consistent with the Kyoto international agreements; finally, on the initiative of the USA, the EU was forced to repeal the directive imposing constraints on the recycling of electronic hardware.

Other questionable decisions in the environmental field may be found in the area of biodiversity protection. We may recall the constraints imposed by the USA on tuna fishing in defense of dolphins in accordance with the Marine Mammal Protection Act, and those on shrimp fishing in defense of marine turtles in compliance with the Convention on International Trade of Endangered Species (CITES) treaty.

As for the laws imposing health constraints contested by the WTO, we can mention the case of the EU ban on the import of beef containing hormones, South Korean regulations on food safety, the Guatemala limitations on advertising powdered milk in accordance with United Nations Children's Fund (UNICEF), and those introduced in South Africa to improve accessibility to anti-AIDS drugs.[100]

As for humanitarian constraints, the WTO forced signatory countries to repeal the AGP agreement prohibiting bids for public contracts by firms that use child labor; in addition, on the initiative of Brazil, the WTO forced the EU to cancel its aid to Andean countries to encourage substitution of coffee plantations for the existing coca cultivations, to the small independent producers of bananas in Caribbean countries, or to avoid the import of furs from animals caught in traps.

Finally, within the WTO there emerged a coalition including the USA and many developing countries aiming to forbid the labeling of products certifying their environmental, health, ethical quality or their origin, and that of their productive processes. This crucial issue, that could jeopardize the CSR (corporate social responsibility) strategies that we are going to discuss in Chapter 7, is still hot on the agenda notwithstanding the firm opposition of the EU.

In the first years of its activity the WTO played a crucial role in extending the principles of free trade to new areas such as the service sector and property rights. Many observers claim that these extensions raise serious problems. In the service sector there are areas, such as education and public health, where there are good reasons (public goods and environmental and social externalities) for avoiding systematic privatization. As for property rights enforced by the TRIPS agreement it was observed that its implementation is bound to redistribute wealth from the countries that have to import patents, i.e. developing countries, towards developed countries that export them (see subsection 2.4 of Chapter 1).

In addition, the current rules implemented by the WTO allow operations that have been called "biopiracy" in the sense that they consent to the privatization of a gene pool which has been selected and refined over millennia by ancient cultures. An example often cited in this respect is that of basmati rice, produced for centuries by Indian peasants, that risks being replaced by a genetically modified variety, almost identical but for its higher resistance to pests. A particularly deplorable aspect of this and similar commercial operations is that the genetically modified variety was engineered as sterile in order to force peasants to buy new seed each year.

The above list of examples refers only to the first five years of activity of the WTO and is by no means exhaustive. It suggests that the interventionist philosophy of the WTO in a few occasions has discouraged local efforts to upgrade the environmental, social and health standards of economic development in order to consolidate its sustainability, imposing convergence of market regulations at a lower level. We believe that the international authorities with the responsibility of regulating international markets should encourage, on the contrary, competition of firms and countries towards progressively improving sustainability standards.

This requires, among other conditions, a radical reform of the WTO aimed at encouraging a more active participation of member states, including the developing ones, in decision procedures, granting greater defense rights to countries under accusation and to other stakeholders.

From this viewpoint, a particularly urgent reform of the WTO concerns the global governance of the intellectual property rights. In our opinion, we should implement a reform of the WIPO (World Intellectual

Property Organization) meant to extend its scope and power of enforcement, and at the same time the power of control of all the stakeholders. For this purpose, the trade-related aspects of intellectual property protection – that are currently regulated by the TRIPS agreements within the WTO – should be transferred back under the jurisdiction of an empowered WIPO with similar powers to those currently possessed by the WTO. It would be desirable, moreover, to replace the TRIPS agreements with a more equitable and effective agreement. This could contribute to shorten the gap between the global market and the ideal model of perfect competition. As a matter of fact, the latter requires free circulation of information to avoid distortional asymmetries, and free circulation of knowledge to avoid gaps that would establish persisting monopolistic rents. Limited and circumscribed deviations from these fundamental rules are acceptable only in the cases in which the costs implied by intellectual property protection are demonstrably inferior to the benefits. Contrary to a widespread opinion, however, this is not generally the case with the pharmaceutical industry. Pharmaceutical patents are difficult to define, often establish monopolistic situations, and impose huge costs to developing countries (as the case of AIDS dramatically shows). As for the alleged benefits (incentive to innovation), pharmaceutical companies invest more in marketing and lobbying than in Research and Development (R&D) that is mainly (90%) focused on lifestyle drugs having a huge market in rich countries rather than on solving the problems raised by the most grave diseases haunting mankind, such as malaria and tuberculosis. It is arguable that we may introduce more efficient and balanced incentives to pharmaceutical innovation following a different approach, for example by awarding substantial prizes to the most relevant innovations for citizens' health (Stiglitz, 2006).

While these considerations call for a reform of the WTO, we believe that its mere suppression advocated by some critics would raise more problems than it would solve, unless a new international authority is established with features similar to those advocated above. Otherwise the consequence could be an undesirable revival of wild protectionism.

5   New globalization and new environmental policies

The analysis developed so far has a few policy implications for enhancing the sustainability of development at the world level. First, global markets cannot be left unregulated, while their mere deregulation is unable to ensure a satisfactory and sustainable performance of the world economy.

Therefore, the international community cannot do without institutions with the power and resources to provide the minimum amount of active regulation necessary for developing competitive global markets and for assuring their smooth functioning.

First of all, the process of new globalization has made it more urgent to establish an authority with the responsibility for regulating e-markets in collaboration with the other regulatory authorities. This unregulated medium offers new opportunities for economic crime that must be promptly thwarted. In particular, the worldwide web offers plenty of new, more efficient, opportunities for evading or eluding existing national regulations. A case in point is the sale of extremely dangerous weapons and devices that may be used by organized crime and terrorist organizations. The control of e-markets should not be used, however, as an excuse to control the liberty of opinion and criticism in the Internet.

In addition, it is urgent to establish an anti-trust authority to repress monopolistic practices at the world level. A firm which is not dominant but influential in many local markets could well be dominant at the world level. In addition, there are monopolist and oligopolist practices that cannot be detected and thwarted by local authorities without a strong co-ordination of efforts with other local authorities.

An authority is also needed to cope with the instability of financial markets. Existing local authorities have been greatly weakened by the new globalization since their powers are local while the genesis and transmission of instability increasingly has an international nature (for a recent restatement of this argument see Eatwell and Taylor, 1999). A crucial role of this authority should be the issue and management of a global reserve money along the lines suggested by Keynes and recently revived and updated by Stiglitz (2006).

Finally, we have to establish an environmental authority designed to enhance the sustainability of world development. This organization, that could be called the International EPA, should intervene to promote: (i) international agreements on a short list of global problems that need C&C (Command and Control) measures, collaborating with local environmental authorities in order to enforce regulations, (ii) international agreements on the equitable exploitation of global commons (see Dasgupta *et al.*, 1997), (iii) international agreements between developed and underdeveloped countries, such as debt swaps, pollution offsets, transfer of technologies, and so on.[101] In addition, it should promote and harmonize green taxation measures whenever they are viable and productive, establish and regulate international markets for environmental permits and derivatives, promote the design and implementation of voluntary agreements between firms and public authorities, promote environmental certification, minimal requirements of environmental safety of products and processes to be certified, and voluntary certification of environmental excellence (ISO 14000, Eco-Management and Audit Scheme [EMAS], ecolabeling, etc.), promote the systematic design and implementation of "knowledge-based" instruments inducing the active participation of stakeholders and local communities, and promote environmental knowledge and education. On the 23 September 2003 President Chirac read at the 58th General Assembly of UN a document signed by 46 countries advocating the institution of the UNEO (United Nations Environmental Organization), a new International Organization on global environmental issues with a larger scope and more power than UNEP, not inferior to that of the WHO, to cope with the growing environmental emergencies of the globe, including global warming. This proposal has been opposed by a few countries led by the USA, Brazil, China and India, but is actively sustained by a group of countries (the so-called "friends of UNEO") that recently held a meeting in Agadir (April 2007) to decide the best strategies to pursue the plan.

The list of international regulatory authorities that are urgently needed is not exhaustive but must be kept as short as possible. In fact the international authorities, which have to be established in order to provide the minimal required regulation to global markets, have to be, as far as possible, light non-bureaucratic organizations. In addition, they must be transparent and accountable democratic organizations assuring the active participation of all countries, including the poorest developing countries (Stiglitz, 2006). Moreover, the international community should establish minimal requirements for local regulations in order to avoid the effects of what could be called "Gresham's law of regulation" according to which, as in the case of currencies, the bad regulation drives away the good regulation. The new globalization is very much reinforcing this phenomenon as is suggested by the very rapid recent development of "fiscal paradises" and offshore centers and by the downgrading of environmental, health, and ethical standards often enforced in recent years by a few international trade agreements (particularly after the establishment of the WTO). A gradual upgrading of the minimal regulations has to be introduced by the international community in order to stop and begin to reverse this process. International agreements on a well-calibrated package of incentives for good regulation and disincentives for deviations from it may be useful to start the process.

We have argued so far that to solve some worldwide problems, including environmental ones correlated with the new globalization, we need a minimal amount of regulation of global markets. What sort of regulation? We will try to sketch a summary answer only for the environmental problems. In the past environmental regulation relied almost exclusively on the legal system and C&C instruments. C&C interventions are necessary whenever the problem faced may involve catastrophic and/or irreversible effects and the action to curb the behavior responsible for these effects must be taken immediately. The prohibition of production and use of DDT and cholorofluorocarbon (CFC) gases by the Montreal Protocol in 1987 has been quite effective in repressing their use and thus in slowing down the accumulation of substances with irreversible catastrophic effects. However, the short-comings of these methods are by now well-known. To actually enforce the required regulations of global markets, the necessary controls must be efficient; however, this is very difficult particularly at the world level. In addition, in order to enforce the sanctions inflicted to curb deviating behavior, the legal system must be efficient, while in most countries this is not generally the case. In any case, the enforcement of controls and sanctions is more likely to be efficient if the prohibitions are kept to a minimum so that environmental and legal authorities may concentrate their attention and resources to enforce them.

In all the other cases, environmental policies should rely on economic and knowledge-based instruments. As for financial and economic instruments, green taxation may play a crucial role to internalize negative environmental externalities but its shortcomings are becoming increasingly evident. In most countries "green taxation" schemes are very difficult to design in an equitable way and even more difficult to enforce effectively; in addition, they are usually very unpopular so that their implementation may bring about not only evasion but also widespread hostility towards any kind of environmental policy intervention. The idea of a global harmonized environmental taxation has been recently advocated by a few influential environmental economists who believe that it is the only instrument that may efficiently cope with climate change (see, e.g., Nordhaus, 2005). Another option is the systematic introduction, also at the world level, of marketable permits schemes. In this case the intervention of environmental authorities may be kept to a safe minimum and is basically concentrated in the initial phase (establishment of the global amounts of permits, initial distribution, and the setting up of the market for their regular trading). As the number and scope of these schemes increase, the initial costs and requirements are bound to diminish; in particular the establishment of a world market where many kinds of emission permits may be traded would encourage the launch of new similar initiatives. In particular, the project of an international permits scheme to meet the Kyoto objectives is very welcome as it would contribute to close the gap between the current trend of environmental indicators and that planned in Kyoto. Once an international market for tradable permits is set for a given environmental problem, it would be much easier to adopt further permit schemes dealing with other environmental issues. Finally, mixed economic instruments, such as deposit-refund schemes, are emerging as powerful instruments of environmental policy since they introduce in the markets effective incentives for environment-friendly behavior without an excessive bureaucratic burden for the public authorities that manage them. In particular, innovative schemes of environmental bonds could be devised in order to prevent and control environmental risks, especially those connected with the introduction of innovations that might have irreversible negative effects in the long period, as often is the case in the field of biotechnologies.[102]

In addition, in the knowledge-based economy progressively established by the new globalization, the focus of policy intervention should be shifted further in the new direction of knowledge-based instruments. Environmental objectives are in the interests of people whether they act as entrepreneurs, consumers or savers, provided that their time horizon is not too short (see Chapter 7). Clarifying this point and its implications to everyone should therefore become an important objective of environmental authorities. This could encourage people to change their behavior in order to reach objectives that are in their self-interest, at least in the longer period. In particular, this may be obtained by means of voluntary agreements with firms that commit themselves to improve the environmental quality of goods, services and productive processes in exchange for advice, know-how, technical expertise and further benefits (e.g. a particular eco-label that certifies the specific environmental concern of the firm) from the environmental authorities.

In addition, in the context of the new globalization – that in principle could eventually enhance the actual sovereignty of consumers – efficient incentives for environmentally sound products and processes have to come from consumers themselves. To the extent that consumers are environmentally aware, they will choose the most eco-compatible products provided sufficient information is available to discriminate between them. This role may be played by environmental certification (such as ISO 14001, EMAS, and ecolabels) that allows consumers to make the right choice. This is basically a transfer of information promoted by environmental authorities that can be made more efficient by utilizing the new opportunities offered by ICT technologies. Certification just proves that a certain aggregate standard has been reached, but the considerations and details underlying it could be made available to interested consumers or associations of consumers via the Internet, greatly enhancing the impact of the certification process.

In general, the field of "knowledge-based" policy instruments is promising, though still almost completely unexplored, territory. A few recent experiments in this direction were quite successful and opened up important new intervention strategies for promoting sustainability in both developing and developed countries. Three examples may be briefly mentioned.

By gathering and disclosing information on the environmental performance of firms and by rating them, the *Proper* program introduced in Indonesia in 1995 succeeded in creating powerful incentives for pollution control ensuring a bargaining equilibrium between firms and stakeholders which was much more consistent with sustainability than before (see Vinod, *et al.*, 2000). Similarly, by gathering and disclosing information on the environmental quality of beaches and rating them, the *Blue flag* campaign in Europe succeeded in soliciting the active participation of stakeholders and private sponsors in order to upgrade the environmental quality of beaches while inducing healthy competition between local communities and authorities in order to obtain an excellent rating (*ibidem*). Finally, the recently introduced obligation for UK Pension Funds (as from 3rd July 2000) to disclose systematically how social, environmental, and ethical considerations are taken into account in their investment policies, is already succeeding in pushing the investment managers and trustees of Pension Funds to address systematically environmental and social issues in their investment strategies (Nicholls, 2000, p.17).

These proposals may appear utopian, as many countries are reluctant to take any step that would seem to involve the transfer of even a small portion of their sovereignty to a supranational agency. However, we stress a logical necessity that of course must be realized to avoid any unnecessary transfer of sovereignty from local authorities to the supranational agency, and to guarantee at the same time transparency, accountability, and democratic participation of member states, local authorities and stakeholders. In any case, the main activity of an environmental agency of this kind should focus on the gathering, processing, and transfer of information, knowledge, know-how, and technical expertise concerning the relationship between economic activity and sustainability in order to upgrade progressively the environmental standards of world development. In the knowledge-based economy spread around the world by the new globalization, these limitations may turn out to be less binding than it might seem at a first sight.

7
The Sustainable Firm: Long-Run Performance and Corporate Social Responsibility

1 The sustainable corporation and its social responsibility

The sustainability of development has been studied, so far, almost exclusively in macroeconomic terms. The development of an economy in its usual macroeconomic sense, however, is sustainable only if the activity of most firms operating within the economy is itself sustainable. It is thus not less important to study the microeconomic side of sustainability. Hence we introduce in this chapter the concept of "sustainable firm" in order to discuss under which conditions a company may survive healthily in the long term. To be as precise as possible we focus on the most important type of firm in industrialized countries: the corporation.

The main point we intend to emphasize in this chapter is that, to be sustainable, a corporation must be socially responsible. Of course, the socially responsible firm is sustainable if it is also reasonably profitable in the long term. Assuring profitability, however, is the task of the entrepreneur and little can be asserted in general without focusing on individual sectors and individual firms and situations. The bulk of our argument refers, thus, to the relationship between CSR and corporate sustainability. To do so we have also to consider the implications for corporate sustainability of the rules of corporate governance (CG) and their evolution through time. In particular we intend to examine what kind of regulation, whether relying on the legal system or on CSR self-regulation or both, may constitute the most effective system of incentives and disincentives to assure and consolidate both CSR and corporate sustainability.

We may say that a firm is sustainable when its activity is compatible with the requirements of sustainable development. Otherwise it runs the risk of compromising its own sustainability contributing to deteriorate that of macroeconomic development. To be more precise we define a corporation as sustainable if it creates *lasting* value for all its *stake-holders*. This definition is characterized by two specifications that we deem strictly connected but not redundant in that they illuminate independent, albeit correlated, aspects of corporate sustainability.

The first specification concerns the traditional aim of corporations, namely creation of value for shareholders or, in economic terms, profit maximization, but it points out that in order to attain corporate sustainability the firm's DMs have to focus on its long-term averages. In this light, exceptional short-term results, much appreciated by stock markets and most shareholders, are not desirable if they are reaped, as often occurs, at the expense of future performance. In recent years, especially during the long boom in the late 1990s, accounting practices have become increasingly common, whereby corporate results are, by legal means or otherwise, inflated to the detriment of future returns. Some of these accounting practices use derivatives to include in the current financial year expected future returns or postpone inclusion of losses by valuing securities at the purchase price instead of at the market price (see, e.g., Rossi, 2003, p.62). Particularly risky is the use of the OTC (over the counter) derivatives that are not liable to regulation and nowadays constitute more than 90% of derivatives in circulation. The "creative" accounting practices have been fueled by excessively optimistic expectations and incentives given to managers, sometimes also to directors, based on short-term results. A significant case in point is the recent diffusion of stock options given to managers and directors as variable compensation in order to strengthen their commitment to produce shareholder value.[103] This has led to manipulations of share prices and a narrowing of the time horizon of economic decisions to the time when the options mature, to the detriment of corporate sustainability (see, e.g., Bebchuk, Fried, and Walker, 2002).

Finally, the growing financialization of the economy which has proceeded parallel to the growing importance of stock markets has made the financial side of balance sheets increasingly important while short-term *trading* has gained greater weight.[104] As was recently emphasized, "the ratio of financial wealth to real wealth, Goldsmith's FIR (Financial Intensity Ratio), doubled between 1980 and the second half of the 1990s in the US, UK and France (where the FIR is between 2.1 and 2.9); it increased by over 50% in Italy and Germany (FIR between 1.3 and 1.4)" (Nardozzi, 2002, p.15). Early on, Keynes observed that:

> as the organization of investment markets improves, the risk of the predominance of speculation [over enterprise] increases... Speculators

may do no harm as bubbles on a steady stream of enterprise. But the position is serious when enterprise becomes the bubble on a whirlpool of speculation. When the capital development of a country becomes a by-product of the activities of a casino, the job is likely to be ill-done. (Keynes, 1936, pp.158–159)

In general, excessive focusing on the short term is fueled by a situation of potential conflict of interest involving a firm's *top managers* and directors on one side and stakeholders on the other side in that career and remuneration of the former actually depend heavily on their short-term results. According to some qualified observers the conflict of interests, which has always been endemic in a market economy, has recently become epidemic (Rossi, 2003).

The second crucial specification of the definition of sustainable firm concerns the key-recipients of value creation on the part of the company. According to the traditional concept, embedded in the civil code of industrialized nations, the sole concern of a corporation should be to increase its profits so as to create value for the shareholders.[105] This point of view has been stated in a particularly rigid and monist way since the 1970s under the name of "shareholder value theory" (SVT: see section 2). An alternative view, often called "*stakeholder* theory", has taken root in the last decades as a reaction to the strictures of the recent versions of the SVT. According to this view, a firm should concern itself with creating value not only for its *shareholders* but also for all the other subjects, called *stakeholders,* who are interested in its performance and its consequences, especially its employees, customers, suppliers and the local communities where it operates. To this purpose new initiatives are being carried out to find alternative incentives to strengthen CSR. In this regard a debate is under way, whether or not it is appropriate to explicitly include *stakeholder* interests among corporate strategic aims. Some experts note that the mono-stakeholder point of view prevailing in the legislation of industrialized economies has been superseded by events and should be updated by taking *stakeholder* interests explicitly into account. To wit, the formulation of tasks and responsibilities of the directors of a public company as acknowledged in the relevant codes in the USA is still based on the codes drawn up at the beginning of the 19th century on the basis of Massachusetts case law (Longstreth, 1986). The views on this issue are rapidly changing also within official institutions. For example in the *Principles of corporate governance* issued by the OECD a whole section (III in the first part) is devoted to the role of the *stakeholders* encouraging active co-operation between corporations and stakeholders in creating wealth, jobs, and the sustainability of financially sound enterprises.

A broad consensus is coalescing among scholars and experts on the need to take shareholder objectives into account *in a long-term approach* (Jensen, 2001). Official documents are beginning to record this need. For example, the self-regulation code of companies listed in the Italian Stock Exchange explicitly states that shareholder interests should be evaluated in a "non-short" time horizon (*Committee for the self-regulation of corporations quoted in the Italian Stock Exchange*, 1999, p.19). This implies more attention for all the stakeholders since "to manage the corporation in the long-term interests of the stockholders, management and the board of directors must take into account the interests of the corporation's other stakeholders" (*American Business Roundtable Report* del 1997). The latter statement is crucial and well grounded. It may be argued that in the long term there is no irreconcilable conflict between a company's specific aims (maximization of sustainable profit) on one side and *stakeholders'* welfare and quality of life on the other side. This is confirmed by a growing number of studies that have applied the most diverse methods (historical, statistical, econometric).[106] The results mostly confirm that companies which have survived longer and have attained higher *average* profitability are precisely those that have attached greater importance to the interests of all *stakeholders* within a far-sighted framework (see Schmidheiny and Zorraquin, 1996).

The two specifications of the definition of sustainable company that we have suggested above are correlated in that the *stakeholders* are often bearers of long-term interests. For example, employees are mainly interested first in the company survival and then in its good economic and financial performance evaluated in a long-term perspective, so that they are guaranteed a job, opportunities of career and remuneration no lower than that prevailing in the market. Similarly, customers are interested in maintaining a lasting fiduciary relationship with the company. The latter may consolidate it by focusing on customer needs, and even forgoing to this end a share of the short-run profits. Finally, society is interested especially in the firm's survival so as to protect jobs over time and ensure lasting social benefits, as well as in the firm's attention to the environment and local social needs.

By the same token, it is in the long-term interests of the company to devote as much attention as possible to *stakeholder* expectations. As regards workers, it is well-known that continuous attention to their needs is fundamental to stimulate commitment and raise their productivity as well as to attract and keep a labor force with maximum professional potential. In the case of customers, an orientation towards their needs so as to maximize their satisfaction is obviously fundamental to gain their loyalty and attract new clients. Lastly, the relationship with civil society is of crucial importance to be able to obtain job orders, reasonable taxation and structural facilities.

The long-term orientation of entrepreneurial choices is a fundamental criterion for guaranteeing a firm's social responsibility. Yet it is not *per se* sufficient. Indeed, there is no objective criterion for determining a clear-cut threshold between short and long period neither a sound criterion to establish how long the "long term" choice horizon should be. The precise choice of the time horizon for decisions has different effects on different stakeholders. This assertion holds even if we restrict our attention only to shareholders since they are motivated by objectives set in different time horizons. The same shareholders who participate in a controlling syndicate do not always have long-term objectives. This also applies to other stakeholders. The employees may exploit their training received or position reached in the firm so as to find a better – or better-paid – position in another company. The customer who entertains an impersonal relationship with the usual supplier does not hesitate to change supplier once she finds an albeit marginal improvement in price/quality ratio. The local community may yield to the temptation of squeezing money out of a firm by applying a heavy tax burden without bothering to create the necessary infrastructures and facilities. Thus the orientation of corporate choices towards value creation for all stakeholders is no guarantee of sufficient long-term attention. It is thus inevitable that there will be negotiations between the company's DMs and stakeholders to agree on an appropriate *reference time horizon,* that is the longest time horizon within which corporate strategic choices are to be made. Obviously, this time horizon must then be segmented into shorter horizons within which the decisions have to take account of unexpected contingencies within the constraints of the strategic aims set for the reference horizon. There are company decisions, for example as regards cash management, which must also be taken for very short periods. What is important is that the decisions taken for different time horizons have to be mutually consistent like the dolls of a matrioska, all held within a larger one, which corresponds to the reference time horizon.[107]

The above remarks should have made it clear that the two qualifying elements of the definition of sustainable corporation herein proposed, that is the reference to long-term value creation and the attention for all stakeholders, are correlated but not redundant.

The deep link between the definition of sustainable development and sustainable firm as defined in this chapter may be better understood by realizing that the stakeholders play in the definition of sustainable firm about the same role that generations play in the definition of sustainable development. We may say that generations are the stakeholders of economic development while the stakeholders are the relevant sections of the overlapping generations of stakeholders concerned with the sustainability of a specific firm. We have also here a distributive conflict between different stakeholders and between current and subsequent generations of them. In both cases the criterion of sustainability is based on a principle of equity that may balance the different interests through time. Also in this case distributional equity guarantees a long-term horizon for managerial and strategic decisions and therefore the environmental and social responsibility of choices.

Having ruled out that there is, in the long term, a systematic insuperable conflict between corporate objectives and development sustainability, we may wonder whether and to what extent this conflict exists in the short term. Up to the fairly recent past, environmental and social issues were often perceived as a barrier to economic development and a threat to employment due to legal constraints and repressive measures taken by public authorities. In recent years, however, the perception of this conflict has greatly subsided for a series of reasons. First of all, there is growing *market pressure* towards greater attention to the environmental and social quality of products and production processes. This stems especially from increasing environmental and social concern on the part of consumers and users. According to recent surveys, at least 75% of consumers prefer to avoid, at least on some occasions, the purchase of goods and services from firms deemed to have little respect for the environment and direct thus their choices towards the most responsible firms. To these stimuli are added those which derive from environmental legislation which in the last three decades of the 20th century became increasingly rigorous so as to provide incentives for respecting the environment and disincentives for wasting resources and pollution. In recent years, this trend has fallen back though, as we hope, only temporarily (see Chapters 1, 3 and 4). It is to be presumed – as well as desired – that with the relaxing of economic and geopolitical tensions connected to the world economic crisis at the beginning of the Millennium and to the terrorist attack of 11 September 2001, issues related to the sustainability of development will resurface in public debate and policy with all their importance and urgency. The recent alarming reports on climate change (Stern, 2006, and

IPCC, 2007) are currently refocusing the attention of public opinion on sustainability issues.

In the last 30 years a growing number of companies have actively undertaken to revise the traditional concept of efficiency, transforming it into the more comprehensive criterion of *eco-efficiency* that includes external environmental costs. This concept should be further generalized in order to consider also external social costs. Contrary to a commonly-held opinion, the traditional criterion of efficiency pursued by companies is *per se* fully compatible with development sustainability. Producing efficiently means producing goods and services at minimum costs, which entails the minimum use of human and natural resources, as well as minimum pollution given that the latter – other conditions being equal – is proportional to resources consumed as productive input. The traditional criterion of economic efficiency, however, is insufficient as not all the environmental or social costs and benefits are recorded by the market (inasmuch as they correspond to negative or positive externalities). Hence the need to draw up a criterion of "sustainable" efficiency that fully allows for implicit environmental and social costs, even before they emerge in consequence of progressive consumer awareness as well as environmental and social policy measures.[108]

Finally, the concern for environmental and social values is increasingly perceived by firms as an *investment opportunity* rather than a simple implicit cost or constraint. Such opportunities partly concern *defensive* investment, as an instrument to defend pre-existing penetration in the market. For example, investments that allow recognized environmental certification (ISO 14000 or EMAS) or ethical certification (SA 8000) are increasingly becoming a *sine qua non* for firms seeking to continue exporting to countries with stricter environmental and social laws, such as northern European countries (including Germany). Moreover, increasing importance is being attached to opportunities for *pro-active* investment in order to design and commercialize new products on new markets. Many firms are becoming convinced that being at the forefront in the CSR field may give them a decisive competitive edge in business operations.

In light of such considerations, the conflict between social and environmental objectives on one side and traditional corporate objectives on the other side boils down to an aspect of the ubiquitous conflict involved in any investment strategy, given that the costs of an investment in physical capital and new technology must be borne immediately while benefits are distributed in various future accounting years. What impedes sustainability-orientated investment is thus chiefly the short-sightedness of economic agents which derives from a speculative rather than entrepreneurial mentality, from a lack of confidence in the future which depresses expectations, or from the lack of imagination concerning future scenarios and opportunities. It is a serious problem which affects the global market in all its aspects, not only in reference to development sustainability, with the difference that in the latter case uncertainty over future investment returns is reduced by the reasonable expectation that, despite ups and downs, the trend towards more rigorous environmental, social and health legislation is bound to continue.

2 The CSR initiatives and stakeholder theory

The rising wave of CSR initiatives and the lively debate on their meaning and scope started in the 1970s, gathered momentum in the 1980s and 1990s and became a very hot topic in the recent years after the appalling financial scandals that inaugurated the new millennium. This is strictly related to the progressive extension and deepening of global market relations since WWII and the new modalities of their (de)regulation since the late 1970s. The deep crisis of the 1970s was interpreted by most contemporaneous observers as the consequence of misguided political interferences on the functioning of markets nurtured by tensions in the industrial relations, by the disruptive consequences of two oil shocks and the systematic failures of a cumbersome welfare state. This interpretation greatly increased the widespread conviction that the remedies to the crisis could be found only by giving more power to markets and corporations through a systematic deregulation of markets and privatization of public goods.

The rekindled faith in the virtues of the market brought about important changes also in corporate behavior and theory. In particular, the objective function of the firm was restated in more reductive terms than it was usual before. The only social responsibility of the firm, it was claimed with unprecedented emphasis, is that of maximizing profits. According to the traditional economic theory of competitive markets, maximization of profits is the only relevant condition for optimizing the social welfare. Any other preoccupation on the part of the firm's DMs would be self-defeating and would just bring about suboptimal results, also from the point of view of social welfare. Milton Friedman was particularly influential in propagating this doctrine not only in his contributions to the learned literature but also in articles written for a larger audience.[109]

According to the SVT the shareholders are the only stakeholder whose interests should be taken into account in the firm's objective function. In this view, the other stakeholders could be taken into account only for instrumental reasons: the clients to the extent that customers satisfaction drives their demand, the employees to ensure smooth industrial relations, the suppliers to guarantee the quality and timeliness of their supply, the local communities to obtain the necessary infrastructures and avoid excessive taxation, and so on. The main justification of this theory is that the shareholders hold the residual rights on the surplus produced by the firm and therefore have a concrete interest in taking the strategic and managerial decisions that assure the persistent production of a satisfactory surplus that guarantees the survival and good financial health of the firm. In this view managers and directors are seen as mere agents of the shareholders. The principal-agent theory applied to interpret their relations restricts the area of potential conflict of interest to the opportunism of the agents who pursue their own aims in a situation of limited information. In order to realign the interests of the agents (managers and directors) with that of the principal (shareholders) it is sufficient in this view to introduce specific economic incentives aimed to the maximization of shareholders value. A case in point is the distribution of stock options to the top managers, and sometimes directors, in order to induce a conduct committed to increase the shareholder value as much as possible.

These arguments raise two sorts of objections. A shareholder may have an interest in value creation in the short period having in mind the sale of revalued shares. Nothing guarantees that within the shareholders always prevails the point of view of those who are more concerned with the long-term performance of the firm. In any case the shareholders should not be seen as a homogeneous subject since they are often divided by a fundamental conflict of interest between those who have a short-term time horizon and those who have a longer-time horizon. The second objection is that the legitimization of shareholders on the grounds of their residual rights highlights the existence of a basic conflict of interest between shareholders and other stakeholders. The shareholders may easily approve strategic and managerial decisions that increase the surplus by damaging other stakeholders: paying low wages or salaries, restricting the rights of workers, holding unfair contractual relations with suppliers, altering the quality of products jeopardizing the health of clients, producing negative externalities in the areas of their operation, and so on. The increasing prestige of the SVT, often entertained in simplistic versions, increased the conflict of interest between shareholders and other stakeholders shifting the balance of power in favor of shareholders. In this light the introduction of CSR initiatives may be seen as a physiological reaction meant to safeguard the interests and values of all the stakeholders.

The previous dominating view was much less monist and extreme, although perhaps more ambiguous. The managers were seen not as simple agents of the property, i.e. in a corporation the shareholders, but as professionals having fiduciary duties in regard to all the stakeholders (Sacconi, 2005). The managers associations defended with success this point of view and the discretionary powers that descend from it until the early 1980s when the SVT succeeded to realign the economic, judicial, social and ethical points of view around the mono-stakeholder approach. This new generalized perspective immediately translated in a different management philosophy. The first and foremost victim was the only stakeholder different from shareholders that had managed to gather a real power in the crucial decisions of the firm: the employees. In particular, the power of trade unions started to be energetically curbed with a novel determination that was absent in the different climate of the period of Bretton Woods. Under the flag of flexibility, by developing processes such as overtime, outsourcing, delocalization, the influence of employees on the strategic and managerial decisions of the firm rapidly declined. It is in this new situation of increasing neglect of the rights and needs of stakeholders that a few scanty CSR initiatives started to be adopted. In a second time they were fairly diffused and coordinated within a CSR philosophy. The rapid diffusion of the CSR initiatives was nurtured by different, partially inconsistent, motivations.

First, the exclusive emphasis on shareholder value provoked the reaction of people and groups with religious motivations who emphasized the ethical dimension of the economic activity. In particular they promoted successful initiatives of so-called ethical finance (see section 6). At the same time people and groups of liberal inspiration, persistently aware of the limits of markets self-regulation argued that the SVD applied in real markets encouraged the social irresponsibility of firms and started to introduce countermeasures (see section 4). The introduction and diffusion of CSR initiatives, however, could be seen as the fruit of market, i.e. spontaneous and decentralized, self-regulation. Interpreted in this way the CSR initiatives were seen with favor also by the rising new liberal stream: the substitution of market self-regulation for judicial, and policy regulation was considered as a progressive evolution, or at least an unavoidable collateral effect of deregulation. Summing up, the growth of CSR initiatives in the last three decades was pushed by cultural and policy streams of different inspiration having in mind different purposes and limitations. This observation contributes to explain why the debate on the meaning and perspectives of the CSR initiatives has been so far particularly ambiguous and confused. In order to put some order in the issues raised by the CSR initiatives we need a theoretical anchor. Most supporters looked for foundations in the so-called "stakeholders theory" (ST), while most critiques focused on its shortcomings.

The emergence of ST that accompanies that of the CSR initiatives provides a multi-stakeholder prospective that may be seen as a reaction to the rigidly monist SVT. Though it is possible, as usual, to find pre-decessors, what is now called ST has been introduced by Freeman in the early 1980s (Freeman, 1984). The basic idea is that shareholders are not the only subject that has a legitimate stake in the performance of the firm and that all the stakeholders should be taken into account in its managerial and strategic decisions. The vast and growing literature stimulated by Freeman's seminal contributions is still characterized by many areas of disagreement. The definition of stakeholder itself is still quite controversial. It is generally claimed that it includes all the people who have a relevant and legitimate interest in the activity of the firm. In particular it includes all the individuals, or groups of indi-viduals, that made a specific investment in the firm. This includes share-holders who invested in total capital of the firm, creditors who invested in its financial capital, employees who invested in their human capital, and clients who invested in trust. It is less clear whether it should include the local communities where the firm operates. Also in this case, however, it is possible to argue that the local communities invested in infrastructures and trust. The subjects listed above may be defined as the stakeholders in strict sense. In what follows we intend by stake-holders only those in strict sense that made a specific investment in the firm.

The second point of disagreement is whether the interests and values of stakeholders different from shareholders should enter in the deci-sion process of the firm as mere constraints or as arguments of the objective function. The role of CSR as constraints is not necessarily denied by the SVT, at least in its more general and sound version, since the proprietors of the firm should take full responsibility of its choices and behavior. The CSR perspective has the dignity of an authentic alternative theory of corporate governance only if it faces the problems raised by the inclusion of the interests and values of the stakeholders in the objective function of the firms, a move that is harshly opposed by the SVT in all its versions.

The third crucial point of disagreement is why the firm should take account of the interests and values of all the stakeholders. There are two basic responses. First we have to acknowledge an ethical reason since all the stakeholders contributed to the performance of the firm; second there is an instrumental reason since a systematic attention for the interests and values of the stakeholders, generally improves the performance of the firm. None of these explanations taken alone is sufficient to justify CSR self-regulation on the part of the firm. A purely instrumental point of view would introduce interests and values of the stakeholders only as a constraint and not in the objective function and would subordinate CSR initiatives to the tenets of SVT. The "enlightened" version of the SVT is ready to agree that serious attention should be given to the stakeholders in order to attain the maximization of the shareholder value in the long period (Jensen, 2001). On the other hand a purely ethical approach to the CSR initiatives would risk to remain rather sterile. A simple exhortation to a more ethical behavior has never been particularly effective and often happened to be counterproductive. In our opinion the ST is interesting to the extent that it succeeds to coordinate ethical and instrumental considerations. The CSR initiatives may have a real impact in the business world to the extent that they succeed, through an apt system of incentives and disincentives, to reduce the gap between the required standard of ethical behavior and self-interested behavior. In what follows we intend to coordinate ethical and instrumental considerations from the viewpoint of firm sustainability, and of CSR initiatives themselves.

Having discussed a few preliminary issues, we have now to survey very synthetically the main uses of this theory (Donaldson and Preston, 1995; Sacconi, 2005). We should mention first its *descriptive* use. The ST suggests and supports a definition of firm as a network of relations between stakeholders that are in part cooperative, mainly in the productive process, and in part conflicting, mainly in the distribution of the surplus and of decision power. This point of view is more comprehensive than the prevailing view that interprets strategic and managerial decisions as a mere implementation of an agency relation in favor of a unique stakeholder, i.e. the shareholders. The second use is *instrumental*, as ST helps individuating the stakeholders' interests to be taken into account in order to improve the performance of the firm. The third use is *prescriptive*, since the analysis of the interests of the stakeholders and of their impact on the performance of the firm leads to prescriptions concerning stakeholder management in an instrumental perspective.

As we have argued before, we cannot neglect the ethical implications of ST. We have thus to consider it also from the normative point of view. As soon as we accept the idea that stakeholders are not only an instrument for a better performance of the firm but ends in themselves of its activity, an ineludible problem emerges. Since the interests of the stakeholders are, at least in part, mutually conflicting, the firm's DMs should promote a dialogue between the stakeholders in order to find a sound criterion to balance them. This is the great challenge of ST. It is often maintained by both supporters and critics that this problem cannot find an exact analytical solution. It is possible to demonstrate, however, that under reasonable assumptions, the strategic conflict between stakeholders, restated as an evolutionary game, under suitable conditions has in principle an exact analytical solution (Sacconi, 2004). In any case, under fully realistic conditions, a systematic and well organized dialogue may produce a deeper awareness of the interests and values involved in strategic and managerial decisions of the firm leading to a reasonable compromise capable to orientate its activity.

Finally, in the light of the preceding considerations, the ST provides a model of corporate governance alternative to the prevailing one based on the SVT. In the latter the firm's DMs are seen as agents of the shareholders having fiduciary duties exclusively in their regard. The ST suggests a different model of CG in which the firm's DMs have fiduciary duties in regard to all the stakeholders. They have to find an equilibrium between interests and values that are likely to be heterogeneous, by promoting a constructive dialogue with and between them. The discretionary power of firm's DMs is therefore limited by the active participation of stakeholders. The more the latter are active and proactive, the less is their effective discretionary power.

The hot debate that has developed on the virtues and limits of ST does not question its contributions from the descriptive and instrumental points of view, but its prescriptive and normative roles. ST can play a role as autonomous theory, alternative to the mainstream approach, only by coordinating its instrumental role with its normative role. While the theory of sustainable firm that we intend to sketch in this chapter may provide microeconomic foundations to the macroeconomic theory of sustainable development, the latter provides a benchmark and solid foundations to the ST and CSR.

The point of view of sustainability is immediately appealing. With the only exception of speculators, the interest of stakeholders and society at large in the activity of a firm is its long-run survival, corporate growth and its capability of obtaining satisfactory average returns. The concept of macroeconomic sustainability is founded on ethical values concerning distributive justice, the value of life and biodiversity. The same values provide the necessary ethical foundation to the sustainability of firms. The point of view of sustainability does not play down the importance of the economic performance of the firm that has to be pursued under the constraint of its long-term durability. In other words, the point of view of sustainability shifts the focus on the long-term performance of the firm and its consequences for the stakeholders and society at large. A firm that aims to be sustainable includes the interests and values of all the stakeholders in the objective function within a long-term time horizon. In order to achieve the most satisfactory sustainable performance, the firm's DMs have strong incentives to take CSR initiatives in order to strengthen a constructive dialogue with the stakeholders.

3   CSR and business ethics

In recent years the issues concerning CSR have attracted growing attention. This is partly due to a progressive awareness of the importance of ethical values in economic and financial relations. For example, increasing awareness of the importance of the environment has driven a growing number of managers, directors and stakeholders to examine the implications of corporate decisions for the environmental sustainability of development. The growing attention to ethical standards, however, may also be interpreted as a reaction to their perceived deterioration in many areas of the business world. For example, the awareness of the crucial role of CSR increased also in consequence of the recent financial scandals: from Enron to Worldcom, from Tyco to Global Crossing, from Vivendi to Asea Brown Boveri Ltd (ABB) and Ahold, from Cirio to Parmalat, and so on. These two explanations are not contradictory. Directors and managers who are more concerned with their own ethical rigor have a short-term comparative disadvantage with respect to those who have fewer scruples, as they are likely to obtain worse results in the short period. They are thus driven by this unfair handicap to defend their convictions and take increasingly effective initiatives to support them. In the case of stakeholders, it is evident that their progressive awareness of the importance of CSR is also reinforced as a reaction to the unprecedented series of financial scandals. A further source of interest in CSR lies in the evident incapacity of the legal system to identify and sanction misbehavior rapidly and efficiently. Many have thus felt that CSR self-regulation may constitute a way out from these problems (see in particular Sen, 1987 and 1991).

To understand issues which are extremely elusive and intricate it is worth taking a step backwards. The initiatives to consolidate CSR aim to promote the so-called business ethics, that is respect for ethics in the economic field. The study of business ethics is a particularly problematic sub-field of ethics (Sacconi, 1991). Beyond general principles that it shares with other sub-fields, it has some peculiarities that create unsolved dilemmas both in theory and practice. In fact economic activity is based on a myriad of market transactions that occur when an equilibrium point is found between the conflicting interests that typically set agents against one another. For example the seller is keen to increase the sale price to the maximum while the purchaser is interested in minimizing it, and so on.

From the legal angle, each transaction between economic agents may be interpreted as the implementation of a contract between them, whether explicit or implicit. There is thus the temptation to consider each transaction as justifiable, in both ethical and juridical terms, since there would seem to be nothing wrong with a contract freely concluded between the parties, in the absence of violence or fraud or other violations of the general principles of ethics or law. However, things are much more complex than they seem at first sight. This is due to the existence of asymmetries between contracting parties which distort the equilibrium point between them to the advantage of only one (Bebchuck, 1989; Posner, 2001). A typical case is that of *insider trading* which depends on information asymmetries between someone who has exploitable private information, and other economic agents. Having more information cannot certainly be censured *per se* from the ethical or legal standpoint. What is improper is to abuse of this advantage for one's own personal gain and hence to the detriment of other persons. This is a crime, however, which is difficult both to ascertain and to sanction. The immense and disparate family of crimes called euphemistically "conflict of interests" is yet more difficult to define and ascertain. As we have seen, conflict of interests is quite common on the market. Behavior called as such, however, is improper only when there is clear abuse of a situation of advantage. The vast set of cases in point that go under the name of monopolistic and oligopolistic practices is a major example of abuse of market power asymmetries.

It is widely held that in recent years, not least during the boom in the late 1990s, business ethics deteriorated considerably. It is difficult to ascertain whether there has been actually a downward trend in the ethical standards on financial markets, even though there is evidence that makes plausible this assertion. We refer in particular to the growing weight of short-sighted, speculative decision strategies whose effects have been often multiplied by herd behavior on globalized markets, to the spread of forms of remuneration and incentives linked to short-term results, the progressive extension of conflicts of interest between listed companies, accountancy firms, analysts, mass media and institutions (Budd and Wooden, 2002; De Nova, 2002). This opinion is shared by some of the foremost experts in economic and corporate governance law (for example, Rossi, 2003). This appears to be confirmed by the wave of unprecedented scandals which has hit stock markets since 2001, that is, as soon as the speculative bubble of Wall Street and other stock markets began to deflate. The boom had concealed a series of flaws which were destined to surface with the crisis.[110]

The growing discomfort due to this "epidemic" did not fail to produce antibodies in the social organism. A growing number of companies launched a myriad of initiatives to reinforce and highlight their socially responsible behavior. At the same time there was a mushrooming of initiatives on CSR by international governmental organizations (UNEP, UNDP [United Nations Development Programme], UNESCO [United Nations Educational, Scientific and Cultural Organization], FAO [Food and Agriculture Organization of the United Nations], the WB itself, etc.), NGOs (consumer associations, such as Nader's *Public Citizen*, environmental associations like *Greenpeace*, humanitarian associations such as *Medicins Sans Frontières*, civil rights groups like *Amnesty International*, voluntary associations, and so on). In turn, national public authorities took various initiatives to support CSR self-regulation, but overall the legislation to sanction ethically improper behavior in the business world may be said to have weakened in recent years. In general, public authorities have favored deregulation, or at any rate decriminalization, of behavior conflicting with business ethics in favor of voluntary self-regulatory instruments judged to be more consonant with market mechanisms.

In addition, legislative measures which have followed the recent financial scandals in the US and elsewhere have been very timid. For example, the final version of the *Commodity Futures Modernization Act* approved in the US in 2000 refused to introduce controls on OTC derivatives advocated by many experts. Also the *Sarbanes-Oxley Act*, passed in 2002 in the US so as to make it more difficult for financial scandals to occur appears destined to fall short of expectations (Rossi, 2003, p.66), as the measures taken seem to be insufficient. For example, as regards the conflict of interests between drawing up financial statements and consultancy for the same firms, it only goes as far as to

require that the accountancy firm declares the consultancy activities
it has performed at the firms whose financial statements they have
certified. In most countries, nothing serious has been done to react
to the recent wave of economic and financial scandals. Sometimes
the deregulation of financial markets further progressed also in recent
years. In Italy, for example, under Law Decree 61/2002 the crime of
false accounting has been decriminalized.

Recent experience shows that this weakening of legislation has favored
the spread of low standards of business ethics, while self-regulatory
initiatives have so far managed only to diminish their virulence
and slow down their spread. We shall attempt to evaluate in the subsequent sections to what extent the CSR business initiatives have been
effective and have managed to halt the epidemic.

4 Initiatives to consolidate corporate sustainability

There is no magic formula to ensure corporate sustainability. In general
we may only say that strategic decisions must be taken within a long-
term approach, bearing in mind the interests of all stakeholders. Yet
there is a series of initiatives which may contribute to consolidate
ceteris paribus corporate sustainability.

The essential logic of CSR initiatives may be represented as a feedback between the system of CSR initiatives taken by the firm and the
active reaction of stakeholders (see Figure 7.1). The system of CSR
initiatives starts in logical terms from the approval of an ethical code
that sets the basic ethical principles to be respected by whoever takes
decisions and acts in name of the firm. In order to translate these principles in managerial rules of conduct, the firm has to adopt a management system that takes into account the environmental and social
values sanctioned by the ethical code. This move by itself corroborates
the long-run sustainability of the firm, particularly if it is coupled with
a systematic program of education. The state of the art and the CSR initiatives taken to upgrade it should then be reported to the stakeholders
and public at large in periodic statements such as the environmental or
sustainability report, the social balance sheet, and so on. The CSR standards reached by the products, services as well as by their productive
and distributive processes may be certified.[111] The reports and
certification documents generate an additional flow of information
at the disposal of stakeholders and public at large that integrates
and complements the information required by law in balance sheets
and budgets. Its role is the more important the more stakeholders react

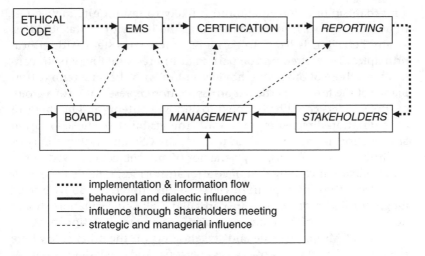

Figure 7.1 CSR initiatives and stakeholders feedback

to it in a continuous and constructive way in order to influence the strategic and managerial decisions of firms. A particularly important reaction is that of socially responsible customers who shift their demand towards the most socially responsible companies. Stakeholders may also react confronting the firm on sensitive environmental or social issues either directly or through representative organizations, such as trade unions, consumers associations, and so on. The confrontation may use more or less aggressive means, from the dialogue with directors and top management to the organized boycotting of products, strikes, denunciation to mass media or courts. Another instrument increasingly used is the exposure of a socially irresponsible behavior in the assembly of shareholders, taking into account that the ownership of one share is generally sufficient to participate in it. The impact of these reactions may be considerable and may induce a deeper ethical awareness on the part of managers and directors and convince them, even if reluctant, to take action in order to strengthen the CSR standards of the firm. In addition, a proactive attitude by stakeholders could induce the firm to improve the quantity and quality of information disclosed and to develop new CSR initiatives.

The representation of the inner logic of CSR self-regulation as a feedback between the firm and its stakeholders clarifies that the success of these initiatives strictly depends on the active and proactive behavior of stakeholders. In its absence, the CSR self-regulation remains without a mechanism of enforcement and is likely to result quite ineffective. In addition we wish to emphasize that the behavior of stakeholders, as any behavior, is liable to be more or less consistent with ethical principles. They often pursue particular interests that may be in conflict with those of other stakeholders and/or with the long-term performance of the firm. In particular an association representative of a group of stakeholders could be tempted to choose contents and methods of confrontation directed more towards the visibility of the association and its short-term success than towards the CSR and sustainability of the firm. In other words, any behavior of any subject involved in the CSR feedback, including that of control authorities, is liable to be evaluated from the ethical point of view. No one should feel above ethical judgment and reprobation. In particular CSR self-regulation should not be seen, as often happens, as an asymmetric relation between the firm's DMs on one side and stakeholders on the other side where the former play the role of accused persons, and the latter the role of judges. The attainment of high ethical standards depends on all the subjects involved and the behavior of each of them may be more or less consistent with crucial ethical principles.

We should conceive of the CSR feedback as a persistent and constructive dialogue between all the subjects involved that progressively increases their awareness of the ethical implications of their behavior and of the options open to improve their ethical standards. This dialogue may be seen as a process of learning that progressively improves the ethical awareness in order to improve the social responsibility of the firm and all its stakeholders and to contribute to the sustainability of its performance.

The economic benefits arising from a commitment to sustainability on the one hand create incentives for reinforcing their sustainability but at the same time, for the same reason, also raise a serious problem of opportunism. Also firms which are not convinced of the importance of improving the social responsibility of their decisions may be tempted to do their utmost to appear so. For example, some of the companies involved in recent scandals, such as *Enron* itself, had succeeded in becoming accredited as companies that were particularly concerned with their social responsibility. Many others are nonetheless camouflaged, "following the vogue" of social responsibility. This has nurtured a widespread skepticism about the real scope and efficacy of these new trends. Some critics have even expressed a negative opinion, believing that CSR self-regulation, whether voluntary or required by law, as it is not subject to legal sanction, may distract attention from the absolute need for appropriate civil and penal legislation backed by sanctions (see section 5).

Such skepticism is only in part justified. In fact there are effective disincentives for those who go for appearance rather than facts. Ethical codes and periodic *reporting* require commitments and make statements whose truthfulness can be verified. Just because some *reports* may be ambiguous or insincere does not mean that reporting in general is pointless. This would be tantamount to deducing from the existence of imprecise or inaccurate economic and financial balance sheets that the latter are pointless, if not misleading, and hence can be, or must be, abandoned. In a certain sense sustainability reporting is nothing but an extension of the balance sheets, with the advantage that, while the ability to interpret balance sheets requires specific skills, checking the credibility of sustainability reporting is relatively less difficult for stakeholders. We may thus conclude that the rules established by self-regulatory and corporate governance codes are not devoid of potential enforcement mechanisms, albeit not of a legal nature, in that they are susceptible to economic and social sanctions on the part of stakeholders. Their application is generally favored by a system of economic incentives and disincentives that depend on stakeholder behavior. The more effectively and continuously stakeholders control the actual standards of CSR, the greater the efficiency of the CSR initiatives. To achieve this goal, sensitization of the firm's DMs, stakeholders and public at large is required: this may be promoted by the education system and by NGO initiatives devoted to such issues.

We should point out, however, the opposite danger that has emerged in many industrialized countries. Stakeholder organizations at times intervene in sensational fashion to attract the attention of a public which is insufficiently aware of the importance of these issues. Such interventions, however, risk being counterproductive in the long term as they may discourage transparency and dialogue on the part of companies, triggering a vicious circle that may further weaken CSR standards. What is therefore required is active stakeholder participation that sets constructive and long-term objectives with a view to starting a virtuous circle between reporting and the initiatives taken by sustainable companies in the field of CSR. Yet the recent globalization process has also jeopardized CSR and hence its sustainability in the long term. Indeed, delocalization of production has made participatory stakeholder control increasingly difficult.[112] Moreover, it has led to progressive shortening of the decision time horizons on international markets which are increasingly linked by the Internet and by deregulation, in the presence of ever more marked herd behavior. This has led many firms to aim towards excellence in short-term results to the detriment of their long-term sustainability (see *retro* Chapter 6).

5 Critiques of self-regulation designed to reinforce CSR

As we have hinted at before, not everyone is convinced that self-regulation initiatives to reinforce CSR are effective. Some observers are convinced that the recent wave of CSR initiatives is a fashion devoid of significant effects, if not even counterproductive for the objectives proposed. In this section we discuss the main general critiques advanced against the CSR approach and the ST that underlies it. We may classify these critiques in two groups, the first one of scholars and experts who have a deep trust in the power of markets self-regulation and interpret CSR initiatives as distorting interferences with the market forces, while the second group of critiques is much more aware of the limits to markets and interprets the CSR initiatives as unduly substitutive of regulation by law.

Within the first group, the most detailed and well-argued critique is probably that recently made, and extensively cited, by M.C. Jensen (2001), emeritus professor of Business Administration at Harvard Business School with a number of business appointments that guarantee first-hand knowledge of the subject in question. According to Jensen, self-regulatory initiatives and standards to strengthen CSR are devoid of sound theoretical foundations and end up becoming counterproductive insofar as they are based on an erroneous theory, the so-called "stakeholder theory". Indeed, in his opinion CSR initiatives would make sense only if it was held that the company should include in the objective function value creation for all stakeholders and not only for shareholders.[113] Jensen raises two objections in sequential order.

First there is a preliminary objection of a "logical" nature. In Jensen's opinion an efficient objective function must have only one argument to allow a thorough assessment of the performance of the company and its directors. Otherwise, corporate behavior could not be appraised on the basis of an unambiguous criterion, and this would leave excessive discretional power to the company's DMs who would thus be in a position of eluding effective control on the part of stakeholders, including the shareholders themselves. This might lead to opportunist behavior by managers and directors to the detriment of stakeholders and corporate interests. The trouble is that, according to Jensen, ST suggests a corporate objective function based on a plurality of goals which correspond to the differentiated and often conflicting interests of the various stakeholders, and is thus unable to propose an efficient objective function. In his opinion this problem is made evident, and at the same time insuperable, by the reluctance of supporters of the theory to indicate the exact nature of the trade-offs between various stakeholder interests. Stakeholder theory is thus unable to propose a credible alternative to the traditional objective function (maximizing total company value) which is backed by two centuries of economic and financial research. Moreover, adds Jensen, there would be no need for an alternative criterion as economic and financial theory have shown that in a competitive market "in the absence of externalities and monopoly" (Jensen, 2001, p.11) maximization of total company value is a necessary and sufficient condition to obtain maximum social welfare which also includes that of the company stakeholders. Thus, if on the one hand public authorities should intervene to eliminate monopolistic practices and internalize externalities, the company for its part should only be concerned with maximizing its total value to obtain much more securely and efficiently the same results which *stakeholder* theory proposes so airily and inefficiently.

Stakeholder theory is given by Jensen a role as heuristic support for long-term profit maximization. He recognizes that maximization of company value, if restricted to the short term, could damage some stakeholders and jeopardize company value in the longer term. He thus points out that the company's objective function has to maximize total value in the long term since "short-term profit maximization is a sure way to destroy value" (Jensen, 2001, p.16). And it is here that, according to Jensen, stakeholder theory may provide a useful contribution, especially as to how to create good relations with customers, employees, financers, suppliers, regulators and the community, since he recognizes that it is not possible to maximize an organization's market value in the long term if the interests of one or more major stakeholder are ignored or harmed (*ibidem*).

This convergence between the two opposing viewpoints of traditional theory and stakeholder theory is defined by Jensen as the "enlightened" version of SVT. This view, without abandoning the traditional objective function, would enable one to take into account many of the arguments – those that are in his opinion acceptable – that motivate stakeholder theory.

Finally, Jensen criticizes management methods of evaluating business performance of individual company employees or divisions based on a "balanced scorecard" due to their inability, as their parent stakeholder theory, to express a single transparent measurement able to ensure actual controllability of corporate behavior. Jensen corroborates his argument with examples taken from the evaluation of sporting performance: to classify competitors unequivocally and identify the winner, a single measurement would be in his opinion necessary (time, height of the bar, length of jump or throw, and so on). On the other hand, also management techniques based on the definition of a "balanced scorecard", like the stakeholder theory that inspires them, are appraised as a useful heuristic support to understand the specific sources of value creation whose measurement and valuation are entrusted to straightforward indexes of value creation such as the well-known EVA (economic value added).

To summarize, even if Jensen does not explicitly discuss the practices and standards of CSR, his position clearly undermines its prescriptive role, though not its supportive role to a more constructive dialogue between company and stakeholder. Nevertheless, in our opinion Jensen's criticisms are not convincing. First of all, the preliminary argument of a "logical" nature which underpins his critique of stakeholder theory and management techniques based on the *balanced scorecard* is definitely groundless. The logical problem of reducing various arguments of a valuation function to a single unit of measurement is a problem which has long been tackled and solved. An obvious example is the index number theory which allows us to measure sets of heterogeneous magnitudes with the same unit. This requires the specification of different weights for each magnitude and the definition of trade-offs between the various arguments of the measurement function, but their determination is not necessarily arbitrary. There are tested techniques to determine weights and trade-offs based on dialogue with stakeholders, which have been examined and applied in multi-criterion analysis and decision procedures based thereon (Munda, 2004). There are also unique benchmarks that may be obtained in each single situation by using game-theoretic models that study strategic interaction between different stakeholders (Sacconi, 2003). The reference itself to the appraisal of sporting merits confirms that Jensen's critique is not well-grounded. Multiple disciplines, such as the decathlon, pentathlon and triathlon, adopt composite measurements that take account of results obtained in the various events without encountering logical difficulties in classifying competitors according to merit. Clearly, procedures to make results homogeneous in a single measurement require the consensus of stakeholders, in this example the public, athletes and their federations, but this does not need to be an insurmountable problem.

In any case, the "logical" problem underlined by Jensen is not wholly avoided by assuming the criterion of maximization of total company value. Indeed, the measurement is destined to change according to the time horizon chosen, as is recognized by Jensen himself. One has to agree with his choice of a long-term time horizon but this does not at all solve the logical problem that he poses. Indeed, how can we univocally determine how "long" should be the long-term? To this problem there is no objective solution that avoids the need for agreement between all stakeholders based on dialogue and consensus. Besides, the previous argument shows a basic logical flaw in Jensen's position. If it is really believed that the company operates in a market with perfect competition, which also implies the completeness of markets (including future ones), the perfect foresight of economic agents and perfect time reversibility of choices, then in this case there could be no conflict between short and long term.[114] Otherwise it is believed that the former hypothesis is not realistic as future markets are not complete, time is not perfectly reversible, and the expectations of economic agents may be systematically mistaken, in which case the conflict between short and long term is ubiquitous. In this second case, however, the traditional objective function would also give ambiguous and arbitrary results until the reference time horizon and the trade-offs between the different time horizons are specified, which would raise the same problems of stakeholder involvement to reach a sound agreement on the reference time horizon and the most appropriate trade-offs among the various time horizons which has the necessary consensus of all stakeholders.

As for the conviction expressed by Jensen that the criterion of maximization of total company value maximizes at the same time also social welfare, this would only hold in a perfectly competitive market (with infinite agents who are all price-takers) in the absence not only of monopolistic practices, externalities, but also of all the further conditions that guarantee the validity of the theorems of welfare economics: the above-cited completeness of the markets (including future ones), perfect foresight or at least rationality of expectations, more generally the unlimited rationality of economic agents, the absence of transaction costs, weak uncertainty, and so on (see Chapter 2). It is precisely the wide gap between the real market and the ideal market of perfect competition (in which, by the way, companies could not exist) which makes it essential to explicitly take account of the interests of all *stakeholders* to reduce as much as possible the distortions in the allocation of resources, especially intertemporal distortions, and maximize social welfare. That this is how things stand is recognized by Jensen himself in reference to the short term. Allocative distortions generated by maximization confined to the short term cannot but stem from shortcomings in real markets. Why they should disappear in the long term remains a mystery. Trade-offs between the interests of the various stakeholders are thus not implicitly fixed in the optimal way by the criterion of maximization of company value either in the short or long term.

Jensen's criticisms of the normative importance of "stakeholder theory" are thus basically groundless even if they rightly recall attention to the requirement that corporate governance should be based on a simple, clear and transparent objective function, which focuses on the long term and gathers a basic consensus on the part of all stakeholders. Particularly in this function, as in the criteria for evaluating individual or division performance, the weights and trade-offs characterizing the interests of individual stakeholders must be made clear. Finally, the operative time horizon of strategic decisions to be agreed upon with the stakeholders should be long term. The necessary short-term maximization should then be performed by the managers of the corporation according to the guidelines provided by long-term maximization.

A different critical position has been taken by the exponents of the second group mentioned above. A good example of this point of view is the critique advanced by Guido Rossi, a well-known expert in corporate law and governance (Rossi, 2003). He argues that self-regulation to reinforce business ethic and CSR is pointless if not counterproductive. Self-imposed rules to reinforce CSR would be futile since, unlike legal regulations, they would have no sanctions or enforcement mechanisms. In his opinion, the illusory fashion of corporate self-regulation aiming at CSR is counterproductive as it provides an alibi for weakening the legal regulation of corporate business. Indeed, in recent years, in line with systematic market deregulation, laws governing the behavior of firms and markets have progressively weakened. The justification for this policy lies partly in the increasingly swift evolution of economy and finance which makes it difficult for legislation to keep pace, and also in the growing complexity of economic and financial questions which makes it ever more difficult to apply the rules and sanctions of deviant behavior. Yet this would not be enough to justify a weakening in the law if there were not the illusion, or excuse, of a better alternative, namely corporate self-regulation.

Even this critical position is not wholly convincing. Rossi is right to stigmatize the opportunistic abuses of ethical issues and social responsibility. The more one believes that it is urgent and potentially productive to address matters regarding ethics and social responsibility concerning economic and financial behavior, the more serious such abuses should be considered. Conversely, the idea that CSR self-regulation would be structurally powerless as it lacks enforcement mechanisms is groundless. As we noted before (see section 4 above), CSR self-regulation may be accompanied by a structure of incentives aimed at compliance and disincentives for non-compliance. The market may give a significant contribution in this direction depending on the sensitivity of end-users of goods and services (consumers and savers) to environmental, social and ethical quality of goods and services supplied by firms and of the production and distribution processes upstream of their commercialization. The system of incentives and disincentives which is thus created may be made more effective through CSR initiatives as long as there is no illusion that the market is able, independently and spontaneously, to start and maintain this virtuous circle between companies and stakeholders. Obviously, the more sensitive consumers are to the ethical, social and environmental quality of goods and services purchased, the more effective is the system of incentives and disincentives. This requires a process of sensitization and education of stakeholders that the market is unable to implement autonomously, but can be promoted by well-designed CSR initiatives. So Rossi is definitely right in rejecting the arguments of those who think that legal regulations should be replaced by corporate self-regulation, but he is mistaken in maintaining that the latter is condemned to lack sanctions or enforcement mechanisms. The nexus between legal regulations and corporate self-regulation should be conceived not as one of competition but as one of synergy. Indeed the process of stakeholders sensitization and education is an important condition for the effectiveness of legal regulation itself. It has long been known that the more regulations are supported by the consensus of civil society, the more effective is the enforcement of legal regulation. This may be considerably strengthened by the virtuous circle of self-regulation assisted by public interventions of citizen sensitization and education.

6   Sustainability and the financial sector

We now intend to discuss the issues related to corporate sustainability in the financial sector for its crucial role in determining the sustainability of other companies and hence of macroeconomic development itself. Indeed, the financial sustainability of companies in all sectors depends crucially on banks. As self-financing is typically insufficient to ensure a fluid rotation of circulating capital and a consistent funding of investment projects, companies often resort, to a greater or lesser extent, to bank credit. Banks are thus the only authentically "transversal" companies as they interact in a crucial way with all the others. In terms of macroeconomic development, banks determine to what extent the flow of savings is channeled towards more sustainable companies and uses.

The crucial role of banks in development sustainability has begun to be recognized only very recently. This stems from the fact that the debate on development sustainability which gained momentum after the publication of the Brundtland Report (1987) focused primarily on environmental issues (see Chapter 1). From this point of view banks do not appear particularly relevant for sustainability as they are not particularly polluting (like the chemical industry) neither they consume large amounts of energy from non-renewable sources (like heavy industry), or both (like the petrochemical industry and paper manufacturers). Yet this view neglects the crucial role of the financial sector in ensuring corporate and macroeconomic development sustainability, not only in financial but also in structural terms.

A pioneering contribution to understanding the crucial role of banks in bringing about development sustainability came from the *Finance Initiative* launched by UNEP just after the World Summit at Rio (1992). The declaration of intent in favor of development sustainability drafted by UNEP was signed by more than 150 banks from various countries, while publications and conferences promoted under the initiative progressively clarified the impact of the financial system on development sustainability. Another significant initiative was that of the World Business Council for Sustainable Development (WBCSD) which groups together some 200 international companies which are particularly sensitive to development sustainability that presented at the Johannesburg World Summit (2002) a document drafted by some important banks regarding their commitment to sustainable development.

Let us now examine in some detail the specific contribution of banks to development sustainability. As regards production processes, we can first of all identify some significant initiatives. As to the measures to reduce consumption of material inputs, it may be sufficient to focus on the case of paper whose production is heavily polluting and compromises forest sustainability. Simple interventions may help, such as to replace printers that use only one side of a sheet with those that print on both sides to halve the consumption of paper. Moreover, it is now possible to organize an office so as to completely avoid all consumption of paper (the so-called "paperless office"), as has already been successfully tested in some major corporations, such as Microsoft and Boeing, using modern electronic technologies (especially linking all employees via an *Intranet*). Much attention should be paid to recycling waste, above all paper and hardware material. Energy consumption can also be significantly reduced with appropriate lighting, heating and cooling systems. New premises, including area branches, should be built according to bio-architectural criteria, and old premises should be progressively renovated by adopting the same principles. Considerable savings on construction and transport costs may be obtained by developing Internet banking. Finally, telecommuting could also be developed: this would permit considerable savings in costs incurred in transport, building, maintenance and air conditioning.[115] Also in this case, initiatives may be appropriately encouraged by certification, whether environmental (such as ISO 14000 and EMAS) or ethical (e.g. SA 8000). Finally, the progress made, its limits and future plans may be fruitfully communicated to stakeholders by means of sustainability reports.

The measures we have reviewed so far follow the same lines as those already mentioned in section 4 for companies in general. Nevertheless, they should assume particular importance due to the "demonstration effect", given the transversal nature of banking. Although lending is not a particularly risky activity for the environment directly, it is crucial in indirect terms insofar as it provides investment finance for companies, which could be hazardous for the environment. Such risks are of huge proportions, as shown by recent episodes. Every one knows the case of the oil tanker Exxon-Valdez charged with a serious pollution episode close to the Alaskan coast and condemned to pay huge compensations over several years. In general, it is calculated that total environmental compensation for damage already caused to be paid in the near future amounts in the US alone to a sum equal to one-and-a-half times the turnover of the entire insurance sector in the USA.[116] This has led to a serious crisis in the insurance sector which has almost entirely withdrawn from the environmental sector, making the risks for individual companies even more serious. Environmental risks may compromise the solvency of the firms financed and the value of collateral assets, which are usually fixed assets whose value is extremely sensitive to pollution.

In particular, environmental risk must be taken seriously into account by banks, especially since in the US and in some northern European countries, the law has established in some cases a principle of *indirect liability* of the company funding the investment that caused environmental damage. By contrast, EU Environmental law (which goes back to the 1993 Lugano Agreement) provides for the principle of *objective liability* on the part of the polluter who must thus compensate for the damage even without proof of fraud or guilt, as long as the cause-effect nexus can be demonstrated, which again considerably increases the indirect risk of banks.

Environmental risks are particularly insidious when the companies financed are *small or medium* enterprises. In this case, knowledge of environmental issues, whose investigation requires the availability of inter-disciplinary *teams* of highly specialized staff, is often lacking, while the difficulty in detecting the polluters in an extensive network of SMEs may create a disincentive for respecting environmental regulations. Banks – like those in Italy – that operate in the framework of an industrial structure heavily dominated by SMEs find it difficult to assess environmental risks, in that case-by-case monitoring of environmental risks would be too burdensome. To overcome such problems, *scoring* models may be set up that give a presumptive score of environmental risk to an SME on the basis of certain objective characteristics (areal, sectional, organizational, and so forth). SMEs that exceed a certain threshold of presumptive risk are those that are analyzed in detail. Moreover, environmental risks must also be considered together with others in the ambit of corporate risk management.

As regards products and services, the financial system still plays a major role of intermediation between savings and investment. With regard to direct intermediation on the part of banks, application of methods for assessing environmental risks and reputation mentioned above allows savings to be channeled towards more sustainable uses.

For banks as for other companies, environmental issues pose not only the urgent need for defensive investment, but also opportunities for pro-active investment so as to open up new markets, consolidate traditional ones, gaining a competitive edge over other banks which are not so advanced on this front. First of all, there is the need to finance the huge environmental investments of industrial companies and local authorities, which will require increased skills and specialist know-how. Interesting opportunities are also emerging in the field of finance. We will confine ourselves to a few examples. Environmental finance was introduced only a few years ago and shows considerable development potential. Negotiable permits introduced in 1992 at the Chicago Board of Trade to achieve the aim of cleaning up the air, as laid down by the Clean Air Act enacted under USA law, reached their established aims in shorter time than predicted and at much lower costs than those foreseen, and were in any case more efficient than the alternative economic policy measures (taxation, administrative bans, etc.). This success is steering the signatory states of the Kyoto protocol to launch an ambitious world program of negotiable permits to control the greenhouse effect. Local markets have been established in Europe and elsewhere (see retro Chapter 4).

Moreover, 2001 saw the launch, once again at the Chicago Board of Trade, of environmental derivatives (*futures* and *options* connected to environmental events) which are beginning to achieve a certain success. Clearly, a bank could steal a march over its competitors by specializing in the negotiation of environmental securities.

There is a long history of ethical funds that typically include respect for the environment among their constraints, and "environmental funds". These ethical funds specializing in environmental securities were established several decades ago and have shown a slow but steady growth rate. In the last few years these funds have enjoyed considerable success, often with growth and performance indexes exceeding those of other funds. In the US the number of ethical funds has trebled in recent years, exceeding US$1000 billion of managed capital, reaching 13% of the total. The 34 main ethical funds in the UK manage assets of more than 67 billion euros. The weight of ethical funds is increasing rapidly in all the major industrialized countries, including France, Canada and Germany. As for *performance*, though subscribers allow for lower returns in exchange for greater ethical transparency, medium-long term results often exceeded market averages (Consolandi *et al.*, 2008). For example, Domini, the second-ranking ethical fund in the US with US$1.5 billion of net asset value, has for several years managed to outperform the general reference indexes (Dow Jones and S&P 500).

What accounts for the success of ethical funds? Initially they were chosen by savers with particular ethical sensitivity to the extent that they were prepared to forgo a possible profit margin in exchange for greater transparency and guarantee of ethical conduct. Then other savers with a low speculative propensity intervened, who were oriented towards a long-time horizon, like institutional investors (pension funds), once they saw that their long-term performance was no lower than the average.

At first sight this seems a paradox: restriction of the set of choices used by ethical filters should reduce performance. This is a preconception that has acted as a barrier to their success. Yet judging from the facts, this preconception is groundless, because, as we have noted, companies that have lasted longer, with higher average long-term profitability are those that have paid particular attention to all stakeholders in a far-sighted perspective (which implies attention to development sustainability). Such results have been recently confirmed by the good performance of ethical funds and by a comparative analysis of the so-called "ethical" indexes. These are indexes that summarize the stock market trend of company shares chosen according to ethical exclusion criteria ("negative filters") or inclusion criteria ("positive filters"). Negative filters exclude from the index the shares of companies that have undesirable features in ethical terms (e.g. because they operate in the tobacco sector, in gambling, pornography or arms, or because they employ, directly or indirectly through holdings or suppliers, child labor or those with no union rights, and so on). The selection criteria (positive filters) seek to identify firms that stand out for their social responsibility. By comparing the medium-long term trend of ethical indexes with that of general stock market indexes, we may gain an idea of the *performance* of more socially responsible companies.

The first ethical index to achieve public recognition was the *Domini 400 Social Index* which was introduced in 1990 by the American fund Domini, one of the largest and most profitable ethical funds (see section 6). This index is based on negative and positive filters and has performed systematically better than the general S&P 500 index from 1990 on. Of particular significance is the *Dow Jones Sustainability Index* (DJSI) introduced in 2001, based on positive filters. This index was calculated retrospectively from 1993. We may thus compare its performance with that of the *Dow Jones Global Index* from 1993 to today. Also in this case there is a systematic out-performance. Finally FTSE4Good, which is based essentially on negative filters and is more oriented towards European companies, has performed marginally better than that of the general FTSE since 1996.[117] The good performance of ethical funds and ethical indices makes it possible to consolidate the virtuous circle between development sustainability and corporate sustainability. The companies included in the ethical indexes are likely to have a better performance than the others. Therefore the demand of their shares should increase more than the average while the exclusion is likely to shift demand towards other shares, in particular the new entrants in the ethical index.

8
Liberalism, Perfect Competition and Real Markets

The argument we have developed in the preceding chapters was focused on the history of selected economic facts concerning the process of globalization and its effects on the sustainability of development. History of facts, however, is strictly linked to history of ideas. Our topic is not an exception. On the contrary, in this case the link is particularly tight, as the evolution of international markets proceeded in parallel with the evolution of liberalism. The latter progressively shaped the attitude towards the process of liberalization of markets, while the consequences of this ever-changing historical process modified the trend of liberal ideas. We cannot thus understand the evolution of globalization without grasping its interaction with the evolution of liberalism. As a premise to this analysis we intend to sketch in this chapter a cursory history of economic liberalism. Its evolution had a crucial impact on the process of globalization and on the sustainability of world development, as it affected the prevailing view on the role of free markets, on the liberalization of domestic and international exchanges, and on the opportunity of state interventions in the economy.

The evolution of liberal ideas is a very complex phenomenon influenced by many intellectual streams, not only economic doctrines but also political philosophy, ethics, international law, and so on, as well as by practical interests and aims. We restrict the attention on what we suggest to call "economic liberalism", i.e. the system of liberal ideas about the properties of markets and their policy consequences explicitly and directly founded on sound economic theory.[118] We wish to emphasize that what we call "economic liberalism" should not be confused with "*laissez-faire*" that we define as an ideological doctrine forbidding any sort of public interference with the spontaneous

working of free markets but lacking sound foundations on rigorous economic arguments. *Laissez-faire* assumes a procedural approach as it advocates an attitude of non-interference in economic matters on the part of
Public Authorities, irrespectively of its specific consequences. Economic
liberalism, on the contrary, is typically characterized by a consequentialist
approach as it prescribes whether the Public Authorities should intervene
or not in economic matters in each specific case on the basis of an analysis of the consequences of each possible intervention in the market. The
latter analysis requires sound foundations on state-of-the-art economic
theory.[119]

1   Classical liberalism

Economic liberalism was initiated by Adam Smith who may be considered as the first scholar who provided rigorous economic foundations
to liberal ideas concerning economic policy.[120] He aimed at providing
sound foundations to liberalism from the point of view of political and
moral philosophy. He argued in particular, as was usual in his time (for
example in Locke, Hume and the Physiocrats), that a free market is
a natural order that should not be perturbed by unjustified human
interferences. We are here exclusively concerned, however, with Smith's
suggested economic foundations that are his specific contribution that
initiated full-fledged economic liberalism.[121] The scientific nature of his
arguments in favor of free markets has been occasionally denied by inter-
preters (see, e.g., Schotter, 1985). In our opinion the "scientific" nature of
Smith's arguments may be questioned from the point of view of the
current scientific standards in economics but not from the point of view
of those of the late 18th century. Smith gave a quite sophisticated causal
account of the working of the invisible hand in the spirit of the most
advanced approach available in his time, the Newtonian method inspiring the Royal Society of which he was a distinguished member.[122]

Smith introduced the basic ideas that were going to characterize political economy and economic liberalism. First, he saw the market as a
coherent system, or "machine", expressing in the economic field the
"obvious and simple system of natural liberty" (Smith, 1776, p.651).
This is the great innovation of Adam Smith that underlies his novel
conception of political economy as an autonomous scientific discipline
based on a systematic investigation of its subject-matter. In other
words he conceives of political economy theory as providing an *ideal
machine*, we would say today a *model*, representing the *real machine*
underlying a market economy.[123]

Second, he introduced the crucial distinction between the ideal model of a market that corresponds to "perfect freedom" (in the sense conveyed today by "perfect competition") and real markets. He was skeptical on the possibility of eliminating the gap between the real markets and the ideal perfect-competition market.[124] He believed, however, that a reasonable approximation to perfect competition was sufficient to realize much of its advantages:

> The uniform, constant, and uninterrupted effort of every man to better his condition...is frequently powerful enough to maintain the natural progress of things toward improvement, in spite both of the extravagance of government, and of the greatest errors of the administration (*ibidem*, 343).

The competitive market is therefore seen as stable, provided that the exogenous disturbances are not too large, exactly as in the case of "the healthful state of the human body... [that] contains in itself some unknown principle of preservation, capable either of preventing or of correcting, in many respects, the bad effects of a very faulty regimen" (*ibidem*, xxx).

Third, he clarified that the properties of a market depend on the prevailing system of prices: the ideal market is characterized by *natural* prices while real markets are characterized by *market* prices. The system of natural prices that characterize the ideal model is seen as an equilibrium towards which market prices gravitate.[125] This equilibrium is considered as dynamically stable in the ideal model of perfect liberty because, as long as there is a gap between market prices and natural prices, self-interest will tend to reduce the gap. Self-interest is thus the centripetal force of the market system and plays the same role as gravity in the Newtonian celestial mechanics (Skinner, 1974, p.7).

In the first three of the five books of the *Wealth of Nations* Adam Smith argued in a fairly rigorous way that a perfectly competitive market allocates resources between alternative uses in the best possible way maximizing the welfare of people. This argument happened to be labeled as the argument of the "invisible hand", although Smith introduced this expression only in the 4th book of his masterpiece.[126] By using this expression he wanted to stress that the reconciliation between the private interests and the interests of society is realized by the market, notwithstanding that the individuals generally pursue their own private interest and are unaware to what extent they contribute to the social interest. This implies that, as a general rule, the state should avoid any unnecessary interference with free enterprise and the free movement in space of goods, services and factors of production. In other words, the liberal policies advocated by Smith aim to approach as far as possible this desirable state of affairs although, as we have seen before, he entertained no illusion on the concrete possibility of fully eliminating the gap between real markets and the ideal model of perfect competition.

Smith advocated the free movement of goods, services, and factors of production (labor and "stock" or capital), both within and between national boundaries. In particular he emphasized the right of individuals of fixing their residence where they wished. He considered freedom of residence a fundamental natural right.[127]

What is characteristic of Smith's approach, however, emerges with clarity also on this point. He did not limit himself to argue that any limitation to the mobility of work is a blatant violation to natural liberty, but he put forward detailed causal economic arguments to show that such a violation is a crucial obstacle to a proper functioning of the market and therefore a serious damage to individual and social welfare. The interferences arising from the Poor Law,[128] in particular, had the effect of maintaining distortional disequilibria: "the scarcity of hands in one parish, therefore, cannot always be relieved by their super-abundance in another" and this brings about "the very unequal price of labor which we frequently find in England in places at no great distance from one another" (*ibidem*, p.142). The argument of Smith shows full awareness of the causal interdependence of markets:

> whatever obstructs the free circulation of labor from one employ-ment to another, obstructs that of stock likewise; the quantity of stock which can be employed in any branch of business depending very much upon that of the labor which can be employed in it (*ibidem*, p. 138).

This example confirms that Smith established with clarity that the free mobility of all factors of production is a crucial prerequisite of free markets.[129] Classical liberalism, thus, provided scientific foundations to the whole of the exhortation *"laissez-faire, laissez-passer"* without omit-ting the second part as often happened later on, in particular in recent times. Free internal and external mobility of labor, besides capital, was considered as an essential part of the liberal policy advocated by them. This exhortation has never been used by Smith in an unqualified manner.

In Smith, in fact, as in most other classical economists, the exaltation of this "providential" role of the market was never disjoint from a lucid awareness of its shortcomings. This is the reason why the liberalism of classical economists, or "classical liberalism" as we call it here, did not deny an important economic role for the state. The invisible-hand argument implies only that the interference of the state in the economy should be considered an exception, not the rule, and that any violation of this rule should be thoroughly justified in each single case. In the 4th and 5th books of the *Wealth of Nations* Smith discussed in some detail the general cases in which the intervention of the state is justified. In particular, he argued that the state has to assure the best possible environment for the full expression of economic freedom by promoting justice, liberty and equality, as well as by introducing and preserving free competition in the markets. Economic freedom, in particular, presupposes personal and property security that must be assured by the state by providing an adequate military defense from external threats and internal defense from crime. This requires an efficient administration of justice to be kept independent of government pressure, as well as an efficient system of education based also on an active cultural policy. Smith attributes to the state, in addition, the task of designing and managing taxation not only to finance public expenditure but also to reduce inequality. He also confers on the state a certain responsibility in monetary policy to avoid fraud and inflationary pressures. Finally, the state should provide efficient infrastructures for the economic activity, caring especially for the network of transports.

In the classical school there were notable advances after Smith only in single aspects of the general argument. Ricardo developed the point of view of classical liberalism and consolidated its influence within the economists, policy-makers and the public opinion. His point of view was narrower than that of Smith but he went deeper on some points, in particular on the issues concerning international trade. In *The Principles of Political Economy and Taxation* (1817) he introduced in particular the celebrated theory of comparative costs which provided the first rigorous argument on the benefits of free trade between countries. This does not imply that his argument was fully correct. John Stuart Mill soon observed that effective exchange ratios do not depend only on the cost conditions but also on the demand functions (1948). We may say, however, that in Ricardo the standard of analytic rigor of the argument was for the first time comparable to that required today in scientific research. On the basis of this and other important contributions to economic theory, such as his theory of rent, he carried on an influential campaign in favor of free trade, advocating in particular the abolition of the *corn laws*. Though the latter were eventually abolished only in 1846, the influence of Ricardo and his pupils and followers was immense on the gradual shift, starting in the early 1820s, of the British economic policy towards a new strategy based on free-trade principles.

At the beginning of 19th century Bentham added an important ingredient to classical liberalism: measure-oriented utilitarianism. From then on the debate on utilitarianism strictly intermingled with the debate on the limits of free markets. Utilitarianism opposed the view maintained by Locke, the Physiocrats and Adam Smith himself that free markets realize a natural order created by God and that for this basic reason the State should not interfere with it. For Bentham and the utilitarians, neither the *status quo* nor any definition of natural order, could be considered as sacred, and government intervention was justified whenever the utilitarian calculus proved that such intervention could increase the happiness of society (on this point see, e.g., Schotter, 1985; Robbins, 1952). The generalized adoption of Benthamite utilitarianism by most classical economists since the early 19th century tended to put the debate on the limits of unfettered markets on a scientific perspective based, case by case, on an accurate evaluation of the costs and benefits of state intervention in single areas.

The synthesis between classical economics (in the Ricardian version) and Benthamite utilitarianism was first systematically sketched by James Mill, mentor, friend and pupil of Ricardo. *The Principles* of Ricardo in its utilitarian reading dominated the intellectual scene until the half of the century when John Stuart Mill published a new updated synthesis of the classical school worked out from a utilitarian point of view in his *Principles of Political Economy* (1848). Mill re-affirmed the general principle of classical liberalism:

> *laissez-faire*, in short, should be the general practice; every departure from it, unless required by some great good, is a certain evil (1848, p.314).

Then he put great effort in defining the cases where these departures may be considered as justified (particularly in book 5, Chapters 1 and 11 of his masterpiece). The "natural" liberty of individuals is passionately defended from any unjustified interference on the part of the state, provided that this does not jeopardize the liberty of other individuals and therefore also the security, stability and prosperity of society:

> as soon as any part of a person's conduct affects prejudicially the interests of others, society has jurisdiction over it, and the question whether the general welfare will or will not be promoted by interfering with it becomes open to discussion (Mill, 1859, p.141).

On the basis of this approach, Mill seemed to be sometimes more restrictive than Smith on the role of the State. In the matter of education, for example, he maintained that the government "must claim no monopoly" on education because "a government which can mould the opinions and sentiments of the people from their youth upwards, can do with them whatever it pleases" (*ibidem*).[130] Mill did not hesitate, however, to add new important areas to the legitimate intervention of the state. A case in point was the preservation of natural commons:

> is there not the earth itself, its forests and waters, and all other natural riches, above and below the surface? These are the inheritance of the human race, and there must be regulations for the common enjoyment of it (*ibidem*, p.148).

John Stuart Mill may thus be considered as a forerunner of the idea of sustainable development, an intuition that, unfortunately, he did not develop and was not as influential as other contributions of his.

Classical economists never liked the slogan "*laissez-faire*" as they perceived it as an unqualified prescription. It is difficult to find this expression in their work. In the late classical economists it is easy to find explicit criticisms to this simplistic slogan (see Robbins, 1962).

A major breakthrough in the analysis of the invisible hand argument, however, came only with Walras's general equilibrium model. He succeeded in representing the general system of transactions that characterizes a certain competitive economy under "pure" conditions, showing that such a system has an equilibrium that realizes the optimal allocation of resources between alternative uses. In addition, in his analysis of the "tâtonnement" he offered an argument to corroborate the plausibility of the dynamic stability of the general equilibrium depicted by the model. He did not exploit, however, the potential of his path-breaking general equilibrium model for advancing systematically economic liberalism.

This potential started to be developed by Pareto, his successor in Lausanne, who was in his youth a fervent liberal militant (see section 3 in Chapter 1).

Classical liberalism extended its influence until the first two decades of the 20th century. The *Principles of Political Economy* by Mill was still the most popular textbook of economics at the end of the 19th century in English-speaking countries, when it was gradually overtaken by the *Principles of Economics* (1891) by Marshall.

2   Updated liberalism

Though Marshall is considered as one of the main exponent of the "marginalist revolution" in economic theory, his liberalism maintained a quite strict continuity with classical liberalism.[131] Writing at the end of the 19th century, however, he recognized with unusually emotional words the negative implications of *laissez-faire* that had emerged in the preceding part of the century when:

> free competition, or rather, freedom of industry and enterprise, was set loose to run, like a huge untrained monster, its wayward course. The abuse of their new power by able but uncultured business men led to evils on every side; it unfitted mothers for their duties, it weighed down children with overwork and disease; and in many places it degraded the race (Marshall, 1891, p.9).

He cleared liberal economists from any responsibility for these deplorable implications of *laissez-faire*:

> the time at which free enterprise was showing itself in an unnaturally harsh form, was the very time in which economists were most lavish in their praises of it. This was partly because they saw clearly, what we of this generation have in great measure forgotten, the cruelty of the yoke of custom and rigid ordinance which it had displaced... Economists therefore treated free enterprise.... as a less evil than such regulation as was practicable at the time (*ibidem*, p.10).

Marshall believed that a deeper knowledge of the effective working of competitive markets and more accountable and competent public authorities made possible a fairly efficient regulation of markets to avoid their experimented failures. He was therefore attracted by the opportunity of bringing "free enterprise somewhat under control, to diminish its power of doing evil and increase its power of doing good." (p.10). This need of an updated liberalism accepted to a certain extent the existing "tendencies towards collective ownership and collective action" since they were "quite different from those of earlier times, because they are the result not of custom...but of free choice" (*ibidem*, pp.4–5).

The new approach to liberalism foreshadowed by Marshall was characterized by two main novelties. First, the boundary between the scope of unfettered markets and legitimate state intervention was discussed not in terms of limits of the state interference in the economy but of limits of unfettered markets. This new attitude reflects the change in orientation of economists and public opinion in favor of free markets and the progressive accumulation of observations on market failures. Second, he was prepared to extend the scope of state intervention in the market beyond the limits of classical liberalism, provided that the new roles attributed to the state were the fruit of free and democratic deliberation based on sound economic arguments. As we have seen, Marshall himself suggested a clear historical explanation of both novelties. While the classical economists were reacting to the negative implications of traditional mercantilist interventionism, the enlightened liberal economists at the turn of the century were reacting to the experience of the negative consequences of insufficiently regulated free markets.

Though the point of view of what we call updated liberalism was already quite clear in Marshall, its rigorous foundations emerged only within the following two generations of economists in the second and third decade of the 20th century. For the sake of simplicity we only stress the crucial role of the two best pupils of Marshall: Pigou and Keynes.[132]

Pigou developed a few seminal contributions of Marshall where he introduced the concepts of external economies and consumer welfare in order to provide sound foundations for "welfare economics" (1920). In particular, he generalized the Marshallian concept of externalities, i.e. costs or benefits not registered by unfettered markets, showing that they are ubiquitous and bring about sizeable distortions of the market allocation. He provided then new microeconomic foundations to public intervention in the economy finalized to the "internalization" of externalities. This clarified the rationale of state intervention prescribed by classical liberalism, such as defense, security, education, and extended the scope of public intervention to new sectors such as environmental economics. The new branch of economic analysis called "welfare economics" was crucial in inspiring the "welfare state" policies that became very influential after WWII, mainly in the 1960s an 1970s.

A bit later, under the influence of the Great Depression, Keynes developed a few intuitions of Marshall on business cycles and liquidity preference in a general theory of unemployment, laying the foundations of countercyclical macroeconomic policies (Keynes, 1936). He argued that the market is unable to auto-regulate itself in such a way to assure the full employment of existing resources, bringing about a huge waste of social welfare. This new limit of the market justified a further extension of the scope of public intervention into the field of macroeconomic policy in order to assure full employment. Whether the Keynesian approach is consistent with the liberal principles has always been controversial. This is a question that Keynes himself raised not only in the well-known essay "Am I a liberal?" (Keynes, 1925) but on many other occasions throughout his life. His own answer has always been substantially affirmative, but we can detect an evolution in his position. Until he conceived and started to write *The General Theory of Employment, Interest and Money* (hereafter known as GT), Keynes's position was not substantially different from that of the "classics". He insisted on the necessity of updating economic liberalism and abandoning the old-fashioned *"laissez-faire"*, but this stance was in line with the attitude of all the best economists since the 1870s (see, e.g., Robbins, 1952).

A radical change of attitude towards classical liberalism clearly emerged, and was emphasized by Keynes, only while he was writing the GT. And it was exactly for stressing the novelty of his own updated position that he introduced the new category of the "classics" that was meant to encompass all the economists belonging to the liberal tradition since Adam Smith. This broad category was meant to emphasize that in the tradition of the "classics" the market failures pointed out by liberal economists were relative to the allocation of resources. They were in this sense microeconomic failures. What Keynes wanted to point out in the GT for the first time in the history of liberalism was the possibility of a macroeconomic failure: the existence of involuntary unemployment.[133] Before the GT structural unemployment was considered the fault not of the market but of restrictions on its working induced by Trade Unions and State interferences. Keynes, on the contrary, wrote the GT to demonstrate that the dire phenomenon of structural unemployment is due to a fundamental market failure, indeed in his opinion much more important than the allocative (or microeconomic) market failures considered up to then.[134]

The introduction of this new crucial variety of market failure was not meant to reject economic liberalism: "but to indicate the nature of the environment which the free play of economic forces requires if it is to realize the full potentialities of production" (Keynes, 1936, p.379). Keynes was aware that it could be contended that "the central controls necessary to ensure full employment will...involve a large extension of the traditional functions of government" but he stressed that "there will still remain a wide field for the exercise of private initiative and responsibility" (Keynes, 1936, pp.379–380). In his opinion, however, this does not imply a reduction of individual liberty for at least two reasons underlined in the GT:

i) Structural unemployment is redefined by Keynes as *involuntary* unemployment, i.e. as a restriction of the set of options available to individuals. Therefore, its removal through state intervention is meant to enlarge the liberty of individuals. In the absence of macroeconomic market failures, the set of possible choices in the market of labor is delimited by the short side of demand and supply of labor so that there is no obstacle to full employment equilibrium. The main purpose of the GT, clearly announced since the second chapter, is to show that the set of options in the market of labor is restricted as a consequence of macroeconomic failures that determine employment exogenously by the "principle of effective demand". Given this constraint, the maximizing behavior of workers selects the optimal point within the restricted set of options, i.e. the point where effective demand crosses the labor demand curve defining the value of unemployment equilibrium characterized by the maximum possible real wage. On the basis of this argument we may say that any measure of macroeconomic policy that succeeds to relax the effective demand constraint at the same time expands the liberty of economic agents.

ii) In any case, this macroscopic but circumscribed enlargement of the functions of government advocated by Keynes is considered by him "as the only practicable means of avoiding the destruction of existing economic forms in their entirety and as the condition of the successful functioning of individual initiative" (Keynes, 1936, p.380). In other words Keynes considered full employment macroeconomic policy as a necessary condition for preserving market capitalism and economic freedom.

In the light of these considerations it is clear that the intention of Keynes was not that of undermining economic liberalism but that of rescuing and updating it in a period of profound crisis. We have thus to recognize a profound continuity between Keynes's and "classical" liberalism. Economic liberalism by its own nature never failed to update its analysis and prescriptions by taking account of the evolution of both economic facts and economic theory. From this point of view we may say that Keynes's liberalism is nothing but a further updating of this tradition of thought. On the other hand, though thoroughly circumscribed, the discontinuity between the liberalism of Keynes and that of the classics is not at all a minor one since in the tradition of economic liberalism no one before Keynes recognized in a rigorous and systematic way the possibility of *macroeconomic* failures and their crucial importance in a monetary market economy. The introduction of this conceptual novelty, however, is not foreign to the spirit of economic liberalism provided that its theoretical foundations are sound.[135]

It has been contended that any sort of public intervention requires a reliable forecast of the reaction of the economic agents (as stressed, e.g., by Hayek and Lucas). Keynes was fully aware that this sort of prediction is condemned to be unreliable since: "in such matters it is rash to predict how the average man will react to a changed environment" (1936, p.377). He used specifically this argument to deny the possibility of controlling the economy through monetary policy. Exactly for this reason Keynes introduced the multiplier in order to shift the analysis on the real side of the economy where state interventions may affect directly aggregate income or employment. In fact, in his opinion, whenever other policy strategies fail to bring about full employment by affecting the marginal propensity to consumption or the volume of private investment, the state may use the last-resort strategy of increasing directly public expenditure by reducing the involuntary unemployment through the mechanism of the multiplier. From the point of view of the hard uncertainty affecting the decisions of economic agents there is no contradiction in Keynes's policy philosophy. We have thus to emphasize that the Keynesian revolution is ultimately based on his peculiar cognitive assumptions. Keynes economic agents have to make choices in a situation of hard uncertainty. They are aware of their ignorance not only about future events but also about the probability distributions of their occurrence. Their expectations are conceived in terms of non-additive probability or multiple probabilities or else elude altogether, in the case of radical uncertainty, any probabilistic formulation.[136] In such a situation economic agents are liable to be influenced by existing conventions that may bring about forms of herd behavior. They may thus suddenly change their expectations or rules of conduct and this translates in unpredictable shifts of the main functions of the model (liquidity preference and marginal efficiency of capital). This prevents the market from self-regulating itself and makes unreliable any effort of monetary policy to help.

Although Pigou and Keynes were both pupils of Marshall, they did not understand nor support each other. As we have seen, Keynes claimed in GT that there was no reason to deny that competitive markets realize a fairly efficient microeconomic allocation of resources, while Pigou denied in his critical review of GT that unfettered markets were unable to recover promptly full employment after a perturbation. Notwithstanding this arguing at cross purposes, due mainly to a different methodological approach, the countercyclical macroeconomic policies advocated by Keynes required a proper microeconomic counterpart to orientate the structure of the budget so that, eventually, their contributions were merged in the policy prescriptions of the "new classical synthesis" (Samuelson, 1947; Modigliani, 1944; Patinkin, 1956), the version of Keynesism that became hegemonic in the 1960s and early 1970s and that inspired the construction of the welfare state in the period of Bretton Woods (1945–1971). This school of thought provided Keynesian macroeconomics with microeconomic foundations in terms of general equilibrium theory. This allowed a merger of the Pigouvian microeconomic approach and the Keynesian macroeconomic approach into an updated version of economic liberalism. In both cases, as is also true with the other exponents of updated liberalism, the role of the state was expanded but only to the extent that the advances of economic theory were better defining the limits of the markets. In our opinion it is difficult to deny that the substantial continuity between classical liberalism and updated liberalism was very profound (see section 4).

The updated liberalism ruling in the period of Bretton Woods inspired the construction of the welfare state meant to reduce inequality, poverty and some of their worse implications, and the systematic adoption of countercyclical policies meant to keep full employment. These policies were quite successful in promoting growth and welfare in the 1950s and 1960s but they had to face serious problems in the 1970s. First of all, the growth of the economic weight of the state, as measured by the share of public expenditure over aggregate expenditure increased in industrialized countries at an unsustainable pace approaching, and sometimes overcoming, the threshold of 50%, hardly consistent with a free market economy (Lindert, 2004). Second, the policies meant to guarantee full employment and social security led, in an environment destabilized by the oil shocks, to persisting stagflation. The inability of the mainstream Keynesism of the time to cope with these problems determined the demise of updated liberalism and the switch of many economists and governments to a new point of view often called "neoliberalism".

3   Neoliberalism

The prestige of updated liberalism was gradually eroded by growing difficulties arising both from within its founding blocks, questioning their soundness, and from different perspectives, questioning its empirical and policy scope. Since the early 1950, the research program of welfare economics was undermined by a growing awareness of its weaknesses. The first serious blow came from the "theorem of impossibility" of Arrow (1951) who proved that individual preferences cannot be aggregated in social preferences through a fully consistent aggregation mechanism. Another paradox was pointed out by Sen (1970) who proved that coherent public choice cannot be based simultaneously on both Pareto optimality and liberalism. Both paradoxes were meant to criticize the narrowness of the traditional approach of welfare economics but were taken by many economists as a criticism of the research program catalyzed by welfare economics in support of updated liberalism.

In the meantime, the philosophy underlying the updated liberalism was challenged by thinkers such as Hayek (1944) and Von Mises (1952). The heterodox contributions by Hayek became eventually particularly influential. He maintained throughout his long and productive life the idea that the only admissible interference with the spontaneous order of the market is the one that establishes or preserves free-market competition. Any other intervention is bound to jeopardize its efficiency, flexibility and pluralism. He rejected, in particular, the general equilibrium Paretian approach that underlay much of the updated liberalism since the early 1950s, denying the alleged independence between distribution and allocation of resources. Hayek maintained, on the contrary, that any interference with the spontaneous distribution of wealth determined by a competitive market would jeopardize liberty (Hayek, 1948) and hinder economic progress (Hayek, 1988). He went so far to consider equalitarianism as immoral since in his opinion it violates the basic ethical principle that every one should be submitted to the same set of rules (Hayek, 1978). The influence exerted by Hayek was more on the philosophical and conceptual side than on the side of his highly controversial scientific approach. In the meantime new analytic contributions paved the way to an alternative approach.

In particular, the market failures attributed by Pigou to the existence of externalities received an alternative explanation in Coase (1960) that rapidly became very influential. He proved that the externalities are likely to depend on inexistent or ill-defined property rights on certain economic goods such as the environmental commons, and that under thoroughly specified conditions it would be enough to attribute well-defined property rights on these goods to one of the subjects involved to overcome the allocative failure through spontaneous recontracting between the agents. Coase pointed out that this argument is valid only under a series of stringent assumptions unlikely to be true in general, but the economists hostile to the tenets of updated liberalism drew from it the conclusion that it is enough to define private property rights on all the goods and systematically deregulate the market to avoid all sorts of allocative market failures.

As for the macroeconomic foundations of updated liberalism, the extension of state interventions advocated by Keynes in order to eliminate involuntary unemployment was challenged from the very beginning by most reviewers and commentators. The younger generation of economists, however, was soon conquered by the new ideas in part because of the persistence of high rates of unemployment observed in the 1930s, in part because the simple Keynesian functions were an ideal field of application for the emerging subdiscipline of econometrics. The construction of multi-equation models of Keynesian inspiration became rapidly a major business financed by public administrations, central banks and big firms. Their use for interpretive and predictive purposes gave a crucial role to economists in public and corporate decision-making. Moreover, the Keynesian models found soon convincing foundations in general equilibrium terms (Hicks, 1937 and 1939; Modigliani, 1944; Samuelson, 1947; Patinkin, 1956) reconciling the new ideas with the traditional ones.

Even when the Keynesian macroeconomic approach became hegemonic in the Bretton Woods era, the existence and relevance of the alleged macroeconomic market failures continued to be energetically denied by many influential economists, including in a prominent position the monetarist economists led by Milton Friedman. They rejected in particular the Keynesian argument that involuntary unemployment (corresponding to excess supply in the labor market) could be interpreted as a persistent equilibrium position, as Keynes did. They denied, in addition, that a value of unemployment inferior to the "natural rate", interpreted as the long-run fundamental equilibrium, could be sustained by expansionary policies without accelerating the rate of inflation. The stagflation of the 1970s, coupled with unexpected upward shifts in the short-run Phillips curve eroded the prestige of the Keynesian approach. Finally, by assuming rational expectations and optimizing equilibrium throughout the cycle, the then emerging school of new classical economists, denied the existence of macroeconomic market failures and therefore also the soundness of macroeconomic policies meant to mend them (see Vercelli, 1991).

4   The evolution of economic liberalism: continuity or discontinuity?

The division in three periods of mainstream scientific liberalism suggested above does not need to be particularly controversial. The distinction within economic liberalism between the original version prevailing in the classical period and the updated version prevailing in the Bretton Woods period after a long period of gradual evolution, is widely recognized (see, e.g., the recent book by Benjamin Friedman, 2006). The distinction between liberalism and neoliberalism is increasingly recognized because of their divergent policy approaches based on a different vision of market properties. Of course, a more detailed analysis of the evolution of economic liberalism should introduce further distinctions between different sub-periods and varieties of economic liberalism and should discuss the crucial influence exerted be many other important economists and streams of economic thought. The chosen level of detail has the advantage of making explicit the basic synchrony between the evolution of economic liberalism and the evolution of globalization. Classical liberalism deeply affected the first period of globalization. Updated liberalism shaped the policy philosophy underlying the Bretton Woods Treaties and the post-war period until the breakdown of the Bretton Woods system in the 1970s. Neoliberalism profoundly influenced the most recent phase of globalization.

What is controversial is the judgment whether the process of evolution of economic liberalism was characterized by a major discontinuity or not, and in the case of an affirmative answer, where exactly this discontinuity should be located. On this issue there are sharply contrasting opinions that have deep implications for the interpretation of the evolution of economic liberalism and of its policy prescriptions.

The main exponents of what we called neoliberalism tend to deny any discontinuity between their point of view and that of classical liberalism while they emphasize the sharp opposition to the point of view that we have called updated liberalism. In fact they interpret the latter as a dangerous deviation from the principles of liberalism that has to be altogether rejected. The point of view maintained in this book, on the contrary, inclines to the opinion that there is a basic continuity between classical liberalism and updated liberalism, since both recognized the existence of insurmountable limits to the markets and stressed the need to define the areas where the interference of the state in the economy is preferable or necessary. The updated liberalism defined better, and extended to some extent, the scope of state intervention on the basis of the advances in economic theory, but it did not change the basic approach: the market should rule the economy unless there are serious reasons, grounded in scientific theory, to call for state intervention.

Ironically, the point of view of continuity between classical liberalism and neoliberalism argued by the latter school may find some support in the simplistic and insufficiently articulated criticism raised against classical economics by Keynes, who blurred the distinction between classical and updated liberalism, and at the same time lost sight of the differences and qualifications of pre-Keynesian liberalism. In particular, what we have here called classical liberalism and pre-Keynesian updated liberalism were unduly merged by Keynes and interpreted as if it were advocating unqualified *laissez-faire*. This simplistic point of view may have helped the Keynesian ideas to find followers when they were first put forward but their superficial articulation eventually backfired against them.[137]

A sharp discontinuity may be seen, on the contrary, between neoliberalism and both classical and updated liberalism. The exponents of neoliberalism emphasized the discontinuity with updated liberalism, as is obvious since they denied its consistency with the principles of economic liberalism. For the same reason, generally they refused to be labeled neoliberal as they believed in the basic unity and continuity of "authentic" liberalism and interpreted their own historical role as that of restoration of genuine liberalism after the misleading detour originated by what we have called updated liberalism. We do not find in neoliberalism, however, the same awareness that characterizes both classical liberalism and updated liberalism of the limits to markets and the necessity of regulating them in order to avoid, or at least minimize, ubiquitous market failures. Neoliberal exponents seem to believe that economic policy could simply rely on the systematic deregulation of markets and privatization of goods and services. Deregulation and privatization, no doubt, characterize any kind of economic liberalism; a full awareness of the limits of markets, however, also implies an alert attention to the limits of deregulation and privatization that define at the same time the scope for collective action. Notwithstanding a conspicuous stream of economic literature that in the last decades has progressively clarified the limits to markets, neoliberalism very often seems to advocate an apparently limitless policy of deregulation and privatization. In this extreme version, it is even doubtful whether such an approach to economic policy deserves to be considered as the latest mainstream version of economic liberalism, since it does not seem to take in due account the theorems and analytic results accumulated by economic theory on the limits to markets. This is particularly surprising since in the last decades many new important contributions on these issues have been published in the best learned journals of economics and most prestigious series of economic books that allow a definition of the legitimate scope of the markets with much more clarity and detail than in the past (see section 3 in Chapter 1 and the Appendix to this chapter). This approach, therefore, could be appraised rather as an updated version of *laissez-faire* that appeals more to ideological convictions than to scientifically-based argument. As we argued before, the neoliberal ideas may claim some support in a few scientific contributions, such as the Coase theorem and new classical economics, but their neoliberal interpretation seems to ignore their presuppositions and therefore also their limits of validity that are generally recognized and emphasized by their proponents. (We refer the reader to the Appendix of this chapter where we try to clarify further the controversial concepts discussed in this section.)

The reconstruction of the evolution of economic liberalism suggested above is admittedly very simplified. First of all we have to emphasize that economic liberalism coexisted with what we have called *laissez-faire* throughout all the historical period considered, and that it is not always easy to distinguish between the two. Many economists have sometimes neglected some of the knowledge accumulated by economic theory and empirical evidence on the limits to markets, falling victim of the ideological tenets of *laissez-faire*, while the advocates of the latter often utilized arguments drawn from economics although in an uncritical and partial way.

The temporal succession of the three basic varieties of economic liberalism is based on what we consider the hegemonic point of view, i.e. the point of view prevailing between the most influential liberal economists of the time, We could say, however, that the three points of view coexisted throughout the period analyzed. For example, to limit ourselves to the early 19th century, Bentham entertained a point of view very similar to that of updated liberalism, while Say and Bastiat entertained a point of view very close to that of neoliberalism.

Looking back to the evolution of economic liberalism we may notice the persistence of long swings between the two extremes of statism and mere *laissez-faire*, where each phase is triggered by a reaction to the negative implications experienced in the preceding phase. The classical liberalism reacted to the statism of the Mercantilists, the updated liberalism reacted to the shortcomings of unbounded *laissez-faire*, neoliberalism reacted to the bureaucratic degenerations of updated liberalism. Analogously, many recent contributions may be interpreted as a reaction to the negative social and environmental implications of neoliberalism (see, e.g., Sen, 2002; Stiglitz, 2002; Friedman, 2006).

These pendulum-like swings are typical in the psychological sphere of individuals or in the cultural sphere of societies where between unilateral thesis and antithesis it is very difficult to find a satisfactory synthesis. The economists, however, should take on themselves the specific responsibility of clarifying both the virtues of markets and their limits and, at the same time, the virtues of collective action and bureaucracy as well as their limits. Both strands of analysis should be then unified in a comprehensive conceptual framework independent of ideological prejudices and emotional overtones. To reach this goal, the economists should fully exploit all the continuous advances on the front of the properties of the ideal perfect-competition market, real markets, collective action, private and public bureaucratic processes, as well as public and corporate governance. This imposes the abandonment of widespread but misleading simplifications. The existence of a market failure does not imply, by itself, the necessity of state intervention, because the latter could be liable to worse failures. In principle, although is very difficult, we should evaluate in each single case the costs and benefits of the different alternatives and the optimal institutional design that can reduce the probability of both kinds of failure in order to maximize the social welfare and the quality of life (see section 3 of Chapter 9).

We have to recognize that we are still quite far from the goal that we have advocated. Since the time of Adam Smith we learned a lot about the properties of a perfect-competition market and something on the properties of monopolistic and oligopolistic markets, but we still know very little on the properties of real markets and of bureaucratic and collective decision-making. What we know, moreover, has not yet been unified in a comprehensive framework, and this goes a long way in the direction of explaining the swings that we have noticed in the history of economic liberalism. In particular, the lucidity of economists' judgment on these matters is still often compromised by misleading correspondences between simplistic dichotomies. The dichotomy state/market is often considered coextensive with the dichotomy centralized/decentralized decision-making, bureaucratic/non-bureaucratic organization, private/ public and, finally, *laissez-faire*/public intervention (or interference). The alleged correspondence between some or all of these dichotomies is widespread but highly misleading. Bureaucratic decisions may be decentralized and organized according to market principles even in the public sector. The bureaucracy of corporations, on the contrary, is often highly centralized and distorted by motivations inconsistent with market efficiency. In the absence of regulation, competitive markets tend to degenerate in oligopolistic or monopolistic markets where the decisions are definitely dominated by the huge bureaucracies of big firms only weakly affected by market constraints (see section 3 of Chapter 9).

Appendix
The Meanings of "Economic" Liberalism: A Conceptual Clarification

The different concepts of liberalism discussed in this chapter are very ambiguous and quite controversial. We think it worthwhile to try to clarify further their meaning in this appendix. The concepts here defined should be understood as *ideal types* that do not necessarily correspond to the opinions entertained by any single person but, by abstracting from individual and minor differences, try to fix a few clear conceptual references (a brief account on the concept of ideal-type as characterized by Max Weber may be found in Bendix, 1987).

In this spirit, we define *laissez-faire* as an approach to economic policy that in principle denies any positive role for the regulation of markets and state intervention. When its arguments are based on economic theory their foundations are typically lacking in acceptable rigor. On the contrary "economic liberalism" may be defined as an approach to economic policy based on sound theoretical arguments rooted in state-of-the-art economic theory.

All the varieties of economic liberalism share the following proposition, although it is expressed in different versions and argued with different degree of sophistication:

1. *Invisible hand postulate.* A perfect-competition market allocates the resources between alternative uses in the best possible way by coordinating the decisions of self-interested rational agents in such a way to maximize their welfare.
   More controversial are the following propositions:

2. *Limits to the invisible hand.* Even an ideal model of perfect competition has strict limits in its power of coordinating the decisions of economic agents. In particular, it cannot solve the distributive problems, in the sense that the distribution of income, wealth and resources does not necessarily correspond to a given standard (ethical or of other nature). In addition the uniqueness of equilibrium and its stability are not granted (see *retro* section 3 of Chapter 1).

3. *Existence of a market gap.* Between real markets and the ideal perfect-competition market there is a significant discrepancy, here called "market gap", that is quite relevant for economic theory and economic policy. As we have seen in section 3.2, markets are incomplete, and characterized by externalities, transaction costs, asymmetric information, and other intrinsic shortcomings.

4. *Foundations of liberal policies.* The ultimate rationale of liberal economic policies may be seen in the progressive reduction of the market gap. In order to provide general foundations to them we have thus to assume that, in principle, there is a monotonous correlation between the size of the market gap and the losses of social welfare brought about by this gap. This postulate is not made explicit but is logically necessary to justify the validity of liberal policies.

5. *Limits to liberal policies.* In principle, there are serious limits in the reduction of the gap between real markets and the ideal perfect-competition market. As we have seen in section 3.2, markets cannot be altogether completed, externalities cannot be completely internalized, transaction costs may be reduced but not fully eliminated, information may become less asymmetric but not fully homogeneous, and so on. The economic agents operating in real markets are boundedly rational and not always self-seeking DMs (see, e.g., Agarwal and Vercelli, 2007).

We are now in a position to define in a more rigorous way the different concepts of liberalism analyzed in this chapter. Classical and updated liberalism accept the five propositions above. From the logical point of view of this Appendix, the distinction between these two types of liberalism is secondary, corroborating the thesis of their continuity advanced in section 3 of this chapter. As maintained in section 1, the updated liberalism is characterized by different economic foundations, a different rhetoric orientated to define the limits of the market rather than its superior virtues, and a cautious and motivated extension of the role of the State to new fields.

If, from the logical point of view of this appendix, we compare classical and updated liberalism with neoliberalism we see a sharp distinction that corroborates the thesis maintained in this book of a marked discontinuity with the preceding evolving tradition of economic liberalism. Neoliberalism, in fact, accepts proposition 1, 3 and 4 but, differently from both classical liberalism and updated liberalism, does not accept or plays down propositions 2 on the limits of the invisible hand, and 5 on the limits of liberal policies.

As for proposition 2, the Paretian approach to welfare adopted by most liberal streams since the 1950s, clarifies that the optimality of market equilibrium is relative to a given initial distribution. According to a common belief in classical and updated liberalism the market performs well when the initial distribution is sufficiently fair, such as to allow access to all the relevant options by all the economic agents. Typically the neoliberal exponents deny this requirement maintaining that redistributive policies are inconsistent with free market individualism.

As for proposition 3, the gap is not denied but its relevance is played down. The neoliberal exponents, for example, typically believe that the monopolistic or oligopolistic deviations from perfect competition in a certain market may be much less relevant than they seem at first sight to the extent that the market in question remains contestable (see, e.g., Baumol *et al.*, 1982). Analogously, they deny the soundness of the distinction between strong and week uncertainty, and the empirical relevance of other distinctions emphasized above such as the distinction between equilibrium and disequilibrium, bounded and unbounded rationality, and so on.

As for proposition 4, we have to stress, however, that – to the best of our knowledge – this apparently plausible postulate is not much more than an act of faith. First, it is not clear how to measure the market gap. Real markets deviate form the ideal model on many accounts that are mutually independent. In order to simplify this delicate issue the monotonicity postulate is routinely applied to each of these deviations. There is no reason to believe that the correlation between the single market deviations, or an eventual aggregate measure of the market gap, and welfare losses is monotonic. There could be trade-offs between the single dimensions of the gap that would forbid a sound aggregation in a comprehensive measure of the market gap. Although this is the weakest postulate of scientific liberalism it is needed to draw unambiguous policy conclusions from knowledge concerning the economic and welfare properties of ideal and real markets. For this reason we also had to adopt it in some of our arguments. We have to keep full awareness of this weakness in order to avoid the degeneration of the argument in ideological statements on these complex and badly understood issues.

As for proposition 5, the neoliberal exponents typically believe: (i) that markets can be completed, e.g. by introducing a congruous number of Arrow securities; (ii) that transaction costs can be reduced at will through institutional reform aiming to enhance the transparency of business decisions or through technological innovations based on ICT; (iii) that externalities may be reduced by defining property rights on free goods, and so on.

The economic policy implications vary according to the acceptance or not of the above propositions. The acceptance of propositions 1, 3, and 4, leads towards the liberalization of markets and their acceptance is the common denominator of the different varieties of economic liberalism. Collectivism and statism, on the contrary, deny the validity of proposition 1. The *laissez-faire* stance, as here defined, is against any sort of interference of the state on the economy in principle, as it entertains the presumption that, in any case, public interference would get things worse.

The neoliberal point of view as here defined, on the contrary, accepts propositions 1 and 3 which, taken together, justify structural policies based on deregulation and privatization in order to approach the ideal model of perfect competition. In addition it holds proposition 4 that assures that the transition towards a more competitive market is beneficial even if the final target is not fully reached. On the contrary, the limits of the invisible hand as well as those of liberal policies are denied or played down. Therefore, the opportunity of countercyclical policies or interventions directed to internalize the externalities is denied. Analogously, the opportunity of redistributive policies aimed to equalize income and wealth and to fight poverty is rejected.

Both classical and updated liberalism accept a stronger version of proposition 3 that requires a cautious application of competitive theory to real markets. Finally both classical and updated liberalism accept proposition 2 on the limits of a perfect-competition market and proposition 5 on the limits to policies directed to reduce the market gap, but updated liberalism accepts a stronger version of both that expand the scope of state intervention.

9

Concluding Remarks:
The Argument in a Nutshell,
its Policy Implications and the
Liberal Dilemma

As we have emphasized in the introduction, about globalization we cannot say anything sensible in general terms. The characteristics of globalization and its impact on the economy depend on the period, the country, the issue analyzed and the approach adopted. In particular, we argued that the impact of globalization on the process of development and its sustainability is potentially beneficial but the benefits may be caught only under well-specified conditions. If one or more of these conditions are absent, the impact of globalization on development may be negative or, otherwise, positive in the short term but unsustainable.

Our analysis confirmed that globalization offers crucial opportunities of development to both industrialized and developing countries. This is true, moreover, not only of development in its strict economic sense, but also of its other dimensions such as welfare, health and economic freedom. It would thus be irrational to thwart the process of globalization to escape its negative implications. The latter should rather be avoided with apt countermeasures meant to implement the conditions for harvesting the beneficial opportunities offered by globalization. The attention should thus focus on which are exactly the conditions for exploiting the beneficial opportunities offered by the process of globalization, minimizing at the same time its side effects. This is what we tried to do in this book in reference to a few selected issues that bear on the sustainability of development. In this concluding chapter we briefly summarize what we have learned from our analysis trying to see whether the results obtained have some useful policy implications.

1 The argument in a nutshell

We started our argument from the assumption that globalization offers important opportunities to participating countries to increase the rate of growth of per capita income. We have ascertained, however, that also this circumscribed assertion is not true in general since well defined conditions are required. Among them we emphasized in particular the crucial role played by the institutional conditions that insure the rule of law and the necessary regulation of markets. In the absence of these conditions a sudden switch from an inward orientation to an outward orientation of economic policy may have, at least in the short period, damaging effects. The recent case of the troubled transition of eastern European countries to the status of market economies open to foreign trade is a clear example of these difficulties. As we have emphasized in many passages of the book, economic globalization is in its essence a process of extension and deepening of markets. More than two centuries of economic analysis have clarified which are the structural, institutional and policy conditions that assure the healthy functioning of competitive markets. What is surprising is that these conditions are still so often overlooked even by serious economists. This has to do with the spreading, since the late 1970s, of an irrational faith on the power of unregulated markets that blurred the necessary awareness of their limits. The damaging effects of this ideology emerged often in many passages of the book. We have analyzed them in reference to the insufficiently analyzed issues concerning the sustainability of economic development. To this end we have distinguished between the social requisites and the environmental requisites of sustainable development.

We analyzed two main requisites of sustainable development: inequality and poverty. The apparent long-run positive correlation between the global index of inequality built by Bourguignon and Morisson (2002) and globalization seems to suggest *prima facie* that globalization has progressively deteriorated this fundamental requisite of sustainability. We have seen, however, that by decomposing this index into its two basic components, inequality between nations and within nations, the picture becomes much more articulated. A positive correlation between globalization and between-country inequality is detectable during the first globalization of 19th century until World War I, but not in the subsequent period. This is consistent with our theoretical expectations. In fact, globalization has two opposite effects on between-country inequality. It tends to reduce inequality within the group of countries which actively participate in the process, at least in the hypothesis of free movement not only of goods and services but also of productive factors. At the same time, however, it increases the gap between the group of globalizers and the group of countries excluded from the process. The second wave of globalization after World War II succeeded in enlarging the group of globalizing countries beyond the limits of the first one, including countries such as India, China and Russia. This shifted progressively the weight of the effects of globalization towards the equalizing effect. No wonder, thus, that the net effect of globalization on between-country inequality has become progressively more favorable, promising to become a negative one in due time.

It is tempting to interpret the available empirical evidence in terms of an international Kuznets-like curve according to which globalization increases between-country inequality in a first phase that broadly corresponds to the first globalization but tends to reduce it after a certain threshold of its expansion. This interpretation is buttressed by plausible theoretical arguments, such as those mentioned above, and some empirical support, but it is too early to be sure that we have really overcome the vertex of the curve (Milanovic, 2005). In any case the favorable effects may materialize and consolidate only at given conditions, some of which are missing or under threat. First, it is required a further enlargement of the group of globalizers; second it is essential an effective free movement of all goods, services and factors of production that is still hindered in many ways even, to some extent, between the group of countries that actively participate in the process of globalization.

More reliable empirical evidence we have on the analysis of the relationship between globalization and within-country inequality. In this case, however, long-run generalizations at the global level are not possible. The existence of a correlation between globalization and within-country inequality is not falsified by the empirical evidence but is scarcely informative and conceals complex short-period patterns for different groups of countries. While inequality tends to increase in the new globalizing countries such as China, India, and Russia, in most OECD countries inequality changed its behavior since the late 1970s, passing from a trend of moderate reduction to a trend of relatively sharp increase. In the first chapters of this book we could go in some depth on this issue because there is a large and rigorous literature on the correlation between within-country inequality and per capita income. Kuznets (1955) was the first who observed that, as per capita income increases, within-country inequality first increases and then decreases, following a characteristic pattern that came to be called "Kuznets curve". Since there is a clear correlation between globalization and the rate of growth of per capita income, we may expect that an unfavorable effect of globalization on within-country inequality is only transitory. This optimist message, however, turned out to be increasingly at variance with the available evidence in OECD. Since the late 1970s the

KC hypothesis became more and more inconsistent with the updated evidence. We have emphasized a good reason for this trend in history. As we have seen in Chapter 1, in most OECD countries within-country inequality that had decreased since WWI started to increase again in the late 1970s *pari passu* with a further increase in per capita income.

We have then considered the time path of poverty that is another important social condition of sustainability. Also the poverty ratio exhibits a Kuznets-type correlation with a composite index of globalization (Chapter 2). In this case, however, the worrying part of the curve appears only in new globalizing countries and seems to be short-lived. In addition we found in general a sharp reduction of the world poverty ratios as globalization proceeds (Chapter 1). These two empirical patterns induced many observers to conclude that "globalization is good for the poor" and that poor countries suffer not from globalization but from insufficient globalization. This may well be eventually true, but we should ask whether the current patterns of globalization indicate the most efficient way to fight poverty. The progressive reduction of the poverty ratio may give the illusion that the existing trends are consistent with a rapid conquest of poverty. We have shown that this optimist conclusion is a hastened one, since in the meantime the absolute head-count number of poor people continued to increase for most of the time so that their number is much higher today than it used to be at the beginning of the globalization process. The reduction of the poverty ratio is the expression of a growth rate of population that greatly exceeded the growth in the absolute number of poor people. Projecting in the future the persisting increase in the total number of the poor and the slowdown in the demographic growth we are led to anticipate that even the ratio of the poor might end up increasing again in the future. These time patterns of inequality and poverty show that the actual process of growth at the global level is inconsistent with the social requisites of sustainability. In order to avoid these undesired consequences we have to fight poverty within the framework of a more egalitarian kind of growth.

As for the environmental condition of sustainability we could not rely on long-run series of comprehensive indexes. We have thus focused on the indirect correlation of globalization, via the effect on per capita income, with a battery of environmental indexes (Chapter 3). In this case the Kuznets hypothesis works only for a few indicators of environmental deterioration the effects of which are local and fall on the shoulders of polluters themselves. Whenever the negative effects may be shifted away from the polluters, as in the case of acid rain, or are diluted evenly at the global level, as in the case of GHGs, polluters typically assume free-riding attitudes, so that the tendency to a reversal after a certain threshold is not clearly detectable or tends to disappear after a while, leading to worrying N-shaped curves. In order to assure environmental sustainability we have to clarify which are its specific requisites. By generalizing the KC within an identity that we have called "Kuznets relationship" we have aimed to clarify the logical conditions of sustainability. In particular, we found that in order to make possible a reduction of environmental degradation over time the rate of reduction of the intensity of environmental deterioration must exceed the rate of growth of global production. The compliance with this condition is not easy at all, particularly in developing countries where the population growth is higher and environmental policies weaker than in developed countries. This suggests that in most countries economic growth is currently inconsistent with the environmental requirements of sustainability.

This is confirmed by our case-study on the current model of production, distribution and consumption of energy. Also in this case the optimists detected in the data the existence of a KC for energy intensity. It appears that in most countries the energy consumed to produce a unit of output increases after the industrial take-off because of the switch of production from agriculture to energy-intensive heavy industry. In a second time, however, the shift towards light industry and services that are less energy intensive, and a growing awareness of the importance of energy saving, inverts the curve. In addition, the newcomers in the club of industrializing countries may profit of the new technologies repeating the same pattern with a lower curve. This empirical evidence is certainly comforting in itself but is insufficient to guarantee an increasing sustainability within the energy sector. We have to take account also of the intensity of environmental degradation and of the scale effect induced by the growth of per capita world GDP and population. Taking account of all these factors we had to record a worrying sustainability gap that risks increasing again after three decades of reduction. The existence of this sustainability gap in the energy sector should not be interpreted as the consequence of excessive growth of the world production, since we still need it to reduce poverty, but as a sign of defective energy and environmental policies. We should thus update with courage and far-sightedness the existing environmental and energy policies in order to make them consistent with the requirements of sustainable development also in the energy sector.

In the first four chapters we investigated the behavior only of the usual monetary indexes of welfare: income and per capita income. We consider this limitation a serious shortcoming of our analysis. We tried to remedy it, although only in part, in Chapter 5 where we examined the behavior of population health that is a fundamental non-monetary index of sustainability. Also in this case the optimists underlined the existence of a KC of health inequality. Even this curve, however, changed direction since the late 1970s. We cannot thus rely on the existence of a trend that tends to reduce this crucial source of income inequality. More in general, we cannot be too confident in the spontaneous improvement of most health indexes in the future. In addition, there are reasons to believe that, in any case, the improvement of health indexes could have been, and could be, much more rapid under different policy strategies. Their adoption would increase both the rate of development and its sustainability. We have stressed in particular the role of absolute per capita income under a quite low threshold of $5000 per year and of relative income beyond this threshold. Recent research has shown that beyond this threshold income inequality becomes a crucial determinant of health, as it generates a disruptive feeling of relative deprivation leading to mistrust and hostility towards other people. This undermines at the same time the psychological and physiological foundations of good health and the social foundations of economic growth. These findings confirm the need of policy measures directed to fighting poverty and inequality at the same time. This policy strategy is all the more important as the social and environmental conditions of sustainability acquired an increasing role in determining population health. The inverse causality between health and economic growth closes a feed-back that plays a crucial role in determining the world development and its sustainability. Great cure should be put in trying to avoid that this feed-back generates a vicious circle, aiming to establish instead a virtuous circle between improving health and more rapid and sustainable growth.

The belief in a Kuznets-type pattern of undesirable social and environmental indicators is typical of observers and analysts who are optimist on the power of market forces to solve the problems raised by economic development. They recognize that the introduction, extension and deepening of free markets may have a disruptive impact on the economy and society but the ensuing evils are considered as transitory as the market forces themselves are expected to remedy them in due time. Unfortunately, this optimist point of view proved to be groundless in most of the cases we have examined. This does not imply that the negative effects of globalization necessarily exceed its beneficial effects but only that the prevalence of the latter is not granted and requires the compliance with a series of conditions.

The analysis developed in the first five chapters did not consider technological and institutional factors in detail, apart from the obvious influence of the extension of markets on the productivity of factors. The analysis of these factors has a different time scale. Since both the technological and institutional factors change very rapidly, we need a finer periodization. We limited this sort of analysis to the period 1995–2000 that we have christened as the period of "new" globalization. This period was characterized, from the technological point of view, by the emergence of the so-called "new economy" based on the systematic application of ICT in the production and distribution of goods and services. The same period was characterized, from the institutional point of view, by the establishment of new regulation rules for international markets managed in particular by the WTO, the new powerful international organization established in 1995.

In principle, the systematic application of ICT could reduce the gap between the actual characteristics of markets (radical uncertainty, strong incompleteness, sizeable transaction costs, extensive externalities, intrinsic instability, and so on) and the desirable characteristics of the textbook perfect-competition model. The impact of the new economy on the process of globalization, however, has also dangerous implications for sustainability. We have classified these risks in two categories: those that impede the realization of the opportunities offered by globalization and further risks. The reduction of information asymmetries is limited by the availability of efficient access to the Internet as well as by the effective expertise and background knowledge of the user. Generally speaking, the excess of information available in the Internet may seriously jeopardize the selection and fruition of the relevant information. Moreover, the effective meaning of the information received depends on the cognitive structures of the users. The diffusion of the ICTs may have naturally increased the cognitive gap between people having a different fruition capacity of the relevant information. As for transaction costs, a sizeable reduction is possible only when the goods and services exchanged are highly standardized and their characteristics are well known to clients. Also the claim of a reduction in barriers to entry in the markets does not seem to be well grounded. The tendency to a reduction of the average firm size was to some extent countered by the emergence of new opportunities of scale and scope economies based on the size of virtual networks, and of software standardization.

For the preceding reasons we argued that the systematic introduction of the ICTs did not succeed in bridging the gap between the real market and the ideal perfect-competition market. The growth in efficiency has occurred mainly because of the growing flexibility of labor markets and industrial relations that in many cases undermined the social sustainability of development. As for eco-efficiency, so far electronic dematerialization did not live up to its promise. Also the environmental benefits arising from the introduction of the new ICTs are not at all automatic but require the implementation of apt policies. In their absence the e-commerce may increase the environmental costs of the distribution of goods (fuel, pollution, waste, and so on) while the systematic use of electronic devices at home and at the workplace may increase energy consumption.

After a brief transition phase during the 1970s, in the early 1980s a new system of policy rules emerged that gave up the Keynesian and welfarist inspiration of the Bretton Woods period. Focusing on the risks of state failures and playing down the risks of market failures the new policy paradigm aimed at the systematic deregulation of markets and at the privatization of all activities with a potential economic impact. The new regulation of international markets was managed by the same international organizations set up at Bretton Woods (*in primis* the IMF and the WB) that in the new circumstances changed quite radically their policy philosophy (see Chapters 1 and 8). It soon became clear that in the new regulatory regime the liberalization of international exchanges required a new organization with more power and operational facilities than the existing GATT rounds. After a long gestation an organization of this kind started to operate on January 1, 1995 under the name of WTO. The new rules of (de)regulation of international markets rapidly revealed their weaknesses. The "one-size-fits-all" policies adopted by the IMF and the WB underestimated the importance of the structural characters of the single economies. In addition, their unqualified reliance on deregulation and privatization, as well as the imposition of deflationary policies to economies characterized by deficient demand was not often consistent with income growth and sustainable development. The WTO soon revealed a few weak points: insufficient transparency and accountability, deficient participation of member countries to the decision process, insufficient respect for the social and environmental requirements of sustainability.

In the first six chapters we have focused on the macroeconomic conditions of sustainability. In Chapter 7 we have turned to the analysis of the microeconomic conditions of sustainability. Both local and global development cannot be considered as sustainable if it is not grounded on a solid network of sustainable firms. To be sustainable, firms have to take into account the interests of all their stakeholders in a long-term perspective. As a result of market evolution, the companies' performance is increasingly evaluated on the basis of their performance over too short a term. This evaluation determines remuneration, promotion and removal of managers, investor portfolio choices, *pricing* of investment, and so forth. This makes the company's decision-making, in the absence of sufficiently robust ethical awareness, seek short-term results that we could call "doped": they are inflated by licit, and at times illicit, means which allow the company to withstand market competition in the short term only by compromising the sustainability of positive results in the longer term and by jeopardizing at times the very survival of the company.

Stakeholders often have long-term interests linked to the development of human, environmental and social capital, not only of the firms but also of the districts where they operate. A major benefit resulting from self-regulation CSR initiatives – such as the adoption of ethical codes, corporate governance rules, periodic sustainability reporting – is that these initiatives may counterweight market-driven decision myopia to ensure corporate sustainability. This may give a crucial contribution also to the sustainability of economic development in the districts where these firms operate. This holds in particular for banks on which the sustainability of other firms and of the very economic system crucially depends. The financial sector has the crucial task of directly or indirectly channeling flows of savings to uses that are more compatible with development sustainability.

In the first seven chapters the main focus of the analysis was on history of facts. In Chapter 8 we have resorted to the history of economic ideas to reconstruct the co-evolution of liberalism and globalization. This is one field in which the interaction between history of facts and history of thought has been particularly influential. In order to understand the reciprocal influence between the two evolutionary processes, we have reconstructed in Chapter 8 the evolution of liberalism since Adam Smith. We distinguished three streams of liberalism that have affected the evolution of globalization. The classical liberalism that was introduced by Adam Smith in his masterpiece, and was further developed and disseminated by the other classical economists, was no doubt a fundamental driving force in the expansion of free markets and in the genesis and diffusion of the first wave of globalization. In the neoclassical economists at the turn of the 19th century we find a different attitude more focused on the limits of markets emphasized by the historical experience. This new attitude emerges clearly in Marshall and finds proper foundations in the contributions of his best pupils: Pigou and Keynes. Pigou generalized and developed the Marshallian notion of market externalities providing the microeconomic foundations for market regulation. Keynes focused on the necessity of macroeconomic regulation in order to stabilize economic fluctuations and to eliminate unemployment. These contributions were merged in what we have called "updated liberalism" that has been very influential since the late 1930s inspiring also the Bretton Woods agreements. This policy paradigm proved unable to cope with the inflationary tensions of the late 1960s and the stagflation of the 1970s. Updated liberalism was eventually ousted in the late 1970s by what we have called "neoliberalism". This policy paradigm rekindled a deep faith in unfettered markets and relied on deregulation and privatization to minimize public interference with them. We may call the period after the early 1970s as the period of neoliberal globalization. The shortcomings of the process of globalization in this recent period are strictly connected with the weaknesses of this policy paradigm. We do not believe, however, that the way out from these shortcomings should be sought simply by reverting to the preceding policy paradigm. This is what we are going to discuss in the next two sections.

2 Policy implications

As we have often emphasized in this book, from the analysis of globalization we cannot draw unqualified general conclusions. This warning regards not only the interpretation of the process of globalization and its impact on world development sustainability, but also its policy implications. The principal policy teaching of our analysis is thus that we should be suspicious of general recipes applied in any circumstances to any country. The IMF and the WB have been criticized exactly for this reason. Many observers noticed that their "one-size-fits-all" policy prescriptions implemented in the last two decades of the 20th century did not prove to be very successful (Stiglitz, 2002; Bhagwati, 2004). All the other teachings are strictly confined in time and space. We briefly summarize here a few of them.

The general logic of the argument developed in the preceding chapters allows one to draw policy guidelines that may be useful to orientate the draft of concrete and targeted policy plans for specific countries in given circumstances. The polar star of the policy strategy suggested is that economic globalization may be beneficial to the extent that it succeeds in establishing a genuine competitive market at the world level. This may be done only if (i) the conditions for a perfectly competitive market are established or at least approximated in the countries involved, (ii) global markets are regulated in such a way to minimize, at the same time, market and state failures. This assertion has a series of general implications, at least in principle, that we now intend to analyze in order to introduce or strengthen the conditions for beneficial globalization.

Free movement across borders

We know, first of all, that the theorems of welfare economics providing the ultimate foundations for the beneficial effects of a competitive market require a full mobility of goods and services. Contrary to these requirements, serious barriers to free trade among countries still exist. Particularly questionable are those maintained by developed countries in the field of agriculture and textiles where the developing countries have a great export potential. As we have seen, the damage produced has the same order of magnitude of global financial help to developing countries. Many commentators lamented the hypocrisy of developed countries that preach free trade and exhibit their help, while they partially finance their aids to developing countries through protectionist measure against them. As for the mobility of services the issue was at the center of the last WTO meetings. Their liberalization is very controversial because it involves sectors such as health care and education the product of which has, at least in part, the nature of public good so that it is not clear to what extent and in which form competition may be beneficial.

The welfare theorems require also full mobility of production factors. Also in this case we have found serious anomalies. The mobility of labor during the second globalization has been restrained even by participating countries, much more than in the case of the first globalization. Since the mobility of people is an effective "last resort" equalizing factor, the obstacles raised against it by most industrialized countries in the last decades contributed to enhance income inequality and poverty.

As for the cross-borders flows of capital, liberalization is by now almost complete. Openness did not discriminate between FDI, i.e. investment abroad in productive capital (plants and machinery) and speculative flows whose beneficial effects are much more controversial. The latter may play a role in making more flexible the use of capital also for productive purposes, but the size of these flows (by now more than 90% of global capital flows) and their composition (mainly OTC derivatives lacking any sort of regulation and control) may unchain formidable disruptive forces. The idea of the Tobin tax starts to find local application. Particularly interesting is the case of Chile. Even IMF recently admitted that these measures may help a reasonable stabilization of the most fragile developing countries.

Although even the ideal model of perfect competition exhibits well-defined limits, the shortcomings of the real markets are much more pronounced. The ideal model of perfect competition assumes complete information for all the economic agents. This implies full mobility of information across countries, in particular on the best available technologies. This requirement is severely limited in the real markets by the existence of intellectual property rights. The enforcement of these rights at the international level, favored by WTO, is one of the causes of persisting inequality between countries. First of all, it implies a sizable transfer of income from developing countries that are typically importers of patents and innovations to developed countries that are typically producers and exporters of them. In many cases the existence of these royalties translates in mere inaccessibility of information and up-to-date innovation that greatly limits the ability of these countries to compete in the international arena. A particularly serious case is that of pharmaceutical products. The inaccessibility of some of these products compromises the health of population in poor countries (the case of AIDS remedies is particularly controversial).

Beyond intellectual property rights, also banking secrecy is another important factor that limits free circulation of information in real markets. From this point of view, it seems advisable to abolish banking secrecy, including that characterizing the operations of Offshore Financial Centers, as it facilitates illegal activities and contributes to international financial instability. Moreover, although this issue is quite controversial (see, e.g., the recent survey published by *The Economist*, 23 February, 2007), one cannot ignore its crucial role in facilitating systematic and organized crime, including routine corruption practices and terrorist activities. The current attitude of adopting a suspension of banking secrecy exclusively for anti-terrorism motivations is hardly viable because it is very difficult to discriminate *ex ante* between the contents of secret operations.

Finally, a perfectly functioning competitive market should require complete markets. Real markets, on the contrary, are heavily incomplete, particularly as regards future markets. Incompleteness produces externalities that distort market allocation. A sound policy should seek to nplete the markets as far as possible by defining property rights, or introducing financial instruments such as Arrow securities or negotiable permits. We know from economic theory that this process of completion of markets has intrinsic limits. In addition, the definition of property rights on public goods is not always easy or opportune.

The environmental condition of sustainability

The available empirical evidence suggests that the *current* process of globalization is environmentally unsustainable also in the long run, unless we introduce new institutions and policies able to govern it. The principal responsibility of making the global process of economic growth consistent with sustainability requirements lies with industrialized countries which use great part of the world natural resources and are the principal polluters of the biosphere. Unfortunately, the neoliberal ideas have been recently evoked in most developed countries in order to weaken the environmental policies that were not always popular with consumers and entrepreneurs. We believe that this new attitude may give economic advantages, if any, only in the very short period undermining the economic performance in the longer period. In addition, it is necessary to encourage the participation in the process of market integration of those countries and regions that have been excluded from the globalization process to date. For this purpose, the industrialized countries should help the developing countries to introduce environmental policies and to access the environment-friendly technologies first developed by them. This should be done from the very beginning of their economic development: although developing countries pollute less than developed countries, they generally do so at a higher rate per unit of production so that the advocated growth of income would have dangerous consequences on the environment. In any case, the process of deregulation of international and national markets should comply with the environmental and social constraints that buttress the sustainability of world development.

Globalization has increased the mobility of information across countries and this may strengthen the pressure of public opinion in favor of improved environmental quality. In a more competitive market consumers are likely to have more alternatives to polluting products and thus more chances to express their environmental demand. This positive impact of globalization on the environment, however, crucially depends on the actual capacity of globalization to increase competition. If greater market concentration comes together with globalization (as occurs in some sectors), then the opposite might be true and consumers might end up with fewer opportunities to express their preferences. Globalization may thus contribute to a more sustainable development also by enhancing the impact of public opinion pressure on governments and market decisions. Market integration alone, however, may not be sufficient to make the pressure of public opinion more effective in practice, unless genuine democracy and effective market competition are globalized along with trade.

In recent years, the growing optimism about the market capacity to resolve spontaneously the problems of energy scarcity and pollution, has manifestly weakened the policies aimed at promoting energy-saving and the use of renewable sources. In particular, the worsening trend of the sustainability gap in the energy sector discussed in Chapter 4 indicates the urgency of changing the model of production, distribution, and consumption of energy in order to accelerate the convergence towards sustainable development. A crucial priority is to take measures to accelerate the transition towards an alternative energy model. We argued that in this model should be based on energy-saving, on incentives to the adoption of renewable sources meant to internalize their external economies, and on the complementary use of hydrogen to stock the energy produced with renewable sources.

Global health

As we have seen in Chapter 5, crucial socio-economic determinants of health are poverty, inequality, social and environmental capital. In principle, any policy that reduces the poverty and the inequality of a population and invests in its social and environmental capital improves its health and life quality contributing to the sustainability of economic development.

The traditional policies aiming at improving population health by addressing its socio-economic factors have so far focused on poverty and its manifestations (unhealthy housing, low education, limited access to medical care, and so on). These policies are no doubt very important and should continue to be pursued with rekindled energy. Besides these policies, however, also those promoting less income inequality would give an important contribution to the average health of the population. As argued in Chapter 5, there are theoretical and empirical reasons to believe that health depends not only on the composition effect of magnitudes referring to isolated individuals, but also on the quality of social interaction among heterogeneous agents. The welfarist policies pursued in the 1950s and 1960s succeeded to some extent in investing in social capital in many countries. In principle, globalization is fully consistent with these policies, but it may raise specific obstacles to their implementation. Since the welfarist policies may increase the cost of labor, investment and production may shift to the countries where the cost of labor is the lowest, thus triggering a sort of race to the bottom in the labor markets, particularly when competition is not sheltered by the use of superior technology. Globalization, therefore, can make welfare state policies more difficult to implement. The factor mobility that characterizes globalization imposes constraints on the instruments that countries may use for redistribution, such as progressive taxation and health security systems. In a globalized world, progressive taxation on capital and labor income is more likely to cause an outflow of capital and the emigration of high-income earners towards countries having lower tax rates. The same may apply in the case of health policies that aim to promote equality in the access to health services.

The higher factor mobility underlying globalization may also hinder other government interventions that promote health like, in particular, some of the health-oriented environmental policies. In fact the "displacement hypothesis" can prevent governments from implementing this sort of environmental policies as their effects on production costs might lead some firms to move abroad to avoid the consequent reduction in the national production and employment levels.

While factor mobility and financial integration tend to reduce the scope of state interventions that promote health, other aspects of globalization make such interventions more strictly needed. Thus, the existence of global environmental problems should induce developed countries to support the introduction of environmental policies and less polluting technologies in developing countries not only for ethical and humanitarian reasons, but also in their own interest. Otherwise, the rising pollution of the South might compromise also the environmental efforts of the North and damage the health of the Northern inhabitants. Similarly, the existing differences in health between countries and their increasing health interdependence call for a more rapid transmission of the new health care technologies from the North to the South of the world and this can contribute to reduce both health and income inequality across countries. The transmission of health care technologies to the South, therefore, should come along with redistribution policies that guarantee equal access to such technologies for people that equally need them, independently of their income level.

Finally, policy interventions capable of curbing short-termism in favor of the consolidation and diffusion of a longer-term horizon would improve global health and the sustainability of the process of globalization. These health policies can be interpreted as an investment that can contribute to reduce other expenditures in the longer run by reducing poverty and thus also future health expenditures for the poor. As any other form of investment, however, health policies take time to produce their returns. Therefore, while the prevailing short-termism determines a further cut in health expenditures, a less myopic perspective would encourage a different path. In this perspective it would be particularly advisable to pursue internationally coordinated policies that exploit the potentialities of globalization (in particular, the diffusion of knowledge and human capital) to fight the diffusion of global diseases and negative health factors such as poverty and inequality. This consideration applies not only to health policies strictly speaking, but also to any policy that can indirectly promote or preserve good health conditions, like environmental policies. These policies, in fact, often involve high costs in the present, but produce considerable benefits in the longer run, sometimes even well beyond the life horizon of the generation that bears the cost. The prevalence of short-termism hinders, therefore, the adoption of environmental friendly measures, while the global nature of many current environmental problems calls for internationally coordinated policies to solve them.

In conclusion, the deep link between psychological, physiological and economic short-termism stressed above suggests a further strategy of investment in health that is generally neglected in the literature. Whatever intervention may react to the growing short-termism, accelerated by the recent process of globalization, will reduce stress, improve health, and corroborate the sustainability of development.

New regulation rules

Market failures are currently brought about not only by the excesses of unjustified regulation of local markets but also by a deficit of direct regulation of global markets in their real, financial and virtual aspects. They are sometimes also nurtured by the process of deregulation of markets, whenever it undermines the social and environmental standards of international trade. The analysis developed in this book suggests that the way out may be found in two different, but mutually consistent, directions. First, while unjustified regulation of local markets should continue to be relaxed, the deficit of regulation of global markets should be countered through multilateral agreements and independent supranational agencies characterized by transparency, accountability, and active democratic participation of member countries and stakeholders.

Therefore, the architecture of the system of international organizations having the responsibility of regulating global markets should be redesigned by increasing their power of intervention as well as the active participation of all member countries to the decision process. This requires a radical reform of the existing organizations. In particular a radical reform of the WTO is quite urgent to avoid a rejection crisis that would undermine the continuation of the process of globalization. This reform should aim at activating the participation of member countries, including developing countries, granting at the same time defense rights to the subjects under accusation and the other stakeholders.

The architecture of institutions meant to regulate the markets should be completed by establishing a restricted number of new supranational authorities with a well-defined jurisdiction. These agencies should be designed in such a way as to minimize at the same time both market and regulation failures, limiting the interventions to the enforcement of a minimal set of rules capable of assuring acceptable worldwide standards. In the knowledge-based economy spread by the process of "new globalization" an important contribution in the direction of this very difficult task may come from the systematic gathering, processing, and dissemination of relevant knowledge. In particular, a supranational agency for the protection of the environment could help to ensure sustainability within a common, and level, playing field by promoting and managing international agreements on global problems that require "command and control" instruments on the equitable exploitation of global commons, on North-South swaps, on the harmonization of green taxation, setting up and regulating the new markets for environmental permits and derivatives. This agency should also gather and elaborate in-depth knowledge on the health of the biosphere. This would facilitate the diffusion of the relevant information through market mechanisms (environmental certification, eco-labels, environmental reporting, and so on), through the transfer of technology and know-how, and through education of producers and final users of goods and services.

The regulation *of markets* by means of local and global public institutions, though necessary for ensuring their smooth functioning and for drawing the best from them, is insufficient and should be complemented by regulation *through the markets* themselves. The more the markets approach the textbook model of perfect competition, the more the ultimate power in directing economic decisions depends on the preferences and values of the final users of goods and services (consumers, savers, and investors). Though the concern for ethical values and long-term goals is insufficient now as it was in the past, there are no solid reasons to believe that it cannot be rekindled. What has been actually observed in the last few decades was a radical change in the prevailing attitude on the most efficient means for pursuing ethical values and long-term goals. Disillusionment with political parties, trade unions and public institutions has led to a breakdown of confidence in them, while at the same time there has been an impressive growth of voluntary service, humanitarian foundations and associations, environmental and social NGOs, non-profit companies, and so on. Even in the private sector, a series of trends has emerged that tends to strengthen the awareness of the crucial importance of ethical values and long-term goals. The persistent concern of people for ethical values and long-term goals would open the door to a systematic development of regulation of the markets *through the markets*. The final users of goods and services should be encouraged to exert their alleged sovereignty in the right direction by choosing eco-friendly goods and services, by putting them in the position of knowing the ethical and environmental implications of goods, services, and productive processes (through reporting, certification, eco-labeling, etc.). This may produce a virtuous circle between the effort of the producer for improving the environmental quality of their products, services and processes – publicized through certification, disclosure and eco-labeling – and the growing demand of customers stimulated by the publicized ecological improvements of a certain firm. This promising perspective may be successfully pursued only if the international negotiations and regulatory institutions agree that environmental standards, like other ethical standards, are not to be interpreted as unjustified non-tariff barriers to trade but as necessary conditions for the sustainability of world development.

Corporate sustainability and CSR

In this book we have emphasized that, in order to ensure a sustainable pace of world development we have to focus not only on its macroeconomic, but also its microeconomic conditions. In particular, we argued that the CSR initiatives may help to corroborate the social responsibility of the firms and therefore also their sustainability. Critics underlined that their diffusion is in danger of becoming little more than a vogue which is unable to change the substance of things. The most skeptical observers fear that its role may degenerate into a mere marketing tool with scarce authentic content. If such skepticism were justified, it would undermine the effectiveness of the CSR initiatives as an instrument of control and incentive of ethical behavior. We must therefore prevent the adoption of self-regulation rules from becoming purely ritual or promotional. This may be obtained, first of all, by means of ethical certification, i.e. detailed control of the truthfulness, completeness and reliability of information on the part of specialized agencies. The ethical certification SA 8000 issued by a specialized American agency is beginning to spread to Europe. The EU is appraising the establishment of its own ethical certification procedure to complete the EMAS environmental quality certification. This step may be very effective but it is not always sufficient, as recent scandals have shown with regard to the reliability of some economic and financial balance sheets, such as that of Enron, which had been unduly certified.

The decisive condition for reliability of all types of self-regulation and reporting, including environmental and social reporting, is the pro-active and participatory control on the part of stakeholders. The CSR initiatives are more useful if they are critically analyzed and compared by those who are interested in the company's business: customers, suppliers, employees, residents in the areas where the company works, both directly, and indirectly through their elective or associative representatives. In particular, a critical appraisal of the information offered in the CSR reports must become a criterion for choosing products and services, investments, working opportunities of one firm rather than another, thus conditioning corporate performance in a very concrete, profitable fashion. A virtuous circle can thus be triggered by CSR initiatives, with progressive sensitization of stakeholders and increasing corporate commitment. It is a learning process in which all the interlocutors must find the most constructive and effective interaction modes and forms. Firms must become glasshouses, opening themselves up to the critical view of stakeholders so as to ensure full transparency and responsible behavior.

Stakeholders must develop constructive and participatory forms of control and incentives, yet carefully avoiding any type of 'pitch invasion' or inappropriate interference, using traditional methods of conflictual opposition only as *extrema ratio* in cases of proven corporate reluctance to take some of their crucial interests into account. The persistence of such methods would be counterproductive as it could force firms, even those which are willing to change, to turn in on themselves.

This does not mean that regulation by law to ensure proper corporate behavior may be replaced by self-regulation. This illusion, or pretext, has led to a weakening of regulation by law in industrialized countries. As a matter of fact, regulation by law has failed to keep pace with increasingly rapid market developments, especially as regards global-ization which unsettles national legal systems, and ICTs that have introduced new commercial channels which are almost completely free of control. This partially stemmed from intrinsic difficulties in defining and sanctioning economic crimes; however, the widespread revival of *laissez-faire* in recent years undoubtedly emerged from an excessive trust in the ability of markets to self-regulate themselves. Moreover, pre-existing regulations have at times been repealed as they were deemed superseded, even when this was not the case. Conversely, CSR self-regulation should be considered not substitutive but complementary to legal regulations. Both regulatory systems generate incentives and disincentives, albeit of a different nature. Moreover the effective-ness of legal regulations presupposes a social consensus that may be progressively generated by the virtuous circle between corporate self-regulation and active *stakeholder* control. It is therefore necessary to set up a strategy of parallel and complementary reinforcement of CSR-oriented legal regulation and self-regulation.

3 The liberal dilemma

The general policy implications underlined in the preceding section are not much more than general guidelines. Can we rely on their adoption by the existing political authorities? We cannot be particularly optimistic on this issue since many countries and powerful pressure groups have vested interests in the status quo or try actively to change it in their favor, and thus in a direction that rarely coincides with the guidelines here advocated. In order to "filter" the positive potentialities of globalization from its disruptive "side effects", we have first of all to find the right balance between the main sources of economic power in order to mini-mize the economic failures originating from their weaknesses and mis-behavior. This issue raises a dilemma. We defined as development the process of expansion of economic freedom. Globalization may contribute to development in this sense only by choosing a policy strategy con-sistent with individual freedom. At first sight this strategy should coincide with "*laissez-faire*" as any intervention of the state seems to interfere with free initiative, i.e. the exercise of individual freedom. The latter, however, may be limited not only by the state but also from other individuals and private organizations. In order to avoid these restrictions to individual liberty it seems convenient to resort to the state, notwithstanding all the risks of substituting the public restrictions of individual liberty for the private restrictions. This is what we call the "liberal dilemma".

Classical liberalism was aware from the very beginning that markets have limits that would involve serious restrictions in individual liberty and that these limits require some sort of public intervention. The obvious case is that of personal security and defense of private property that require the administration of justice, a police and a defense apparatus. Also education was considered by some liberal thinker a task that should not be left to the market because a good basic instruction for every one is fundamental to assure their effective freedom of choice. Analogously, health was considered as a precondition for the exercise of freedom, and so on (see Chapter 8). The trouble is that the liberal dilemma has been, and still is, generally conceptualized in simple binary terms, as a zero-sum game between the state and the market. In this view, if a certain activity, say education, is subtracted to the market, the decision power on this matter is transferred to the state, and there is no guarantee that the discretionary power of public authorities will be exercised for the public good, and vice versa. In order to define the correct demarcation between the economic power attributed to the market and that attributed to the state we should evaluate the costs and benefits of each possible allocation of economic power. The result is likely to be quite different in different countries and different circumstances.

In this book we have interpreted economic globalization as a process of extension and deepening of markets at the world level. In particular, in the parallel history of economic markets and of liberal ideas we have detected an alternation between two policy paradigms (Chapter 8). A paradigm in favor of the systematic intervention of the state in the economy was typically followed by a policy paradigm committed to transferring economic power, or substantial portions of it, back to the market, and vice versa. The rationale for this alternation is quite straightforward. A paradigm in favor of a systematic intervention on the part of the state is based on its alleged superior performance in the areas of intervention for some reason believed to be structural. Of course this orientation of economic policy is bound to increase the production of "state failures", i.e. economic failures originating in the abuse or mismanagement of public power. This is due to arouse, sooner or later, a growing reaction against public intervention calling for a transfer of economic power in the hands of private initiative. Also the birth of economic liberalism and its subsequent evolution may be seen in this perspective. David Hume, the Physiocrats and Adam Smith reacted to the then prevailing "mercantilism" that justified protectionism and systematic state intervention over the economy. They advocated restraint of public intervention and shift of power to free initiative. The progressive success of liberal ideas in the 19th century and the parallel development of markets did not stop, however, the alternation of policy paradigms, even within liberalism itself. The growing impact of markets on economic decisions showed that even the latter have limits and may originate economic failures that were eventually called "market failures". As we have seen in Chapter 8, liberal thinkers such as John Stuart Mill, Jevons and Marshall started to recognize the crucial importance of this source of economic failures. The reaction against simplistic *"laissez-faire"* coalesced in the first decades of the 20th century in what we have called "updated liberalism". This new paradigm became dominant since the late 1930s when the extraordinary size and extension of economic failures brought about by the Great Crisis, were interpreted by most observers as a consequence of market failures and convinced most people that a systematic regulation of the markets is unavoidable.

This pro-regulation paradigm was dominant until the early 1970s when the heavy regulation failures observed in the late 1960s and 1970s nurtured a new reaction against the excessive and distorted interventions of the state spreading a policy paradigm founded on privatization and deregulation: what has been often called the neoliberal paradigm. Since the 1990s a new reaction against market failures emerged in consequence of financial crises in Mexico, Far East Asia, Argentina, and other countries, as well as of the stock exchange collapse in 2001 and the ensuing outbreak of particularly serious corporate scandals. This reaction may lead to a new shift towards a policy paradigm more prone to regulating markets. Notwithstanding the official endorsement of the necessity of further globalization on the part of governments and international organizations, the new awareness of the limits to markets spreading in the public opinion is taken by many governments and firms as a pretext to raise new obstacles to free trade that in most cases would not solve the problems but would just aggravate them.

The alternation of policy paradigms described above is the consequence of a simplistic, unilateral and misleading vision of the main sources of economic power that are also the main sources of economic failures. One of the crucial shortcomings of both basic paradigms that alternated within the liberal tradition is their binary nature that gives the impression that power subtracted to the state is necessarily given to the market and vice versa. On the contrary, we have to consider explicitly a third fundamental source of economic power that is also, inevitably, a crucial source of economic failures: the firms.[138] They are generally considered as part of the market but this view is highly misleading since the exercise of corporate power is based upon different foundations.

While the market operates according to an impersonal and decentralized principle of authority, the firm operates according to a centralized and hierarchical principle of authority. The visible hands of the firms (mainly the CEO, the top management and the board of directors) should not be confused with the invisible hand of the market. This crucial difference has been clarified since the path-breaking article by Coase (1937) who observed that "the distinguishing mark of the firm is the supersession of the price mechanism" (Coase, 1937, p.388), i.e. of the market principle of coordination of exchanges. The firms coordinate the economic activity that goes on within their reach and interact strategically with both the market and the state in their own interest. It can be contended that to survive and prosper a firm has to comply with market constraints. This is certainly true but market pressures and desiderata have to be interpreted and this leaves a concrete and quite large discretionary power to the firms' vertices. In particular, as we have emphasized in Chapter 7, firms may interpret the market constraints within a short or long time horizon and this makes a huge difference.

We may observe, moreover, that also the state has to take into account market constraints. The discretionary power of public authorities is strongly limited by their monetary receipts. In addition, the extent and structure of both public income and expenditure must take account of market desiderata since a persisting and systematic conflict with them would seriously jeopardize re-election. Both the firms and public authorities do not lose, however, a genuine discretionary power that is exercised according to bureaucratic, i.e. centralized and hierarchical, guidelines. A few experts contend that firms should mould their bureaucratic organization in such a way to imitate the market. This led to more decentralized decisions and evaluation of performance but did not eliminate the gap between market and corporate decision-making. Also the state tried to imitate the market organizational principles, decentralizing its decision process. In both cases, however, there is an intrinsic boundary that limits the imitation of the market inside a public or private organization. In the case of a firm or a public authority, also the subject in charge of evaluating the performance of individuals that determines their ultimate success or failure is visible: the constituency in the case of a public authority and shareholders (or stakeholders in the alternative view that we have discussed in Chapter 7) in the case of the firm. This underlines also the crucial difference between the firms and public authorities. In the first case the source of power is the electorate at large while in the second case it is a small section of it that comprises the much more limited subset of stakeholders (or, in the prevailing view, the subset of shareholders). This is also what determines the gap between public and private economic interest. The gap is significantly reduced if we adopt a system of corporate governance based on the empowerment of all the stakeholders but it is not altogether eliminated.

Having ascertained that the firms are an agent of economic power different from both the state and the market, we may wonder whether they are a source of economic failures comparable to the other two sources. The answer is positive. We have seen in Chapter 7 how difficult is to avoid conflicts of interest between management, board of directors, shareholders and other stakeholders. These conflicts distort the allocation of resources within the firm jeopardizing its sustainability. Moreover, bigger firms that can affect market prices are in the position of manipulating the market for their own sake. Finally, big firms as well as official or unofficial coalitions of firms may lobby with the government to obtain favorable decisions. The problem is aggravated by the increasing short-termism of firms enhanced by financial deepening and globalization (Chapter 6).

We should thus evaluate the existing policy paradigms in the light of the more complex threefold model sketched above that represents and connects the three main sources of economic power and failures (see

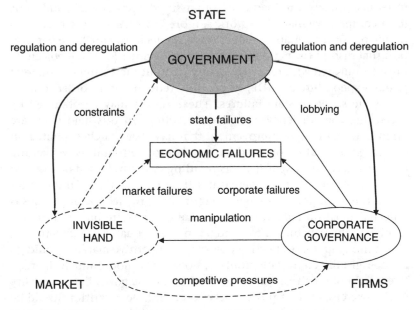

Figure 9.1   The three sources of economic failures

Figure 9.1). In this vision the zero-sum power game should be conceived between three subjects so that a reduction of state power does not imply more power to the market and more freedom for economic agents, and vice versa. In this book we had the occasion of criticizing the neoliberal paradigm that dominated, and still dominates, since the late 1970s. In the light of the conceptual framework suggested in this book we may further underline that, contrary to the declared intentions, the alleged systematic policy of deregulation and privatization often did not shift economic power from the state to the market but rather to the firms, or rather only to some of them having links of interest or friendship with powerful exponents of the government. As underlined by many observers, "crony capitalism" is not at all the hallmark of developing countries but is a pest common also in the most advanced countries (see, e.g., Bhagwati, 2004). Finally, we have to emphasize that the new liberal policies did not succeed in reducing the size of the state but, in the best cases, only in slowing down its growth.

The shortcomings of neoliberalism, however, should not lead us to a simple shift back to the preceding policy paradigm inspired by updated liberalism. We have to recover a few basic ideas from it without falling back in the utopia, or practice, of the "big government". The idea underlying the welfare state was a sound one. Not only it contributed to reduce poverty and inequality but assured a few crucial conditions for a competitive market to work: a more fair access to the basic economic opportunities and a reduction of the feelings of relative deprivation that disrupt trust and social relations (Chapter 5). These objectives must be pursued with renewed energy without increasing the share of public expenditure on GDP, or possibly reducing it, in order to minimize the scope of state failures. These results may be obtained by increasing the efficiency of collective action. In this field there are often huge margins of improvement that have been rarely exploited. In any case the solution of the dilemma cannot be found by weakening the social security system. The dismantling of the welfare state inspired by the neoliberal point of view is not the right solution. On the other hand, the main policy change brought about by neoliberal policies is reflected not in a reduction of the size of the state but in a radical change in the structure of the budget in a less equalitarian direction.

Summing up, more effective power to competitive markets would go in the right direction. The problem, however, is not so much the relative weight of the three main sources of economic power but the quality of the exercise of their power. Between the three polarities should be established a system of check and balances avoiding collusion and prevarication between them. This may be obtained by enhancing market competition and avoiding collusion between firms and public authorities. State failures may be avoided by assuring corporate democracy that presupposes the transparency of the firm and the active participation of citizens to the decision process. Democratic elections are a necessary but not sufficient condition. Analogously, the firms' failures may be avoided by assuring the transparency and participation of stakeholders (see Chapter 7).

A serious analysis of what we have here called the liberal dilemma would require another book. We end this one by observing that we may exploit the opportunities offered by globalization for expanding the economic liberty of people around the world only by strengthening effective democracy, not only political democracy but also corporate democracy.

Notes

1   Not by chance the House of Lords set up an official inquiry to clarify the meaning of this elusive concept (House of Lords, 2002).

2   The process of globalization that occurred in the last two centuries has its ultimate roots in the development of trade and mercantile relations in the classical times and their resumption and further development in Communal Europe in the Middle Age. Milestones of its further progress in the Modern Age have been the explorations of the 16th and 17th centuries, which unified the world in terms of physical accessibility, and, above all, the industrial revolution at the end of the 18th century which expanded the scope of market exchanges.

3   The Corn Laws introduced import tariffs aiming to protect the British agriculture against competition from less expensive corn imports. They were introduced in 1815 and repealed in 1846 after a long campaign by liberal exponents.

4   The Bretton Woods system started disintegrating at the end of the '60s as a result of differentiated inflationary pressures in industrialized countries. It collapsed after the suspension of the convertibility of the dollar by President Nixon in 1971. A transition period lasting about 10 years followed until a new regulation system of international markets emerged.

5   Some authors call "Washington Consensus" the system of regulation of the world economy which has emerged since the early 1980s. Bloom *et al.* (2001b) maintain that this term was originally coined by Williamson (1999) to designate the policy rules agreed by the international organizations sitting in Washington and by the American Treasury.

6   We define development as the progressive expansion of individual freedom. This process depends not only on economic indices, above all per capita income, but also on health as well as on social and cultural indices (see Sen, 1999). In this book we will focus almost exclusively on income per capita and indexes of health.

7   This point was emphasized by Adam Smith and other founding fathers of "classical" liberalism (see Chapter 8).

8   Social and political instability is only one possible way in which inequality may affect economic growth. See Barro (2000) for a discussion of other theoretical effects of inequality on economic growth.

9   The consensus on the growth effects of globalization is large but not unanimous. Rodriguez and Rodrik (2000), for instance, argue that the results of a positive link between trade liberalization and growth are systematically biased by the use of inappropriate indicators of trade policy.

10   The introduction of free exchange areas, such as the EEC (European Economic Community, established in 1958), the Mercosur (Southern Common Market, 1991), the NAFTA (North American Free Trade Agreement, 1994), or the COMESA (Common Market for East and Southern Africa, 1994), has

been motivated by the attempt at seeking the above mentioned economic advantages which have been to some extent realized in practice.

11 Exchange rates, for instance, are likely to affect inequality between countries more than inequality within them.

12 Casual observation supports this conclusion: the Baltic countries, for instance, used to have income levels similar to Denmark before the adoption of inward-oriented policies by their governments after World War II. On the other hand, globalization is likely to have reduced the gap between outward-oriented countries, in particular between OECD countries after World War II (cf. Lindert and Williamson, 2003). The two empirical findings are not in contradiction since post-war trade liberalization has occurred mainly intra-OECD rather than between the OECD and the other countries.

13 The data suggest, in addition, that the increase in between-countries inequality depends only weakly on the process of globalization, at any rate in the last century, while it is likely to depend more on other aspects of the expansion of industrial capitalism. Otherwise, we could not explain why inequality between countries has increased so much in the period of de-globalization (1915–1945). A plausible explanation is that the more inward-oriented and conflicting attitude of industrialized countries raised obstacles to the beneficial transmission of information and technology between countries.

14 According to the classification of inequality measures suggested by Wade (2001), the increase in inequality is quite evident from all the most widespread measures used excluding those which weight countries with their population and simultaneously measure incomes in terms of purchasing power parity. There are strong arguments, however, in favor of the latter measure. Even in this case, sophisticated statistical analysis detects a trend towards a progressive increase in inequality between 1988 and 1992 (see Milanovic, 2002; Dikhanov and Ward, 2001). For the time being, the period covered by this methodology is too short to allow a generalization of these results to a longer period.

15 In addition this side effect is sometimes considered as potentially benign in itself: "the consequences of increased inequality, in any event, might be paradoxically benign, rather than malign" (Bhagwati, 2004, p.66).

16 An individual is defined as poor when her income is inferior to $2 a day, and extremely poor if her income does not exceed $1 a day, expressed in purchasing power parity. The data and the definitions used here come from the WB. The comparison of different ways of measuring poverty raises delicate methodological problems (see, e.g., Brandolini, 2002) that are discussed in more details in Chapter 2.

17 Indices of this nature have been proposed lately. They are, however, controversial and available only for the most recent years (an example is the *Environmental Sustainability Index* published by the *World Economic Forum*). They thus do not allow for the identification of significant medium/long-term trends.

18 Given the non-linearity of the interaction between environmental and economic variables, there may be a threshold above which irreversible destabilizing processes may be set off (see Daily and Ehrlich, 1992).

19 For a broader analysis of this issue see Chapter 3.

20 We must point out, however, that even in this period the speed of reduction in poverty and inequality was insufficient to comply with ethical standards and safeguard "social stability".

21 On the prerequisites of economic causality, see, e.g., Vercelli (1991, 1992), and the literature there cited.

22 The reader who is not familiar with the welfare economic theorems can easily find the correspondent proofs in any microeconomic text book (see, e.g., Varian, 1996).

23 The structural nature of recent financial instability is stressed, e.g., in Vercelli (2000).

24 The stakeholders are all the subjects directly interested in the activity of a corporation. They include shareholders as well as employees, clients, suppliers and all those who live in the areas where the corporation is active (see Chapter 7).

25 Some of the early critiques are summarized in Blaug (1968). See also Garegnani (1960).

26 See Vercelli (1991) for a discussion of the different concepts of instability.

27 A well-known example is the following. Let us assume that police captures two suspect individuals who have effectively stealed goods which however are not in their hand, so that there is no objective proof of their guilt. In this example the best individual strategy is to confess to obtain immunity; if both confess, however, they go to jail. If they act in a co-operative way, on the contrary, the best strategy is not to confess so that both are condemned to a shorter period of jail.

28 See Vercelli (1997, 1998a) and Basili and Vercelli (1998).

29 See, for instance, Temple (1999). See also O'Rourke (2001) for a survey of the studies on the link between openness and intranational inequality.

30 Although their observation period stops earlier (1992), the estimates of Bourguignon and Morisson (2002) are pretty similar to those of Chen and Ravallion (2004) (see retro Chapter 1 and Figures 1.3 and 1.4).

31 See, for instance, Panayotou (2000); Borghesi (2001); Dasgupta *et al.* (2002); Dinda (2004); Brock and Taylor (2006) for some critical surveys of the literature on this topic.

32 See Table 1 in Borghesi (2001) for a comparison of the results that emerge in different studies on single environmental indicators.

33 Ansuategi and Escapa (2002) point out that the negative impact of GHGs like CO_2 is not only international but also intergenerational. The possibility of transferring the negative impact of pollution to future generations, therefore, may have been another important factor that prevented the implementation of emissions abatement measures in the past.

34 We are here referring to the estimates of the "high scenario" described by the IPCC (2007), "low scenario" forecasts being about the half.

35 More than 60% of the world's proven oil reserves is concentrated in only five countries (Saudi Arabia, the United Arab Emirates, Iraq, Kuwait and Iran). The remaining percentage is mainly concentrated in areas of high tension and political instability such as the west coast of Africa, Libya, Algeria, Russia and the post-Soviet republics of the Caspian Sea.

Similarly, about 55% of global gas reserves is currently located in just three countries (Russia, Iran and Qatar). This concentration in a few areas causes some world regions (Europe, North America and Asia) to rely heavily on gas imports to meet their energy demand. In particular, by 2030 the EU is expected to depend on imports for 80% of its gas needs (IEA, 2004).

36   Using the terminology adopted by British Petroleum (2007), the term "proven reserves" indicates those quantities that, on the basis of the geological and engineering information available, can be recovered in the future with reasonable certainty from the known reserves under existing economic and operating conditions.

37   The expected lifespan T is calculated by British Petroleum as the ratio between the remaining proven reserves at the end of the year and that year's output, assuming that output will continue at the same level in the future.

38   Similarly, the observation that the productive capacity of the North Sea could have reached its upper limit led OPEC to cut its own production by about 1.7 million barrels a day in the period 1999–2000. Together with the embargo on Iraq, this increased the price from 15 to over 34 dollars a barrel. The relationship between the OPEC cartel and the non-OPEC countries (the so-called "cartel-fringe" relationship) has been the object of numerous theoretical models that analyze the OPEC's production decisions in relation to those of its competitors and the consequent changes in the leadership of the productive market (see for example Ulph and Folie, 1980; Geroski *et al.*, 1987).

39   For an analysis of the causality links between energy consumption and income growth see, for instance, Cleveland *et al.* (2000) and Soytas and Sari (2003).

40   These observations point out a crucial weakness of the projections based on the lifespan of fossil fuels (see Table 4.1 and the correspondent footnote). About one third of the fuel contained in oil (or gas) fields is not recoverable at a reasonable cost with known technologies. Even before this limit, the increase in the cost of extraction could be sufficient to stop the exploitation of the field.

41   Some of these non-conventional oil sources have already become much more competitive in recent years and they might play a central role in the future since they are largely available also outside the OPEC area, which may contribute to reduce the vulnerability of the current geopolitical situation. Thus, for instance, large reserves of oil sands are concentrated in the Canadian region of Alberta whose production is expected to triple in the period 2003–2012 (IEA, 2004).

42   Coal generates more CO_2 emissions per unit of consumption than oil and than natural gas. Moreover, it also contributes to other pollutants, such as SO_2 and N_2O (that cause acid rains), particulates and mercury.

43   In the case of the US energy market, for instance, Koplow (1993) estimated that nuclear and fossil fuels received 88.5% of total energy subsidies, whereas only 5.4% of the whole subsidy policy was devoted to emerging renewables (non-ethanol biomass, solar, wind, geothermal etc.) and to increasing demand efficiency.

44 See, IPCC (2001) for an exhaustive classification of the numerous GHGs, their lifetime and their global warming potential expressed in terms of CO_2 emissions equivalent (henceforth $GtCO_2$.e).

45 Similar results apply if we use the forecasts of the International Energy Agency (IEA, 2006).

46 Notice that if we exclude biomass, which is often used in an unsustainable way, the other renewable sources (i.e. hydropower, solar, geothermal, wind, tidal and wave energy) will account for only around 4% of global energy demand in 2030 (IEA, 2004).

47 The emissions abatement requirement would actually be even more demanding if one takes into account the increase in the other GHGs (different from CO_2) that occurred since 1990.

48 As Deaton (2004, p.6) observed, "health is most notable by its absence from even critical discussion of globalization in the economics literature".

49 Differently from a "proper" KC, Figure 5.1 measures time rather than per capita income on the horizontal axis. Given the continuous growth at the global level of per capita income that have been observed in the last decades, however, one can consider time as a reasonable proxy for the world average per capita income.

50 See Tarlov and St. Peter (2000).

51 The same pattern was followed by developing countries with a variable lag related to their degree of economic development. As outlined by Deaton (2004, p.11), "Africa is now the only continent in which the majority of deaths are from infectious diseases, rather than from heart diseases and cancer".

52 According to historical epidemiological studies a better nutrition determined most of health gain since 1700. This trend accelerated with economic growth since the second part of the 19th century (see Fogel, 1986).

53 In this case, of course, causality is preventive or inhibitory.

54 See arrows 1, 2 and 3 in Figure 5.2. The signs along the arrows in the block-diagram indicate the prevailing sign of the correlation between the variables examined.

55 The recent phase of globalization has also enhanced the spread of medical knowledge through the Worldwide Web. Internet, in fact, allows on-line access to specialized journals and web sites that have updated information on the most recent developments in health research.

56 The regression line in the diagram describes how a logarithmic curve fits the data.

57 Regressing life expectancy on per capita GNP and on the income share going to the least well off 70% of the population, Wilkinson (1992) finds that the former variable explains less than 10% of the variance of life expectancy, while the latter accounts for most of the variance. Moreover, the correlation coefficient between life expectancy and the income share to people below the 7th decile of the population is basically unchanged when controlling for per capita GNP, shifting from 0.86 to 0.90 with p-value below 0.001 in both cases.

58 Kaplan *et al.* (1996) found that the correlation coefficient between the age-adjusted mortality rates and the income proportion that goes to the

least well off 50% of the population is high and basically unchanged when median income is also taken into account among the explanatory variables, shifting from 0.62 to 0.59 with $p < 0.001$ in both cases. On the contrary, the correlation coefficient between total mortality and median income is much lower and falls drastically from 0.28 ($p < 0.05$) to 0.06 ($p > 0.05$) when adjusted for income inequality.

59 Lynch *et al.* (2000), for instance, observed that higher inequality has been related to lower mortality rates in Britain during the period 1962–1990. On these issues see section 3 in this chapter.

60 Deaton (2002) argues that this psychological mechanism plays a crucial role in causing stress to the agents and sets up a model assuming that each individual's stress is proportional to the total amount of income that goes to richer people in the community.

61 For example, the great French sociologist Durkheim documented more than one century ago in his classical work on suicide the crucial importance of the sudden change in social status on the health of individuals (Durkheim, 1897).

62 Wilkinson (2002) claims that the psycho-social factors are "the most important etiological factors". The gradual emergence of the RIH in the last 30 years or so is reconstructed in the introduction to Kawachi *et al.* (1999).

63 See Kawachi *et al.* (1997) for a detailed description of these indicators. The authors take also poverty into account since the latter variable can be a potential confounder in the relationship between social capital and mortality, being related to both these variables. All the coefficients presented in this study, however, were basically unchanged when adjusted for poverty.

64 Hostility rates were based on the scores obtained through a telephone poll conducted on about 200 persons residing in each of the ten US cities taken into account.

65 See Uslaner (2001, p.29, footnote 22) for a description of how the latter variable is constructed from the data set of the World Values Study.

66 As Deaton (2002) points out, however, the link between inequality and crime is an object of debate. In principle, high inequality may coexist with little crime since very rich individuals may afford defensive expenditures to protect themselves against potential crimes (Wittenberg, 2000). However, these sorts of repressive measures are rarely sufficient to thwart the crime arising from social tension, while they may end up nurturing it even further.

67 For example, Wilkinson (2002, p.14) remarks that "the United States, although it is richer and spends more on medical care than any other country, has poorer health than almost all western European countries and comes 22nd in the international league tables of life expectancy. On the other hand, countries such as Greece, despite having just under half the level of income per head, have substantially higher life expectancy than the United States. More egalitarian countries such as Japan, Norway and Sweden have among the best health in the developed world".

68 Much of the relevant research has been collected in one volume (Kawachi *et al.*, 1999).

69   The inference of mistaken assertions about individual-level relationships from aggregate data is often called in this literature "ecological fallacy".

70   These three forms of pollution are not the only ways in which environmental degradation influences a population's health status. Consider, for example, noise pollution which affects many big cities even during the night, making it increasingly difficult for people to sleep and thus reducing workers' concentration and productivity. Here we consider only three forms of pollution – those regarding air, water and food, i.e. the channels through which human health is most directly exposed to environmental risks.

71   WHO (1997) estimates that atmospheric pollution is also directly responsible for 2% of cases of cancer and that the highest number of deaths by tumour involve the respiratory tract (trachea, bronchial tube, and lungs).

72   Atmospheric pollution also tends to increase the incidence of acute respiratory infections such as pneumonia which is today the main cause of infant death worldwide (WHO, 1997).

73   It has been estimated (WHO, 1997) that 88% of deaths due to intestinal diseases involve children under 15 years of age, a much higher incidence than the average number of deaths under 15 years of age due to other diseases (30%).

74   See, e.g., Conservation Foundation (1992).

75   Thirty years on from the conflict, a recent study carried out in the Bien Hoa area found that 95% of the resident population has extremely high levels of dioxin (sometimes as much as 200 times more than normal values) which causes damage to the liver, birth defects and the appearance of tumors (*The Economist*, 2002b).

76   This may contribute to explain, for example, the high incidence of neonatal tetanus in the poorest areas of the developing countries.

77   Barro and Sala-i-Martin (1995); Bloom and Sachs (1998); Bhargava *et al.* (2001).

78   It should be noted that life expectancy in the rich countries is today around 77 years as against 49 years in the poor countries. This difference can therefore help to explain the large and expanding gap that we find today between the economies of the North and South of the world.

79   As argued by Fogel (1997), the improvement of medical techniques and the increase in the number of calories available to workers have played an important role in supporting growth in Europe in the last two centuries.

80   Besides the three channels described above (investment in physical capital, investment in human capital, and individual productivity), there are other ways in which the health of a population may influence economic growth. For example, a worsening of population health leads to an increase in government spending in the health sector. This can generate high public deficits and an increase in public debt which may cause macroeconomic instability that is likely to be harmful to economic growth in the country.

81   See retro Chapter 3.

82   A strong correlation between these two rates emerged, for example, from the analysis of 148 countries in 1995 carried out by WHO's Commission

on Macroeconomics and Health (WHO, 2001, p.36, Figure 3). In general, this study found that the average number of children increased from two to six as the child survival rate fell from 95% to 75%.

83 See the WHO report (2001, p.37, Figure 4). This study found that the infant mortality rate accounts for 85% of the variation in the population growth rate of a country.

84 The current level of labor mobility, however, is the object of debate. While immigration has increased in some industrialized countries such as in the EU area, some authors (e.g. Sandmo, 2002; Woodward *et al.*, 2001) argue that labor migration is lower in the present phase of globalization than in the previous one (1870–1914), also because developed countries have partly closed their borders to unskilled workers.

85 It is estimated that most of the infectious disease epidemics are of special relevance to Sub-Saharan Africa and Asia that account for the poorest 20% of the world's population (Beaglehole and McMichael, 1999).

86 Lindert and Williamson (2003), for instance, argue that there is no positive correlation between globalization and the use of child labor and that during the last globalization phase (since 1950) the rates of work by children under 15 have been reducing in all member countries of the International Labor Organization.

87 In consequence of the commitments taken in Kyoto on the reduction of CO_2 emissions, the environmental regulations are expected to become much stricter (and the implementation costs much higher) than those adopted by single countries in the past.

88 A few policy implications of the analysis developed in this chapter will be discussed in Chapter 9.

89 We use this expression throughout the paper not in the specific sense of a set of activities directly concerned with the supply of ICT hardware, software, and services, but in the systemic sense of a new organization of the economy as a whole resulting from the systematic application of ICT.

90 Significant exceptions are two books on the "roaring nineties" published by very eminent economists (see Krüger and Solow, 2001; Stiglitz, 2003).

91 As is well-known, the size of networks is characterized by increasing returns. According to Metcalfe law of networks, the economic value of a network is equal to the square of the number of users.

92 This point has been emphasized by Rifkin (2000).

93 See Woodall (2000, p.14), and for a critical point of view Krüger and Solow (2002) and Stiglitz (2003).

94 Though in principle sustainability may be measured (see Vercelli, 1998a), reliable sustainability measures at the world level are still beyond state-of-the-art capabilities.

95 Where this process has been recently strengthened, very promising results have been rapidly obtained: in the eastern European countries in all the fields, in the case of China and most developing countries in the field of water processing (see Vinod, *et al.*, 2000).

96 An example is the incentives offered in the USA by the EPA for the adoption of microchips that switch off automatically when not in use.

97 On this point the analysis made by Keynes in GT (1936, mainly in the celebrated Chapter 12) is still quite up-to-date.

98   The fact that East Asia experienced in the 1990s at the same time the fastest growth rates of GDP, the fastest rate of deforestation, and the highest CO_2 emissions per capita is a case in point (see Vinod, *et al.*, 2000, p.9 and Chapter 4).

99   This fact is emphasized also by many experts (e.g. Rossi, 2003) and is confirmed by insiders such as Soros (1998). See Chapter 7 for a more detailed analysis.

100   As is well-known, the ensuing dispute recently found a controversial compromise solution.

101   A growing literature has recently emerged on the political economy of the international environmental agreements. See, for instance, Haas (2003), Kelleher (2006) and the literature there cited for an analysis of the recent theoretical developments in this field and related applications to major policy debates.

102   The case for the systematic introduction of environmental bonds for controlling environmental risks was first argued by Perrings (1989), while a critical assessment of the literature may be found in Torsello and Vercelli (1998). The basic idea here suggested is that the would-be innovator in certain well-defined areas characterized by high environmental risks which cannot be easily assessed *ex-ante* (such as biotechnology), may be authorized to introduce a new good, say a new transgenic vegetable, only after having paid a sizeable environmental bond which may be recovered (with interest) to the extent that, after a congruous number of years, the feared risks did not materialize. This would slow down the pace of innovation in certain environmentally sensitive areas without stopping it altogether, selecting less dangerous innovations and stimulating further research before the implementation of innovations, while the funds thus accumulated by the environmental authorities managing the scheme could be used for compensating eventual damages, fostering environmental research and realizing environmental projects.

103   As is well-known *stock options* are option rights over the company's shares that may be exercised on maturity.

104   A significant, albeit extreme, example was that of Enron. As explained by Frank Partnoy, professor of commercial law at the University of San Diego in his hearing at the US Senate, "Enron may have been just an energy company when it was created in 1985, but by the end it had become a full-blown OTC derivatives trading firm. Its OTC derivatives-related assets and liabilities increased more than five-fold during 2000 alone" (Partnoy, 2002). On the Enron case, see also Salter (2002).

105   This position has been confirmed on many occasions by courts. In 1919 the sentence Dodge vs. Ford Motor Co. of the Michigan Supreme Court maintained that Ford had to build automobiles in the exclusive interest of its shareholders, without letting itself be "distracted" by concerns for the interests of others, including consumers. Indeed, the sentence declared that the corporation exists for the benefit of the shareholders; therefore all the powers of those who manage it should be used for this purpose (see Rossi, 2003, p.123). This line of reasoning has subsequently been reaffirmed not only by law, but also by authoritative experts and scholars (Cary, 1969). Among the better known contributions in this sense, the

reader is referred to the article by Milton Friedman (1970) with a particularly explicit title: "The social responsibility of business is to increase its profits".

106   For an econometric study which demonstrates the existence of a positive correlation between attention to the environment shown by a firm and its medium-long-term returns see, for instance, Butz and Plattner (1999).

107   To be fully consistent with the requirements of sustainable development, the reference horizon should be infinite, as this would be the only time extension that would take account of all future generations. In a too long time horizon, however, sound assumptions cannot be made on future preferences, so that an infinite time horizon does not allow a motivated choice between numerous and considerably differentiated decision strategies. Thus we must assume a reference time horizon, which we could call "operative", based on well-defined preferences (Vercelli, 1998b). The *operative* reference time horizon cannot thus be extended beyond a few decades, and normally it does not stretch beyond 5–10 years. This poses no problems if the strategies that are taken into consideration have passed long-term sustainability *screening*. In this chapter we use the term "reference time horizon" to denote what we have specified here as *operative* reference time horizon.

108   The eco-efficiency criterion has been taken up by various influential associations of business people sensitive to development sustainability (as the WBCSD). See the survey by Schmidheiny and Zorraquin (1996) published on behalf of the WBCSD.

109   He originally divulgated his point of view in a famous newspaper article (Friedman, 1970) and confirmed his position many years later (Friedman, 1993).

110   Something similar happened after the Black Friday of 1929. On that occasion there emerged widespread behavior vitiated by "conflicts of interest" on the part of lending banks on the eve of the collapse: to avoid the emergence of the financial difficulties of their corporate borrowers, they had systematically purchased their shares to keep market quotations artificially buoyant (Rossi, 2003, p.53). To prevent the repetition of such anomalies the *Glass-Steagall Act* was introduced in 1933 to separate credit supply from investment in listed company shares. The untimely *Gramm-Leach-Bliley Act* of 12 November 1999 partially abrogated the *Glass-Steagall Act* favoring the spread of conflicts of interest which has led to a series of scandals without precedent and the outbreak of a serious stock market crisis.

111   Particularly popular are the environmental certification (ISO 14,000 or EMAS) and the ethical certification (SA 8000).

112   On this point see, for example, Hertz (2001).

113   Total company value includes not only share values but also the market value of all other "financial claims" including debt, preference shares and warrants.

114   In this case the principle of intertemporal coherence that underlies classical theories of intertemporal decisions (axiom of independence in the Morgenstern-Von Neumann theory and the so-called "Sure-Thing Principle" in Bayesian theory) ensure the absence of conflict between short and long term (Vercelli, 1998a).

115   More than half the employees of large companies such as ATT and Boeing take part in telecommuting programmes.

116   See Schmidheiny and Zorraquin (1996, p.xxiii.).

117   In recent years there have been signs of decline in this comparative advantage observed in previous years. This is partly due to the collapse of *high-tech* companies which were over-weighted in these indexes, and partly to the boom of companies operating in the sectors of arms and fossil fuels, which stems from hopefully temporary geopolitical and military factors.

118   We could be tempted to call the "economic liberalism" as "scientific liberalism", in the sense of a system of assertions soundly grounded in "scientific" economic arguments. This terminology, however, would raise the controversial issue whether, and in what sense, economics may be considered a "science". This issue, often discussed in the past, has been recently revived by a group of scientists and opinion leaders who questioned the legitimacy of the Nobel Prize in economics on the ground that the latter discipline is not a science. We do not need to discuss this issue here; therefore, throughout this book, by "scientific" argument we just mean an argument based on state-of-the-art economic theory.

119   The distinction between the procedural and consequentialist approach is similar to the distinction between process-oriented and end-state-oriented arguments: see Nozick (1976) and Schotter (1985, p.4). In our opinion the arguments of economic liberalism are to be based not only on the properties of the desired end-state, i.e. the perfect-competition market, but also on the properties of the initial state (the real market) and of the intermediate states between the two (see the Appendix for a more thorough discussion of this point). The nexus between successive states requires a causal analysis of the effects of each category of intervention.

120   It is tempting to consider the Physiocrats as the first school of economics that argued in favor of "economic" liberalism. The school of the Physiocrats, no doubt, introduced an unprecedented level of rigor in the economic reasoning deeply influencing Adam Smith, but their support for free trade was only weakly related to their own scientific arguments. In addition the Physiocrats advocated *laissez-faire* mainly to support the establishment of favorable trading conditions for French farmers in order to allow them to achieve, in particular, high exports of primary products (see Vagor, 1987, p.874). Although it is always possible to find predecessors for single parts of innovative contributions, *The Wealth of Nations* being no exception, we believe that it is fully legitimate to consider Smith as the real founder of economic liberalism.

121   This was clearly perceived by his contemporaries. His first biographer, for example, maintained that "the merit of such a work as Mr. Smith's is to be estimated less from the novelty of the principles which it contains, than from the reasoning employed to support these principles, and from the scientific manner in which they are unfolded in their proper order and connection" (Dugald Stewart, in Smith, 1795, pp.68–69).

122   Smith distinguished between Aristotelian method and Newtonian method and declared his sympathy for the latter: "in the manner of Sir Isaac Newton, we may lay down certain principles, primary or proved, in the beginning, from whence we account for the several phenomena, connecting all

together by the same chain. This latter, which we may call the Newtonian method, is undoubtedly the most philosophical, and in every science, whether of Morals or Natural Philosophy, etc., is vastly more ingenious, and for that reason, more engaging, than the other" (Smith, *Rhetoric*, p.140).

123 This approach was clarified by Smith since his Early Writings: "systems in many respects resemble machines. A machine is a little system, created to perform, as well as to connect together, in reality, those different movements ad the effects which the artist has occasion for. A system is an imaginary machine invented to connect together in the fancy those different movements and effects which are already in reality performed" (Smith, 1967, p.66).

124 This is made explicit in passages such as the following: "to expect, indeed, that the freedom of trade should ever be entirely restored in Great Britain, is as absurd as to expect that an Oceana or Utopia should ever be established in it" (Smith, 1776, p.471).

125 Smith did not use the word equilibrium in a systematic way, but we find in its place the metaphors that are at the basis of its introduction and fortune in economics: (i) the physical metaphor evoked when he discusses the "gravitation" of market prices towards natural prices, (ii) the dynamic metaphor according to which the center of gravitation is a "center of repose and continuance" (Smith, 1776, p.75), i.e. a resting state persisting until an exogenous shock disturbs it, and (iii) the physiological metaphor of health already introduced by Physiocrats (*ibid.*, p.343 and pp.673–674).

126 The relevant passage is quite well-known: "Every individual necessarily labors to render the annual revenue of the society as great as he can. He generally neither intends to promote the public interest, nor knows how much he is promoting it...By preferring the support of domestic to that of foreign industry, he intends only his own security; and by directing that industry in such a manner as its produce may be of the greatest value, he intends only his own gain, and he is in this, as in many other cases, led by an invisible hand to promote an end which was no part of his intention. Nor is it always the worse for society that it was no part of his intention. By pursuing his own interest he frequently promotes that of the society more effectually than when he really intends to promote it. I have never known much good done by those who affected to trade for the public good" (Smith, 1776, vol. iv, p.456).

127 See, e.g., the following passage: "the property which every man has in his own labor, as it is the original foundation of all other property, so it is the most sacred and inviolable. The patrimony of a poor man lies in the strength and dexterity of his hands; and to hinder him from employing this strength and dexterity in what manner he thinks proper without injury to his neighbor, is a plain violation of this most sacred property. It is a manifest encroachment upon the just liberty both of the workman, and of those who might be disposed to employ him" (pp.123–124).

128 In the 18th century England, a crucial obstacle to the liberty of residence was introduced by the Poor Law that obliged parishes to take care of people without property in case of necessity (accident, illness or unemployment) and prevented them to change residence without a written permission by

the parish of origin. The latter often denied the required certificate for its financial costs. Smith considered the growing number of poor people *sans papier* as an emblematic case of what we would call today "state failure".

129   This is because "the whole of the advantages and disadvantages of the different employments of labor and stock must, in the same neighborhood, be either perfectly equal or continually tending to equality" (*ibidem*, p.101).

130   He agreed with Smith, however, that in the field of education "the intervention of government is justifiable, because the case is not one in which the interest and judgment of the consumer are a sufficient security for the goodness of the community" (*ibidem*, p.321).

131   In fact he emphasized that "Ricardo and his followers developed a theory of the action of free enterprise (or, as they said, free competition), which contained many truths, that will be probably important so long as the world exists" (Marshall, 1891, p.10).

132   Of course Marshall is not the only illustrious ancestor of updated liberalism. Another influential ancestor was Wicksell. In the words of Samuelson: "Wicksell, better than Marshall or Mises or Walras, realized from the beginning that competitive equilibrium...does not necessarily achieve or approximate to a state of maximal social welfare or equity...; so, with the aid of feasible-best prior redistribution of people's endowments, the competitive market mechanism might be used to contrive a state of ethical optimality" (Samuelson, 1987, p.910).

133   Of course, it is always possible to find predecessors. Keynes himself cites Malthus. We find hints on the possibility of macroeconomic failures also in other classical economists. This is the case of Bentham himself (see Robbins, 1952). However, Keynes was the first to provide a systematic analysis of this possibility emphasizing at the same time its crucial practical importance.

134   See, e.g., the following passage: "When 9,000,000 men are employed out of 10,000,000 willing and able to work, there is no evidence that the labor of these 9,000,000 men is misdirected ... It is in determining the volume, not the direction, of actual employment that the existing system has broken down" (Keynes, 1936, p.379).

135   Keynes struggled to show in the GT that the acknowledgment of the existence of this crucial macroeconomic failure had been inhibited by the adhesion of mainstream economists to the Say's law, and that the latter is not necessarily verified. Did he succeed? We cannot provide a full-length discussion of this issue on this occasion (see, e.g., De Vroey, 2004).

136   On this point Keynes takes advantage from the insights reached in the *A Treatise on Probability* (1921) that he explicitly recalls in a few crucial passages of the GT.

137   A detailed defense of the complexity and openness of classical liberal economists on the issue of state intervention may be found, e.g., in the classical book by Robbins (1952).

138   We could easily extend the list of economic powers adding other subjects having some relevant decision power in economic matters. None of them, however, can be put at the same level of the three mentioned here. In the 1960s and early 1970 one could have had the temptation to add the

trade unions as fourth independent source of economic power and failures, but this crucial role did not last long. It is possible that NGOs may
acquire a prominent role in the future but this is not yet the case.

References

Agarwal, B. and A. Vercelli (eds) (2007) *Psychology, Rationality and Economic Behavior. Challenging Standard Assumptions* (New York: Palgrave Macmillan).

Agenor, P.R. (2003) "Does globalization hurt the poor?", *Policy Research Working Paper*, Series 2922 (Washington D.C.: The World Bank).

Ahluwalia, M. (1976) "Income distribution and development", *American Economic Review*, 66 (5): 128–135.

Alesina, A. and R. Perotti (1996) "Income distribution, political instability and investment", *European Economic Review*, 81 (5): 1170–1189.

Ali, A.G. and I. Elbadawi (2001) *Growth could be good for the poor*, manuscript (Washington D.C: The World Bank).

American Business Roundtable (1997) *Statement on Corporate Governance* (Washington: American Business Roundtable).

Anand, S. and S.M.R. Kanbur (1993) "The Kuznets process and the inequality-development relationship", *Journal of Development Economics*, 40: 25–52.

Anderson, A. (2001) "Technical Progress And Pollution Abatement: An Economic View of Selected Technologies and Practices", *Environment and Development Economics*, 6 (3): 283–311.

Ansuategi, A. and M. Escapa (2002) "Economic Growth and Greenhouse Gas Emissions", *Ecological Economics*, 40 (1): 23–37.

Arrow, K. (1951) *Social Choice and Individual Value* (New York: Wiley and Son).

Arrow, K. (1987) "Rationality of Self and Others in an Economic System", in R.M. Hogarth and M.W. Reder (eds) *Rational Choice: The Contrast between Economics and Psychology*, pp.201–216 (Chicago: University of Chicago Press).

Arrow, K. (1999) "Notes on Sequence Economies, Transaction Costs, and Uncertainty", *Journal of Economic Theory*, 86: 203–218.

Atkinson, A.B. (2003) "Income inequality in OECD countries: data and explanations", *CESifo Economic Studies*, 49, 4/2003, 479–513.

Baldini, M. and S. Toso (2004) *Diseguaglianza, povertà e politiche pubbliche* (Bologna, Italy: Il Mulino).

Baldwin, R. and R. Forslid (2000) "Trade liberalization and endogenous growth", *Journal of International Economics*, 50: 497–517.

Banerjee, A. and E. Duflo (2003) "Inequality and growth: what can the data say?", *Journal of Economic Growth*, 8: 267–299.

Barbier, E. (1997) "Introduction to the environmental Kuznets curve special issue", *Environment and Development Economics*, 2: 369–381.

Barro, R. (2000) "Inequality and growth in a panel of countries", *Journal of Economic Growth*, 5 (1): 5–32.

Barro, R. and X. Sala-i-Martin (1995) *Economic growth* (New York: McGraw-Hill Inc).

Basili, M. and A. Vercelli (1998) "Environmental option values, uncertainty aversion and learning", in G. Chichilnisky, G. Heal and A. Vercelli (eds) *Sustainability: Dynamics and Uncertainty* (Dordrecht: Kluwer).

Bates, D. (2002) "Environmental refugees? Classifying human migrations caused by environmental change", *Population and Environment*, Human Sciences Press Inc., 23 (5): 465–477.

Baumol, W.J., J.C. Panzar and R.D. Willig (1982) *Contestable Markets and the Theory of Industry Structure* (New York: Harcourt Brace Jovanovich).

Beaglehole, R. and A.J. McMichael (1999) "The future of public health in a changing global context", *Development*, 42: 12–16.

Bebchuk, L.A. (1989) "Limiting Contractual Freedom in Corporate Law: The Desirable Constraints on Charter Amendments", in *Harvard Law Review*, XII, 1820–1860.

Bebchuk, L.A., I.M. Fried and I. Walker (2002) "Managerial Power and Rent Extraction in the Design of Executive Compensation", *The University of Chicago Law Review*, LIX, 751–846.

Beckerman, W. (1992) "Economic growth and the environment: whose growth? Whose environment?", *World Development*, 20 (4): 481–496.

Bendix, R. (1987) "Weber, Max", *International Encyclopedia of the Social Sciences*, 16: 493–502 (London: Macmillan and New York: The Free Press).

Benhabib, J. and A. Rustichini (1996) "Social conflict and growth", *Journal of Economic Growth*, 1 (1): 129–146.

Bentham, J. (1952–54) *Jeremy's Bentham's Economic Writings*, 3 vols., ed. W. Stark (London: George Allen and Unwin).

Bhagwati, J. (2004) *In Defense of Globalization* (Oxford: Oxford University Press).

Bhargava, A. and J. Yu (1997) "A longitudinal analysis of infant and child mortality rates in developing countries", *Indian Economic Review*, 32: 141–151.

Bhargava, A., T. Dean, L.J. Jamison and C.J.L. Murray (2001) "Modeling the effects of health on economic growth", *Journal of Health Economics*, 20: 423–440.

Blaug, M. (1968) *Economic Theory in Retrospect* (Homewood, Illinois: Richard D. Irwin).

Bloom, D.E. and J.D. Sachs (1998) *Geography, Demography and Economic Growth in Africa*, Brookings Papers on Economic Activity, 2: 207–295.

Bloom, D.E., D. Canning and B. Graham (2001a) *Health, Longevity and Life-cycle Savings* CMH Working Group Paper n. WG1 (p.9).

Bloom, D.E., D. Canning and J. Sevilla (2001b) *Economic Growth and the Demographic Transition*, NBER Working Paper n. 8685, Cambridge, MA, USA.

Borghesi, S. (2001) "The environmental Kuznets curve: a critical survey", in M. Franzini and A. Nicita (eds) *Economic Institutions and Environmental Policy* (Aldershot: Ashgate). Previously published as Nota di Lavoro No. 85.99, Fondazione ENI Enrico Mattei, Milano.

Borghesi, S. and A. Vercelli (2003) "Sustainable globalization", *Ecological Economics*, 44 (1): 77–89.

Borghesi, S. (2005) "The Kuznets curve and the environmental Kuznets curve: a simple steady-state analysis", *International Review of Economics and Business*, VII (1): 35–61.

Borghesi, S. and A. Vercelli (2006) "Global Health", in F. Farina and E. Savaglio (eds) *Inequality and Economic Integration*, 107–136 (London: Routledge).

Bourguignon, F. and C. Morisson (2002) "Income among world citizens: 1820–1992", *American Economic Review*, 92 (4): 727–744.

Bowles, S. and H. Gintis (2001) "The inheritance of inequality", *Journal of Economic Perspectives*, 16 (3): 3–30.

Brandolini, A. (2002) "A Bird's-Eye View of Long-run Changes in Income Inequality", Paper presented at the IEA World Conference in Lisbon.

Brandolini, A. and T. Smeeding (2007) "Inequality patterns in western-type democracies: cross-country differences and time changes", Luxembourg Income Study Working Paper No. 458, Luxembourg.

British Petroleum (1995) *BP Statistical Review of World Energy*, BP p.l.c. (London: UK).

British Petroleum (2006) *BP Statistical Review of World Energy*, BP p.l.c. (London: UK).

British Petroleum (2007) *BP Statistical Review of World Energy*, BP p.l.c. (London: UK).

Brock, W. and S. Taylor (2006) "Economic growth and the environment: a review of theory and empirics", in S. Durlauf and P. Aghion (eds) *Handbook of Economic Growth* (Amsterdam: Elsevier). Available at: http://works.bepress.com/taylor/36/

Brundtland Report (see WCED, 1987).

Brunner, E. and M. Marmot (1999) "Social organization, stress, and health", in M.G. Marmot and R.G. Wilkinson (eds) *The Social Determinants of Health* (Oxford: Oxford University Press).

Bruno, M., M. Ravallion and L. Squire (1998) "Equity and growth in developing countries: old and new perspectives on the policy issue", in V. Tanzi and K. Chu (eds) *Income Distribution and High-Quality Growth*, 117–146 (Cambridge, MA: MIT Press).

Budd, M. and S. Wooden (2002) "Analysts' Conflicts of Interest", *Review of Securities and Commodities regulation*, XXXV: 119–136.

Bunker, J.P., H.S. Frazier and F. Mosteller (1994) "Improving Health: Measuring Effects of Medical Care", *The Milbank Quarterly*, 72 (2): 225–258.

Bunker, J.P. (1995) "Medicine Matters After All", *Journal of the Royal College of Physicians*, 29 (2): 105–112.

Burniaux, J.M., T.T. Dang, D. Fore, M. Forster, M. Mira D'Ercole and H. Oxley (1999) "Income distribution and poverty in selected OECD Countries", *OECD Economic Studies*, 29: 55–94.

Butz, C. and A. Plattner (1999) *Sustainable Investment: An Analysis of Returns in Relation to Environmental and Social Criteria* (Basel: Sarasin Basic Report).

Campbell, C.J. (2004) *The Coming Oil Crisis* (Brentwood: Multi-Science Publishing).

Cantarero, D., M. Pascual and J.M. Sarabia (2005) "Effects of income inequality on population health: new evidence from the European Community Household Panel", *Applied Economics*, 35: 87–91.

Carson, R.T., Y. Jeon and D.R. McCubbin (1997) "The relationship between air pollution emissions and income: US data", *Environment and Development Economics*, 2: 433–450.

Cary, W.L. (1969) *Cases and Materials on Corporations*, 4th edn, p.1580 (Mineola: Foundation Press).

Chen, S. and M. Ravallion (2004) "How have the world's poorest fared since the early 1980s?", *The World Bank Research Observer*, 19 (2): 141–169.

Chichilnisky, G. (1997) "What is Sustainable Development?", *Land Economics*, 73 (4): 467–491.

Chomsky, N. (1999) *Profit Over People* (New York: Seven Stories Press).

Clark, J.B. (1899) *The Distribution of Wealth: A Theory of Wages, Interest and Profits* (New York: The Macmillan Company).

Clarke, G.R.G. (1992) *More Evidence on Income Distribution and Growth*. Policy Research Working Paper WPS 1064, The World Bank, Washington.

Cleveland, C.J., R.K. Kaufman and D.I. Stern (2000) "Aggregation and the role of energy in the economy", *Ecological Economics*, 32: 301–317.

Coase, R.H. (1937) "The nature of the firm", *Economica*, 4: 386–405.

Coase, R.H. (1960) "The problem of social cost", *Journal of Law and Economics*, 3: 1–44.

Cole, M.A., A.J. Rayner and J.M. Bates (1997) "The environmental Kuznets curve: an empirical analysis", *Environment and Development Economics*, 2: 401–416.

Collier, P. and D. Dollar (2002) *Globalization, Growth, and Poverty: Building an Inclusive World Economy*, World Bank (New York: Oxford University Press).

Common, M.S. (1995) *Sustainability and Policy* (Cambridge, UK: Cambridge University Press).

Conservation Foundation (1992) *State of the Environment*, Washington D.C.

Consolandi, C., A. Jaiswal-Dalo, E. Poggiani and A. Vercelli (2008) "Global standards and ethical stock indexes: the case of the Dow Jones sustainability stoxx index", *Journal of Business Ethics*, forthcoming.

CSA – Canadian Securities Administrators (2003) National Instrument 51–101.

Daily, G.C. and P.R. Ehrlich (1992) "Population, sustainability and Earth's carrying capacity", *Bioscience*, 42: 761–771.

Dasgupta, P., K. Mäler and A. Vercelli (1997) *The Economics of Transnational Commons* (Oxford: Oxford University Press).

Dasgupta, S., B. Laplante, H. Wang and D. Wheeler (2002) "Confronting the environmental Kuznets curve", *Journal of Economic Perspectives*, 16 (1): 147–168.

Deaton, A. (2002) "Health, inequality and economic development", *Journal of Economic Literature*, 41: 113–158.

Deaton, A. (2004) "Health in an age of globalization", *Brookings Trade Forum*, edited by Susan Collins and Carol Graham, Washington DC. The Brookings Institute. Research Program in Development Studies Center for Health and Wellbeing, Princeton University.

Debreu, G. (1959) *The Theory of Value: An Axiomatic Analysis of Economic Equilibrium*, Cowles Foundation For Research in Economics at Yale University, Monograph 17 (New Haven and London: Yale University Press).

De Bruyn, S.M., J. Van den Bergh and J.B. Opschoor (1998) "Economic growth and emissions: reconsidering the empirical basis of environmental Kuznets curve", *Ecological Economics*, 25: 161–175.

Deffeyes, K.S. (2001) *Hubbert's Peak: The Impending World Oil Shortage* (Princeton: Princeton University Press).

Deininger, K. and L. Squire (1996) "A new data set measuring income inequality", *The World Bank Economic Review*, 10 (3): 565–591.

De Nova, G. (2002) "Conflict of interest and the Fair Dealing Duty", *Rivista di diritto Privato*, pp.5–37.

De Vogli, R., R. Mistry, R. Gnesotto and G.A. Cornia (2005) "Has the relation between income inequality and life expectancy disappeared? Evidence from Italy and top industrialised countries", *Journal of Epidemiology and Community Health*, 59: 158–162.

De Vroey, M. (2004) *The History of Macroeconomics Viewed Against the Background of the Marshall-Walras Divide*, Université catholique de Louvain, Institut de Recherches Economiques et Sociales (IRES).

Dikhanov, Y. and M. Ward (2001) *Measuring the distribution of global income*, manuscript, The World Bank, Washington.

Dinda, S. (2004) "Environmental Kuznets Curve Hypothesis: A Survey", *Ecological Economics*, 49: 431–455.

Dollar, D. (2000) Letter to the *Financial Times*; June 20, 2000.

Dollar, D. and A. Kraay (2002) "Growth is good for the poor", *Journal of Economic Growth*, 7 (3): 195–225.

Donaldson, T. and L. Preston (1995) "The stakeholder theory of the modern corporation concepts: evidence and implications", *Academy of Management Review*, 20: 65–91.

Drever, F., M. Whitehead and M. Roden (1996) "Current Patterns and Trends in Male Mortality by Social Class", *Population Trends*, 86: 15–20.

Durkheim, E. (1897) *Suicide*, English translation by J.A. Spaulding and G. Simpson, 1951 (New York: The Free Press).

Easterly, W. (2001) "The middle-class consensus and economic development", *Journal of Economic Growth*, 6: 317–335.

Eatwell, J. and L. Taylor (1999) *The Case for International Regulation* (Cambridge: Polity Press).

El-Hinnawi, E. (1985) *Environmental Refugees* (Nairobi: United Nations Environment Programme).

EIA – Energy Information Administration (2006) *International Energy Outlook 2006*, Office of Integrated Analysis and Forecasting (Washington D.C.: U.S. Department of Energy).

Esty, D. (2001) "Bridging the trade-environment divide", *Journal of Economic Perspectives*, 15: 113–130.

FAO – Food and Agriculture Organization of the United Nations (2006) "The State of Food Insecurity in the World", Rome, Italy.

Fiscella, K. and P. Franks (1997) "Poverty or income inequality as predictor of mortality: longitudinal cohort studies", *British Medical Journal*, 314: 1724–1728.

Fishlow, A. (1995) "Inequality, poverty and growth: where do we stand?", in M. Bruno and B. Pleskovic (eds) *Annual World Bank Conference on Development Economics*, pp.25–39 (Washington D.C.: The World Bank).

Flemming, J.S. and J. Micklewright (2000) "Income distribution, economic systems and transition", in A. Atkinson and F. Bourguignon (eds) *Handbook of Income Distribution*, pp.843–917 (Amsterdam: Elsevier).

Fogel, R.W. (1997) "New findings on secular trends in nutrition and mortality: some implications for population theory", in M.R. Rosenzweig and O. Stark, *Handbook of Population and Family Economics*, vol. 1a, pp.433–481 (Amsterdam: Elsevier Science).

Fogel, R.W. (1986) "Nutrition and the Decline in Mortality Since 1700: Some Preliminary Findings", in S.L. Engerman and R.E. Gallman (eds) *Long-Term Factors in American Economic Growth*, pp.439–555 (Chicago: Chicago University Press).

Forster, M. and M. Pearson (2002) "Income distribution and poverty in the OECD area: trends and driving forces", *OECD Economic Studies*, No. 34, pp.7–39.

Francioni, F. (ed.) (2002) *Environment, Human Rights and International Trade* (Oxford and Portland, Oregon: Hart Publishing).

Frankel, J.A. and D. Romer (1999) "Does trade cause growth?", *American Economic Review*, 89: 379–399.

Freeman, E. (1984) *Strategic Management: A Stakeholder Approach* (Boston: Pitman).

Freeman, R. and R. Oostendorp (2000) *Wages around the world: pay across occupations and countries*. NBER Working Paper No. 8058, Cambridge, MA.

Friedman, B.M. (2006) *The Moral Consequences of Economic Growth* (New York: Alfred A. Knopf).

Friedman, M. (1970) "The Social Responsibility of Business is to Increase its Profits", *New York Magazine*, 13 September 1970.

Friedman, M. (1993) "The social responsibility of Business is to Increase its profits", G.D. Chrissides and J.H. Keler (eds) *An Introduction to Business Ethics* (London: Chapman).

Galassi, C. (2002) "Fattori di rischio ambientali e disturbi respiratori nell'infanzia: i risultati dello studio SIDRA", *AIST* (Associazione Italiana per lo Studio della Tosse) National Congress, Bologna, 8–9/02/2002.

Garegnani, P. (1960) *Il capitale nelle teorie della distribuzione* (Milano: Giuffré).

Gates, W.H. (1999) *Business @ the speed of thought* (New York: Warner Books).

Geroski, P., A. Ulph and D. Ulph (1987) "A model of the crude oil market in which conduct varies", *Economic Journal*, 97: 77–86.

Glassman, J. (1992) "Counter-insurgency, ecocide and the production of refugees: warfare as a tool of modernization", *Refuge: Canada's Periodical on Refugees*, 12: 27–30.

Glenn, B.S., J.A. Foran and M. Van Putten (1989) "Summary of quantitative health assessments for PCBs, DDT, dieldrin and chlordane", *National Wildlife Federation*, Ann Arbor, MI.

Goodstein, D. (2004) *Out of Gas: The End of the Age of Oil* (New York: Norton).

Gravelle, H. (1998) "How much of the relation between population mortality and unequal distribution of income is a statistical artifact?", *British Medical Journal*, 316: 382–385.

Grossman, G.M. (1995) "Pollution and growth: what do we know?", in I. Goldin and L.A. Winters (eds) *The Economics of Sustainable Development*, pp.19–45 (Cambridge: Cambridge University Press).

Grossman, G.M. and A.B. Krueger (1995) "Economic Growth and the Environment", *Quarterly Journal of Economics*, 110: 353–377.

Gwatkin, D.R. (2000) "Health inequalities and the health of the poor: what do we know? What can we do?", *Bulletin of the World Health Organization*, 78 (1).

Haas, P.M. (ed.) (2003) *Environment in the New Global Economy* (Cheltenham, U.K. and Northampton, Mass.: Elgar).

Hayek, F.A. (1944) *The Road to Serfdom* (London: Routledge).

Hayek, F.A. (1948) *Individualism and Economic Order* (Chicago: The University of Chicago Press).

Hayek, F.A. (1978) *New Studies in Philosophy, Politics and the History of Ideas* (London: Routledge).

Hayek, F.A. (1988) *The Fatal Conceit: The Errors of Socialism* (London: Routledge).

Hertz, N. (2001) *La conquista silenziosa* (Roma: Carocci).

Hettige, H., R. Lucas and D. Wheeler (1992) "The Toxic Intensity of Industrial Pollution: Global Patterns, Trends and Trade Policy", *American Economic Review* 82(2): 478–481.

Hicks, J.R. (1937) "Mr. Keynes and the 'Classics'. A suggested Interpretation", *Econometrica*, 5: 147–159.

Hicks, J.R. (1939) *Value and Capital* (Oxford: Clarendon).

Hirsch Report: Hirsch, R.L., R. Bezdek and R. Wendling (2005) *Peaking of World Oil Production. Impacts, Mitigation and Risk Management* (Washington: US Department of Energy).

Hirsch, R.L. (2005) "The Inevitable Peaking of World Oil Production", *Bulletin of the Atlantic Council of the United States*, 16 (3): 1–10.

Holdren, J.P. and P.R. Ehrlich (1974) "Human population and the global environment", *American Scientist*, 62: 282–292.

Hoover, K.D. (2001) *Causality in Macroeconomics* (Cambridge: Cambridge University Press).

House of Lords (2002) *Globalization*, Select Committee on Economic Affairs, Session 2002–03, 1st report, London, U.K.

Hsieh, C.C. and M.D. Pugh (1993) "Poverty, income inequality, and violent crime: a meta-analysis of recent aggregated studies", *Criminal Justice Review*, 18: 182–202.

Hubbert, M.K. (1956) "*Nuclear Energy and the Fossil Fuels*", paper presented at the Spring Meeting of the Southern District, American Petroleum Institute, San Antonio, Texas, 7–9/3/1956.

IEA – International Energy Agency (2004) *World Energy Outlook 2004*, Paris: OECD/IEA.

IEA – International Energy Agency (2006) *Key Statistics*, Paris: OECD/IEA.

IPCC – Intergovernmental Panel on Climate Change (2001) *Third Assessment Report*, Geneva, Switzerland.

IPCC – Intergovernmental Panel on Climate Change (2007) *Fourth Assessment Report*, Geneva, Switzerland.

Irwin, D.A. and M. Tervio (2002) "Does Trade Raise Income? Evidence from the Twentieth Century", *Journal of International Economics*, 58: 1–18.

Italian Stock Exchange (1999) Comitato Per la Corporate Governance delle Società Quotate, *Rapporto e codice di autodisciplina* (Milano: Borsa Italiana).

Jensen, M.C. (2001) "Value maximization, Stakeholder Theory, and the Corporate objective Function", *Journal of Applied Corporate Finance*, pp.8–21.

Judge, K. (1995) "Income distribution and life expectancy: a critical appraisal", *British Medical Journal*, 311: 1282–1285.

Kanbur, R. (2001) "Economic Policy, distribution and poverty: the nature of disagreements", *World Development*, 29 (6): 1083–1094.

Kaplan, G.A., E.R. Pamuk, J.W. Lynch, R.D. Cohen and J.L. Balfour (1996) "Inequality in income and mortality in the United States: analysis of mortality and potential pathways", *British Medical Journal*, 312: 999–1003.

Kaufmann, R.K., B. Davidsdottir, S. Garnham and P. Pauly (1998) "The determinants of atmospheric SO_2 concentrations: reconsidering the environmental Kuznets curve", *Ecological Economics*, 25: 209–220.

Kawachi, I. and B.P. Kennedy (1997) "The relationship of income inequality to mortality – Does the choice of indicator matter?", *Social Science and Medicine*, 45, 1121–1127.

Kawachi, I. and B.P. Kennedy (2002) *The Health of Nations: Why Inequality Is Harmful to Your Health* (New York: The New Press).

Kawachi, I., B.P. Kennedy, K. Lochner and D. Prothrow-Stith (1997) "Social capital, income inequality and mortality", *American Journal of Public Health*, 87, 1491–1498.

Kawachi, I., B.P. Kennedy and R.G. Wilkinson (1999) *Income Inequality and Health*, Vol. I. The Society and Population Health Reader (New York: The New Press).

Kaya, Y. (1990) *Impact of carbon dioxide emission control on GNP growth: interpretation of proposed scenarios*, paper presented to IPCC Energy and Industry Sub-Group, Response Strategies Working Group.

Kelleher, D. (2006) "Alternative theoretical perspectives on the political economy of international environmental policy", *Journal of International and Area Studies*, 13 (1): 1–21.

Kennedy, B.P., I. Kawachi and D. Prothrow-Stith (1996) "Income distribution and mortality: cross-sectional ecological study of the Robin Hood Index in the United States", *British Medical Journal*, 312: 1004–1007.

Keynes, J.M. (1921) *A Treatise on Probability* (New York: Macmillan).

Keynes, J.M. (1925) "Am I a liberal?", *The Collected Writings of John Maynard Keynes, XVI: 304–315* (London: Macmillan).

Keynes, J.M. (1936) *The General Theory of Employment, Interest, and Money* (London: Macmillan).

Koplow, D. (1993) *Federal Energy Subsidies: Energy, Environmental and Fiscal Impacts* (Lexington MA: The Alliance to Save Energy).

Krueger, A.B. and R. Solow (eds) (2001) *The Roaring Nineties. Can Full Employment Be Sustained?* (New York: The Russel Sage Foundation and the Century Foundation Press).

Kuznets, S. (1955) "Economic growth and income inequality", *American Economic Review*, 45: 1–28.

Legrain, Ph. (2002) *Open World: The Truth about Globalization* (London: Abacus).

Leigh, A. and C. Jencks (2007) "Inequality and mortality: long run evidence from a panel of countries", *Journal of Health Economics*, 26: 1–24.

Li, H., L. Squire and H. Zou (1998) "Explaining international and intertemporal variations in income inequality", *Economic Journal*, 108: 26–43.

Lindert, P.H. and J.G. Williamson (2003) "Does globalization make the world more unequal?", in M.D. Bordo, A.M. Taylor and J.G. Williamson (eds) *Globalization in Historical Perspectives*, pp.227–270 (Chicago: University of Chicago Press).

Lindert, P.H. (2004) *Growing Public. Social Spending and Economic Growth Since the Eighteenth Century* (Cambridge: Cambridge University Press).

Lomborg, B. (2001) *The Skeptical Environmentalist. Measuring the Real State of the World* (Cambridge: Cambridge University Press).

Longstreth, B. (1986) *Modern Investment Management and the Prudent Man Rule* (New York: Oxford University Press).

Lucas, R.E. (1976) "Econometric Policy Evaluation: A Critique", Carnegie-Rochester Conference Series on Public Policy, 1: 19–46.

Lucas, R. (1990) "Why Doesn't Capital Flow from Rich to Poor Countries?", *American Economic Review*, 80: 92–96.

Lynch, J., G.A. Kaplan, E.R. Pamuk, R.D. Cohen, K.H. Heck, J.L. Balfour and I.H. Yen (1998) "Income inequality and mortality in metropolitan areas of United States", *American Journal of Public Health*, 88: 1074–1080.

Lynch, J., G.D. Smith, G.A. Kaplan and J.S. House (2000) "Income inequality and mortality: importance to health of individual income, psychosocial environment, or material conditions", *British Medical Journal*, 320: 1200–1204.

Marmot, M.G. and R.G. Wilkinson (eds) (1999) *The Social Determinants of Health* (Oxford: Oxford University Press).

Marshall, A. (1891) *Principles of Economics* (London: Macmillan).

McKeown, T. (1976) *The Modern Rise of Population* (London: Edward Arnold Ltd).

Meadows, D.H., D.L. Meadows, J. Randers and W. Behrens (1972) *The Limits to Growth* (New York, USA: Universe Books).

Milanovic, B. (2002) "True world income distribution, 1988 and 1993: first calculation based on household alone", *The Economic Journal*, 112: 51–92.

Milanovic, B. (2005) "Half a world: regional inequality in five great federations", World Bank Policy Research Working Paper 3699.

Mill, J.S. (1848) *Principles of Political Economy* (Fairfield: A.M. Kelley).

Mill, J.S. (1859) *On Liberty* (London: Longman, Roberts and Green).

Modigliani, F. (1944) "Liquidity Preference and the Theory of Interest and Money", *Econometrica*, 12: 45–88.

Munasinghe, M. (1999) "Is environmental degradation an inevitable consequence of economic growth: tunneling through the environmental Kuznets curve", *Ecological Economics*, 29 (1): 89–109.

Munda, G. (2004) "Social multi-criteria evaluation: Methodological foundations and operational consequences", *European Journal of Operational Research*, 158 (3): 662–677.

Myers, N. (1993) "Environmental refugees in a globally warmed world", *Bioscience*, 43: 752–761.

Myers, N. (1997) "Enviromental refugees", *Population and Environment*, 19: 167–182.

Nardozzi, G. (2002) (ed.) *I rapporti tra finanza e distribuzione del reddito: un'interpretazione dell'economia di fine secolo* (Roma: Luiss Edizioni).

Nicholls, M. (2000) "Pension sector shows green tinge", *Environmental Finance*, May, p.16.

Niehans, J. (1987) "Transaction costs", *The New Palgrave: A Dictionary of Economics*, ed. J. Eatwell, M. Milgate and P. Newman, vol. 4, pp.676–679 (London: Macmillan).

Nordhaus, W. (2005) "Life After Kyoto: Alternative Approaches to Global Warming Policies", *NBER Working Paper No. W11889*, Yale University, Department of Economics; National Bureau of Economic Research (NBER).

Nozick, R. (1976) *Anarchy, State, and Utopia* (New York: Basic Books).

Obstfeld, M. (1994) "Risk Taking, Global Diversification and Growth", *American Economic Review*, 85: 1310–1329.

O'Rourke, K.H. (2001) "Globalization and inequality: historical trends", CEPR Discussion Paper No. 2865, London.

O'Rourke, K.H. and J.G. Williamson (2000) "When did globalization begin?", NBER Working Paper 7632, Cambridge, Mass.

Oxfam (2002) "Rigged rules and double standards" (URL: www.oxfam.org).

Panayotou, T. (1993) "Empirical tests and policy analysis of environmental degradation at different stages of economic development", World Employment Programme Research, Working Paper No. 238, International Labour Office, Geneva.

Panayotou, T. (2000) "Economic growth and the environment", Working Paper No. 56, Center for International Development, Harvard University. Forthcoming in *Handbook of Environmental Economics* (edited by Karl-Goran Mäler and Jeffery Vincent) a volume in the series *Handbooks in Economics*, edited by Kenneth Arrow and Michael D. Intrilligator.

Papanek, G. and O. Kyn (1986) "The effect on income distribution of development, the growth rate and economic strategy", *Journal of Development Economics*, 23 (1): 55–65.

Pareto, V. (1906) *Manuale di economia politica. Con un'introduzione alla scienza sociale* (Milano: Società editrice Librario).

Partnoy, F. (2002) www.financialsense.com/editorials/2002/partnoy.htm.

Patinkin, D. (1956) *Money, Interest and Prices*, 2nd edn (New York: Harper & Row).

Pearson, P. (1994) "Energy, Externalities and Environmental Quality: Will Development Cure the Ills It Creates?", *Energy Studies Review*, 6 (3): 199–215.

Perotti, R. (1996) "Growth, income distribution and democracy: what the data say", *Journal of Economic Growth*, 1: 149–187.

Perrings, C. (1989) "Environmental Bonds and Environmental Research in Innovative Activity", *Ecological Economics*, 1: 95–110.

Pigou, A.C. (1920) *The Economics of Welfare* (London: Macmillan).

Piketty, T. (2005) "The Kuznets' Curve, Yesterday and Tomorrow", in A. Banerjee, R. Benabou and D. Mookherjee (eds) *Understanding Poverty* (Oxford: Oxford University Press).

Piketty, T. and E. Saez (2003) "Income inequality in the United States, 1913–98", *Quarterly Journal of Economics*, CXVIII (1): 1–39.

Piketty, T. and E. Saez (2006) "The evolution of top incomes: a historical and international perspective", NBER Working Paper, No. 11955, Cambridge, MA.

Pollitt, E. (2001) "The developmental and probabilistic nature of the functional consequences of iron-deficiency anemia in children", *The Journal of Nutrition*, 131: 669S–675S.

Porter, R. (2006) Book Reviews, Section Q, *Journal of Economic Literature*, 44 (1): 186–190.

Posner, R.A. (2001) *Frontiers of Legal Theory* (Cambridge, Mass.: Harvard University Press).

Preston, S.H. (1975) "The changing relation between mortality and level of economic development", *Population Studies*, 29: 231–248.

Radetzki, M. (1992) "Economic growth and environment", in P. Low (ed.) *International Trade and the Environment*, World Bank DP-159, pp.121–136, Washington D.C.

Ricardo, D. (1817) *The Principles of Political Economy and Taxation* (London: John Murray).

Rifkin, J. (2000) *The Age of Access* (New York: Penguin/Putnam).

Robbins, L. (1952) *The Theory of Economic Policy in English Classical Political Economy* (London: Macmillan).

Roberts, J.T. and P.E. Grimes (1997) "Carbon Intensity and Economic Development 1962–91: A Brief Exploration of the Environmental Kuznets Curve", *World Development*, 25 (2): 191–198, Elsevier Science Ltd.

Robinson, S. (1976) "A note on the U-hypothesis relating income inequality and economic development", *American Economic Review*, 66 (3): 437–440.

Roca, J., E. Padilla, M. Farré and V. Galletto (2001) "Economic growth and atmospheric pollution in Spain: discussing the environmental Kuznets curve hypothesis", *Ecological Economics*, 39: 85–99.

Rodriguez, F. and D. Rodrik (2000) "Trade policy and economic growth: a skeptic's guide to the cross-national evidence", in B. Bernanke and K. Rogoff (eds) *NBER Macroeconomic Annual 2000* (Cambridge, MA.: MIT Press).

Romm, J., A. Rosenfeld and S. Herrmann (1999) *The Internet Economy and Global Warming. A Scenario of the Impact of E-commerce on Energy and the Environment* (New York: The Center for Energy and Climate Solutions).

Rossi, G. (2003) *Il conflitto epidemico* (Milano: Adelphi).

Sacconi, L. (1991) *Etica degli affari* (Milano: Il Saggiatore).

Sacconi, L. (2003) "Responsabilità sociale come *governance* allargata di impresa: una interpretazione basata sulla teoria del contratto sociale e della reputazione", manuscript.

Sacconi, L. (2004) "Incomplete Contracts and Corporate ethics: A Game Theoretical Model Under Fuzzy Information", in F. Cafaggi, A. Nicita and U. Pagano (eds) *Legal Orderings and Economic Institutions* (London: Routledge).

Sacconi, L. (ed.) (2005) *Guida critica alla responsabilità sociale e al governo d'impresa* (Roma: Bancaria Editrice).

Sala-i-Martin, X. (2002) "The world distribution of income (estimated from individual country distributions)", NBER Working Paper No. 8933, Cambridge, Massachusetts.

Salter, M.S. (2002) *Innovation corrupted. The rise and fall of Enron*, draft paper, Harvard Business School, Cambridge (Mass.)

Samuelson, P.A. (1947) *Foundations of Economic Analysis* (Cambridge, MA: Harvard University Press).

Samuelson, P.A. (1987) "Wicksell and Neoclassical economics", in *The New Palgrave*, 4: 908–910.

Sandler, T. and D. Arce (2002) "A conceptual framework for understanding global and transnational public goods for health", *Fiscal Studies*, 23(2): 195–222.

Sandmo, A. (2002) "Globalization and the welfare state: more inequality – less redistribution?", *Discussion Paper 4/2002, Department of Economics, Norwegian School of Economics and Business Administration*, Bergen.

Sapolsky, R.M. (1998) *Why Zebras Don't Get Ulcers: A Guide to Stress, Stress-Related Disease and Coping*, 2nd edn (New York: W.H. Freeman).

Saunders, P.A. (1996) "Income and Welfare: Special Article – Poverty and Deprivation in Australia", in *Year Book Australia 1996*, ed., Commonwealth of Australia, Canberra.

Schmidheiny, S. and F. Zorraquin (1996) *Financing Change: The Financial Community, Eco-efficiency and Sustainable Development* (Cambridge, Mass.: The MIT Press).

Schotter, A. (1985) *Free Market Economics: A Critical Appraisal* (New York: St. Martin's Press).

Selden, T.M. and D. Song (1994) "Environmental Quality and Development: Is There a Kuznets Curve for Air Pollution Emissions?", *Journal of Environmental Economics and Management*, 27: 147–162.

Sen, A.K. (1970) *Collective Choice and Social Welfare* (San Francisco: Holden Day).

Sen, A.K. (1987) *On Ethics and Economics*, Oxford (trad. it., 1988, *Etica ed economia*, Laterza, Bari).

Sen, A.K. (1991) *Denaro e valore: etica ed economia della finanza* (Roma: Edizioni dell'Elefante).

Sen, A.K. (1999) *Development as Freedom* (New York: Alfred A. Knopf, Inc.).

Sen, A.K. (2000) *Lo sviluppo è libertà* (Milano: Mondadori).

Sen, A.K. (2002) *Globalizzazione e libertà* (Milano: Mondadori).

Senior, S. (2008) "Agriculture and world trade liberalization", in P. Della Posta, M. Uvalic and A. Verdun (eds) *Interpreting Globalization: European Perspectives* (London: Palgrave Macmillan).

Shafik, N. (1994) *Economic development and environmental quality: an econometric analysis*. Oxford Economic Papers, 46: 757–773.

Shiller, R.H. (2000) *Irrational Exuberance* (Princeton: Princeton University Press).

Skinner, A.A. (1974) *Adam Smith and the Role of the State* (Glasgow: University of Glasgow Press).

Smith, A. (1776) *An Inquiry into The Nature and Causes of the Wealth of Nations* (London: W. Strahan and T. Cadell).

Smith, A. (1795) *Essays on Philosophical Subjects to which is prefixed An Account of the Life and Writings of the Author by Dugald Stewart*, J. Black and J. Hutton (eds) (London: T. Cadell, jr.).

Smith, A. (1963) *Lectures on Rhetoric and Belles Lettres delivered in the University of Glasgow by Adam Smith, Reported by a student in 1762–63*, edited by J.M. Lothian (London: Nelson).

Smith, A. (1967) *The Early Writings of Adam Smith*, edited by J.R. Lindgren (New York: A.M. Kelley).

Smith, A.H., E.O. Lingas and M. Rahman (2000) "Contamination of drinking-water by arsenic in Bangladesh: a public health emergency", *Bullettin of the World Health Organization*, 78 (9): 1093–1103.

Soros, G. (1998) *The Crisis of Global Capitalism. Open Society Endangered* (New York: Public Affairs, Perseus Book Group).

Soytas, U. and R. Sari (2003) "Energy consumption and GDP: causality relationship in G-7 countries and emerging markets", *Energy Economics*, 25: 33–37.

Stern, D.I., M.S. Common and E.B. Barbier (1996) "Economic growth and environmental degradation: the environmental Kuznets curve and sustainable development", *World Development*, 24 (7): 1151–1160.

Stern, N. (2006) *Stern Review on the Economics of Climate Change* (London: HM Treasury).

Stiglitz, J. (2002) *Globalization and its Discontents* (London: Allen Lane).

Stiglitz, J. (2003) *The Roaring Nineties. Seeds of Destruction* (London: Allen Lane (Penguin Group)).

Stiglitz, J. (2006) *Making Globalization Work* (New York: W.W. Norton).

Storey, D.J. (1994) *Understanding the Small Business Sector* (London: Routledge).

Tarlov, A.R. and R.F. St. Peter (eds) (2000) *The Society and Population Health Reader, Volume II: A State and Community Perspective* (New York: The New Press).

Temple, J. (1999) "The new growth evidence", *Journal of Economic Literature*, 37: 112–156.

The Economist (2000) "Growth is good", U.S. Edition; May 27.

The Economist (2001) "A nation poisoned", December 22, p.75.

The Economist (2002a) "The right to drive or the right to breathe?", March 9, p.54.

The Economist (2002b) "A killer still", March 9, p.59.

Tisdell, C. (2001) "Globalization and sustainability: environmental Kuznets curve and the WTO", *Ecological Economics*, 39: 185–196.

Tobin, J. (1999) "Interview with James Tobin: Reigning in the Markets", *Information Access Company/Unesco*, February 1st.

Toniolo, G. (2005) "The Global Economy in the 1990s: A long-run perspective", in P. Rhode and G. Toniolo (eds) *The Global Economy in the 1990s. A long-run perspective* (Cambridge: Cambridge University Press).

Torras, M. and J.K. Boyce (1998) "Income, inequality, and pollution: A reassessment of the environmental Kuznets curve", *Ecological Economics*, 25: 147–160.

Torsello, L. and A. Vercelli (1998) "Environmental Bonds: A Critical Assessment", in G. Chichilnisky, G. Heal and A. Vercelli (eds) *Sustainability: Dynamics and Uncertainty* (Dordrecht: Kluwer).

Ulph, A. and M. Folie (1980) "Exhaustible resources and cartels: an intertemporal Nash-Cournot model", *Canadian Journal of Economics*, 13(4): 645–658.

UNECE – United Nations Economic Commission for Europe (2004) *UN Framework Classification for Fossil Energy and Mineral resources*. Available online at: http://www.unece.org/ie/se/pdfs/UNFC/UNFCemr.pdf

UNEP (United Nations Environment Programme) and C[4] (Center for Clouds, Chemistry and Climate) (2002) "The Asian brown cloud: climate and other environmental impacts" (Nairobi: UNEP).

Unruh, G.C. and W.R. Moomaw (1998) "An alternative analysis of apparent EKC-type transitions", *Ecological Economics*, 25: 221–229.

Uslaner, E. (2001) *The Moral Foundations of Trust* (Cambridge: Cambridge University Press).

Vagor, G. (1987) "Physiocrats", in *The New Palgrave: A Dictionary of Economics*, p.874, ed. J. Eatwell, M. Milgate and P. Newman (London: Macmillan).

Varian, H.R. (1996) *Intermediate Microeconomics: a Modern Approach* (New York: W.W. Norton and Co.).

Vercelli, A. (1989) "Uncertainty, Technological Flexibility and Long Term Fluctuations", in M. Di Matteo, R. Goodwin and A. Vercelli (eds) *Technological and Social Factors in Long Term Fluctuations* (New York: Springer).

Vercelli, A. (1991) *Methodological Foundations of Macroeconomics. Keynes and Lucas* (Cambridge: Cambridge University Press).

Vercelli, A. (1992) "Probabilistic causality and economic analysis: a survey", in A. Vercelli, N. Dimitri *Macroeconomics: A Survey of Research Strategies* (Oxford: Oxford University Press).

Vercelli, A. (1997) "Sustainable Development, Rationality, and Time", in S. Faucheux, M. O'Connor and J. van der Straten (eds) *Sustainable Development: Analysis and Public Policy* (Dordrecht: Kluwer Academic Publishers).

Vercelli, A. (1998a) "Hard uncertainty and environmental policy", in G. Chichilnisky, G. Heal and A. Vercelli, *Sustainability: Dynamics and Uncertainty* (Dordrecht: Kluwer).

Vercelli, A. (1998b) *Operational Measures of Sustainable Development and the Freedom of Future Generations*, ibid.

Vercelli, A. (2000) "Structural financial instability and cyclical fluctuations", *Structural Change and Economic Dynamics*, 11: 139–156.

Vercelli, A. (2004) "Updated Liberalism vs. Neo-liberalism: Policy Paradigms and the Structural Evolution of Western Industrial Economies after W.W. II", in R. Arena and N. Salvadori (eds) *Money, Credit and the State: Essays in Honour of Augusto* (Aldershot: Ashgate).

Vercelli, A. (2005) "Rationality, Learning and Complexity", in B. Agarwal and A. Vercelli (eds) *Psychology, Rationality and Economic Behaviour: Challenging Standard Assumption* (New York: Palgrave Macmillan).

Vercelli, A. (2006) "Globalization and Sustainable Development", in M. Basili, M. Franzini and A. Vercelli (eds) *Environment, Inequality and Collective Action* (London: Routledge).

Vincent, J.R. (1997) "Testing for environmental Kuznets curves within a developing country", *Environment and Development Economics*, 2: 417–431 (Cambridge: Cambridge University Press).

Vinod, T. *et al.* (2000) *The Quality of Growth* (New York: Oxford University Press).

Von Mises (1952) *Planning for Freedom and Other Essays and Addresses* (South Holland, Ill.: Libertarian Press).

Wade, R. (2001) "Winners and losers", *The Economist*, April 28th, 79–82.

Wallach, L. and M. Sforza (1999) *Whose Trade Organisation? Corporate Globalization and the Erosion of Democracy* (New York: Public Citizen Foundation).

WCED (The World Commission on Environment and Development) (1987) *Our common future. ("Brundtland Report")*, Oxford University Press.

Weisbrot, M., D. Baker, R. Naiman and G. Neta (2001) *"Growth may be good for the poor. But are IMF and World Bank policies good for growth?"*, Center for Economic and Policy Research, Washington D.C.

WHO – World Health Organization (1997) *Health and Environment in Sustainable Development: Five Years after the Earth Summit*, Geneva.

WHO – World Health Organization (2001) *Report of the Commission on Macroeconomics and Health*, Geneva.

Wicksteed, P.H. (1894) *An Essay on the Co-ordination of the Laws of Distribution*, 1932 edition, Reprint No. 12 (London: London School of Economics).

Wilkinson, R.G. (1992) "Income distribution and life expectancy", *British Medical Journal*, 304: 165–168.

Wilkinson, R.G. (1994) "The epidemiological transition: from material scarcity to social disadvantage?", *Daedalus*, 123: 61–77.

Wilkinson, R.G. (1996) *Unhealthy Societies: The Afflictions of Inequality* (London: Routledge).

Wilkinson, R.G. (2002) "Socioeconomic status and health", *Studies on social and economic determinants of population health*, 1: 13–31, WHO Regional Office for Europe, Copenhagen.

Williams, R.B., J. Feaganes and J.C. Barefoot (1995) "Hostility and death rates in 10 U.S. cities", *Psychosomatic Medicine*, 57 (1): 94.

Williamson, J. (1999) *What should The Bank think about the Washington Consensus?*, background paper for The World Bank's World Development Report 2000.

Wittenberg, M. (2000) *Predatory equilibria: systematic theft and its effects on output, inequality and long-run growth*, Department of Economics, University of the Witwatersrand, Johannesburg.

Wolf, M. (2000) "Kicking down growth's ladder: Protesters against the Word Bank and the IMF are in Effect Seeking to Deny the Poor the Benefits of a Liberal World Economy", *Financial Times*; April 12, 2000, p.23.

Wolf, M. (2004) *Why Globalization Works, The Case for the Global Market Economy* (New Haven: Yale University Press).

Wood, A. (1994) *North-South Trade, Employment and Inequality* (Oxford: Clarendon Press).

Wood, A. (1997) "Openness and wage inequality in developing countries: the Latin American challenge to East Asian conventional wisdom", *World Bank Economic Review*, 11: 33–57.

Woodall, P. (2000) "Untangling e-conomics. A Survey of The New Economy", *The Economist*, September 23rd–29th 2000.

Woodward, J. (1997) "Explanation, invariance and intervention", *Philosophy of Science*, 64: 26–41.

Woodward, D., N. Drager, R. Beaglehole and D. Lipson (2001) *Globalization and Health: A Framework for Analysis and Action*, Commission on Macroeconomics and Health, Working Paper No. WG4: 10, WHO, Geneva.

World Bank (1992) *World Development Report 1992* (New York: Oxford University Press).

World Bank (2000) *Bangladesh air quality management project*, Project Appraisal Document, Report n.20573-BD, Environment Unit South Asian Region (Washington D.C.: The World Bank).

World Bank (2007a) *Global Monitoring Report*, (Washington D.C.: The World Bank).

World Bank (2007b) *World Development Indicators* (Washington D.C.: The World Bank).

Worldwatch Institute (1990) *State of the World 1990* (New York: Norton).

Yamaji, K. Y. Matsuhashi, Y. Nagata and Y. Kaya (1991) *An integrated system for C02/Energy/GNP analysis: Case studies on economic measures for C02 reduction in Japan*, Workshop on CO2 Reduction and Removal: Measures for the Next Century, 19–21/3/1991 (Laxemburg, Austria: International Institute for Applied Systems Analysis).

Author Index

Subject Index